Sterling A. Brown

Photograph of Sterling A. Brown in 1980 by Roy Lewis. Used with permission.

Sterling A. Brown

BUILDING THE BLACK
AESTHETIC TRADITION

Joanne V. Gabbin

CONTRIBUTIONS IN AFRO-AMERICAN AND
AFRICAN STUDIES, NUMBER 86

Greenwood Press
WESTPORT, CONNECTICUT · LONDON, ENGLAND

Library of Congress Cataloging in Publication Data

Gabbin, Joanne V.
    Sterling A. Brown: building the Black aesthetic
tradition

    (Contributions in Afro-American and African studies,
ISSN 0069-9624; no. 86)
    Bibliography: p.
    Includes index.
    1. Brown, Sterling Allen, 1901-   —Criticism and
interpretation. 2. American literature—Afro-American
authors—History and criticism. I. Title. II. Series.
PS3503.R833Z66 1985   811'.52   84-19777
ISBN 0-313-23720-4 (lib. bdg.)

Library of Congress Catalog Card Number: 84-19777
ISBN: 0-313-23720-4
ISSN: 0069-9624

First published in 1985

Greenwood Press
A division of Congressional Information Service, Inc.
88 Post Road West
Westport, Connecticut 06881

Printed in the United States of America

10 9 8 7 6 5 4 3 2 1

Lawd I wanna be one o' dat nummer
When de saints goa ma'chin' home.

This book is dedicated to the memory of my parents, Joseph Veal and Jessie Smallwood Veal, who are surely in that number.

It is also dedicated to the memory of my mentor George E. Kent, who guided my work at the University of Chicago.

The Mentor

Silvered hair
Intense eyes
Jaunty step
Wizard words
Gentle wit
Quiet confidence

I will remember all these pieces of you.
Yet, when I find you again, I will know you
By your steadfast faith.

CONTENTS

SERIES FOREWORD

The paucity of creative and scholarly works available for library and classroom use remains a crucial barrier to the adequate study of African and Afro-American arts and letters. Despite a flood of hastily conceived and rashly executed monograph and bibliographical series that ostensibly meant to address this quandary, students, scholars, and librarians agree that African and Afro-American materials continue to be either inadequate as research tools or, more often, simply unavailable at all.

Despite the intention of well-meaning publishers and eager Afro-Americanists, the 1880 lament of the Black critic, Richard T. Greener, retains its poignancy as an account of knowledge of Black arts and letters: "It would be interesting, were it not painful, to observe how little even educated Americans, judging from articles in current literature, know of the capacity, disposition, achievements, services, or sacrifices of the Negro in general and the Negro American in particular." The American academy has only a limited notion of the manner in which Black writers and scholars have structured their responses to the complex fate of institutionalized racial and economic discrimination. Nor does the academy have a sufficient idea of the peculiar manner in which Black texts respond to considerations raised in other, related, texts, which responses themselves constitute an aspect of intellectual history. What's more, there exists no systematic publishing venture that has addressed this problem intelligently, by commissioning major Africanists and Afro-Americanists to prepare sophisticated studies on the vast and challenging subject of the Black arts and letters.

To sharpen the definition of African and Afro-American studies and to present a more coherent view of the continuum of Black thought and action, a new departure is necessary. This series is designed to fill this need. Often inter-disciplinary and cross-cultural, it seeks to address not only the complexities of the cultural and aesthetic confrontation of Black cultures with non-Black ones, but also the nature and function of African and Afro-American arts and letters themselves.

By 1931, when Sterling Brown published *Southern Road*, his first book of poems, the use of Black vernacular structures in Afro-American poetry was controversial indeed. Of all the arts, only through music had Blacks invented and fully defined a tradition both widely regarded and acknowledged to be uniquely their own. Black folktales, while roundly popular, were commonly thought to be the amusing fantasies of a childlike people, whose saga and anecdotes about rabbits and bears held nothing deeper than the attention span of a child, à la Uncle Remus or even *Green Pastures*. And what was generally called "dialect," the unique form of English that Afro-Americans spoke, was thought by whites to reinforce received assumptions about the Negro's mental inferiority.

Dorothy Van Doran simply said out loud what so many other white critics thought privately. "It may be that [the Negro] can express himself only by music and rhythm," she wrote in 1931, "and not by words."

Middle-class Blacks, despite the notoriety his dialect verse had garnered for Paul Laurence Dunbar and the Negro, thought that dialect was an embarrassment, the linguistic remnant of an enslavement they all longed to forget. The example of Dunbar's popular and widely reviewed "jingles in a broken tongue," coinciding with the conservatism of Booker T. Washington, was an episode best not repeated. Blacks stood in line to attack dialect poetry. William Stanley Braithwaite, Countee Cullen, and especially James Weldon Johnson argued fervently that dialect stood in the shadow of the plantation tradition of Joel Chandler Harris, James Whitcomb Riley, and Thomas Nelson Page. Dialect poetry, Johnson continued, possessed "but two full stops, humor and pathos.'' By 1931, Johnson, whose own "Jingles and Croons" (1917) embodied the worst in this tradition, could assert assuredly that "the passing of traditional dialect as a medium for negro poets is complete.''

Just one year after he had performed the post-mortem on dialect poetry, James Weldon Johnson, in the "Preface" to Sterling Brown's *Southern Road*, reluctantly admitted that he had been wrong about dialect. Brown's book of poetry, even more profoundly than the market crash of 1929, truly ended the "Harlem Renaissance," primarily because it contained a new and distinctly Black poetic diction, and not merely the vapid and pathetic claim for one.

To the surprise of Harlem Renaissance's New Negroes, the reviews were of the sort one imagines Heywood Broun's redeemer-poet was to have gotten. The *New York Times Book Review* said that *Southern Road* is a book "the importance of which is considerable. It not only indicates how far the Negro artist has progressed since the years when he began to find his voice, but it proves that the Negro artist is abundantly capable of making an original and genuine contribution to American literature." Brown's work was marked by a "dignity that respects itself . . . there is everywhere art." Louis Untermeyer agreed, "He does not paint himself blacker than he is. . . . " Even Alain Locke, two years later, called it "a new era in Negro poetry." *Southern Road*'s artistic achievement ended the Harlem Renaissance, for that slim book undermined all of the New Negro's assumptions about the nature of the Black tradition and its relation to the individual talent. Not only were most of Brown's poems composed in dialect, but they also had as their subjects distinctively Black archetypal mythic characters, as well as the Black common man whose roots were rural and Southern. Brown called his poetry "portraitures," close and vivid detailings, of an *action* of a carefully delineated subject to suggest a sense of place, in much the same way as Toulouse-Lautrec's works continue to do. These portraitures, drawn "in a manner constant with them," Brown renders in a style that emerged from several forms of folk discourse, a Black vernacular matrix that includes the blues and ballads, the spirituals and work songs. Indeed, Brown's ultimate referents are Black music and mythology. His language, densely symbolic, ironical, and naturally indirect, draws upon the idioms, figures, and tones of both the sacred and the profane vernacular traditions, mediating between these in a manner unmatched before or since. Although Langston Hughes had attempted to do roughly the same, Hughes seemed content to transcribe the popular structures he received, rather than to transcend or elaborate upon them, as in "To Midnight Nan at Le-Roy's".

But it is not merely the translation of the vernacular that makes Brown's work of major importance, informed by these forms as his best work is; it is, rather, the deft manner in which he created his own poetic diction; by fusing several Black traditions with various models he provided the Anglo-American poets with a unified and complex structure of feeling, a sort of song of a racial self. Above all else, Brown is a regionalist whose poems embody William Carlos Williams' notion that the classic is the local, fully realized. Yet Brown's "region" is not so much "the South," or Spoon River, Tilbury, or Yoknapatawpha as it is "the private negro mind," as Alain Locke put it, "this private thought and speech," or "how it feels to be colored me," as Zora Neale Hurston put it, the very textual milieu of Blackness itself. Boldly, Brown merged the Afro-American vernacular traditions of dialect and myth with the Anglo-American poetic tradition and, drawing upon the example of Jean Toomer, introduced the Afro-American modernist lyrical mode into Black literature. Indeed, Brown, Toomer, and Zora Neale Hurston comprise three cardinal points on a triangle of influence out of which emerged, among others, Ralph Ellison, Toni Morrison, Alice Walker, and Leon Forrest.

Michael Harper has collected nearly the whole of Brown's body of poetry, including *Southern Road*, *The Last Ride of Wild Bill* (1975), and the previously unpublished *No Hiding Place*, his second book of poems which was rejected for publication in the late thirties because of its political subjects, and which seems to have discouraged Brown from attempting another volume until 1975. This splendid collection at last makes it possible to review the whole of Brown's works, after years when his work remained out-of-print or difficult to get. Forty-two years separated the first and second editions of *Southern Road*. Rereading Brown, we were struck by how consistently he shapes the tone of his poems by the meticulous selection of the right word to suggest succinctly complex images and feelings "stripped to form," in Frost's phrase. Unlike so many of his contemporaries, Brown never lapses into pathos or sentimentality. The oppressive relation of self to natural and (Black and white) man-made environments, Brown renders in the broadest terms, as does the blues. Yet Brown's characters confront catastrophe with all the irony and stoicism of the blues and Black folklore. Brown's protagonists laugh and cry, fall in and out of love, and muse about death in ways not often explored in Black literature. Finally, his great theme seems to be the relation of being to the individual will, rendered always in a sensuous diction, echoing what critic Joanne Gabbin calls "touchstones" of the blues lyric, such as "Don't your bed look lonesome/When your Babe packs up to leave," "I'm gonna leave heah dis mawnin' ef I have to ride de blind," "Did you ever wake up in de mo'nin', yo' mind rollin' two different ways—/One mind to leave your baby, and one mind to stay?" or "De quagmire don't hang out no signs." What's more, he is able to realize such splendid results in a variety of forms, including the classic and standard blues, the ballad, a new form that Stephen Henderson calls "the blues-ballad," the sonnet, and free verse. For the first time, we can appreciate Brown's full range, his mastery of so many traditions.

The profession urgently needs a book on Sterling Brown's life and works. After a painfully long lacunae (forty-two years separated the first and second editions of *Southern Road*), Sterling Brown's poetry is once again being widely read and studied in the classroom; indeed, Brown is now a permanent part of the Afro-American and the American literary canons. Joanne Gabbin's superb bio-critical study shall serve to underscore Brown's considerable achievement in letters and to make Brown's work even more readily accessible to students and scholars alike.

Gabbin's approach is both biographical and textual. She traces his life from Washington to Harvard and back to Washington again. More than any other scholar, she shows how secure and extensive was the Black upper middle-class at the turn of the century. (Both Frederick Douglass and Paul Laurence Dunbar were Brown's father's close friends.) From "the" Black academic school at Washington, Brown went off to Williams (B.A.) and to Harvard (M.A.) before returning South to teach and to write.

It is her study of Brown's writing that makes Gabbin's work so important, for her book serves as a perfect introduction to Brown's poetry. Gabbin places Brown's poetic heritage in both the Black folk and the Anglo-American poetic traditions. Both English department courses on modern poetry and Black Studies courses could use her book as a central source.

Joanne Gabbin's work is a model of critical sophistication unhindered by contemporary jargon. Her analysis of Brown's work is sustained, sensitive, and scholarly. It is fitting that such a great poet has been explicated by such an intelligent critic.

John W. Blassingame
Henry Louis Gates, Jr.

ACKNOWLEDGMENTS

Sterling Brown asked me a while before this book was published, "Am I in the book?" Fortunately, I was able to answer "yes" because of the many people who helped to breathe life into this seed piece on his career as a poet and critic.

First of all, I am grateful to Sterling Brown, who has become more than the subject of this study, and to the late Daisy Turnbull Brown, who shared with me a wisdom distilled from her rich and meaningful life. The hours I spent with them never failed to inspire in me a renewed enthusiasm for this book.

I am especially indebted to all those who generously shared their insights on Brown's life and work. They include Stephen Henderson, Arthur P. Davis, Sterling Stuckey, Eugenia Collier, John Hope Franklin, Amiri Baraka, the late Larry Neal, Sonia Sanchez, Jerre Mangione, Michael Winston, Michael Harper, Eloise Spicer, the late Allison Davis, Herman Branson, Richard Barksdale, Ethelbert Miller, Gwendolyn Brooks, Haki Madhubuti and Darwin Turner.

In 1972 I began the research on this book at the University of Chicago. There I met George E. Kent who encouraged me to do this study and helped me to develop my critical perspective. It is appropriate that this work is dedicated to him and his legacy of Afro-American literary criticism. I also appreciate the assistance of James E. Miller and the faculty of the English Department at the University of Chicago who broadened my knowledge of American and English literature.

I want to thank the staffs at the Langston Hughes Memorial Library at Lincoln University, the Morris Library at the University of Delaware, the Moorland-Spingarn Research Center at Howard University, the Regenstein Library at the University of Chicago, and the Schomburg Collection in New York for making their facilities and materials available to me during my research.

I am especially grateful to Sidney Williams, one of our ablest griots, and his devoted wife Ruth Williams. Their example provided the additional impetus to complete a project of this magnitude. I am also deeply grateful to my sister, brothers, and their families who have given me support and encouragement. Though I would like to call the roll of those relatives, friends, colleagues, and students who have encourged me in my work, they are legion. Therefore, I must extend a collective thank you which is meant to express my appreciation to each one.

Through it all, two people have given freely of their love and understanding: my husband, Alexander Gabbin, and my daughter Jessea Nayo. Because of them, the entire process was full of joy.

Sterling A. Brown

1

INTRODUCTION: STERLING A. BROWN AND BUILDING THE BLACK AESTHETIC TRADITION

O de ole sheep dey knows de road,
Young lambs gotta find de way. (Spiritual)

With these lines from an old spiritual, Sterling A. Brown opens his first book of poems, *Southern Road*.[1] By the force of their meaning, he foreshadows the nature of the spiritual journey he will take and suggests the aesthetic connections that bind folk culture with contemporary Black life. These lines acknowledge Brown's indebtedness to the "ole sheep" who, steeped in the informing spirit of the folk tradition, have instilled in him an awareness of his cultural inheritance. Their music, their humor, their irony got into his poetry and inevitably influenced its form and feeling. Their tough grip on reality and their clear-eyed view of the past informed his critical perspective. Their suffering, tenacity, faith, and courage got into his being and deepened his life. Out of these lines also emerge the dynamics that suggest Brown's own career that extends from his early years as a writer in the 1920s to the present when he is recognized as the Dean of Afro-American Literature. The "young lamb," after a long process of absorption, has become the inveterate "old sheep," whom Amiri Baraka describes as "a respository of information and inspiration."[2] And most important, during his distinguished career as poet, critic, scholar, and teacher, he has quietly but surely built the foundations of the Black aesthetic tradition.

As a poet, Brown's most significant achievement is his subtle adaptation of song forms, especially the blues, to the literature. Experimenting with the blues, spirituals, work songs, and ballads, he invents combinations that, at their best, retain the ethos of folk forms and intensify the literary quality of poetry. Like his fellow traveler Langston Hughes, Brown discovers how to enable one form to release the power of another.

With a remarkable ear for the idiom, cadence, and tones of folk speech, Brown absorbs its vibrant qualities in his poetry. Rescuing dialect from the wastebins of minstrelsy and the overzealous mimicry of the Dunbar school, Brown naturalizes Black dialect and captures the inflection, the timbre, the racial sound of the vernacular. The genius of his achievement is amplified when one hears him perform his poetry. The hearer becomes intensely aware that the poem takes on added dimensions because of his voice. His words vibrate with new nuances and depth. Brown becomes the African voice, the eloquent griot who makes the past emerge into the present by dint of his virtuoso skill. Brown becomes the Afro-American voice, the elegant trickster, the bodacious badman, the heroic strong man, juggling wit, understatement, irony, and humor with inimitable style.

Brown's poetry is also a testament to the continuity of Black expression. Exploring both the folk and literary traditions, he recognizes the shared concerns, the values, the ways of thinking and feeling about the world that remain bridges from one generation to the next. Because his poetry succeeds in expressing these lasting vestiges, it has a timeless quality. Poems that appeared in *Southern Road* in 1932 have a strong sense of contemporaneousness when read today.

One reason for the lasting appeal of his poetry is his ability to limn some of the most memorable portraits in American literature. Like Langston Hughes, Edwin Arlington Robinson, and Robert Frost, Brown reveals the triumphs, failures, hopes, foibles, and strengths of America's everyman. Because of his skillful portrayal, Sporting Beasley, Slim Greer, Sister Lou, Old Lem, Joe Meek, Big Boy, and Crispus Attucks McKoy are now national treasures. Brown achieves in these portraits truth in representation because of his willingness to restrain from idealizing his subjects and his insistence upon an approach that eschews sentimentality and special pleading. Invariably Brown's poetry reveals an exploration of self-hood, a celebration of the strength and stoicism of Black people, and an abiding faith in the possibilities of their lives. Brown becomes myth-maker, keeper of the images, preserver of values and definitions.

In all, Brown conscientiously masters his craft and accomplishes his goal of creating poetry that is "simple, sensuous, and impassioned." [3] As vivid and vibrant as a Romare Bearden collage, Brown's poetry displays strikingly imaginative, metaphoric language somehow kin to that of the unknown bards and yet somehow different. His poetry communicates and elicits intense feelings. Because of his genius for writing expressive language that is controlled and balanced, Brown makes his readers shout, cry, scream, laugh, and yell, without telling them to do so. He is so well acquainted with the vigorous demands of structure that his handling of narrative, dramatic dialogue, the sonnet, folk idioms, and a variety of experimental forms appears effortless.

The study of Brown's poetry reveals a complex sensibility which experiments with the diverse elements in literature and culture, amplifies understanding through performance, confronts the tragic-comic conditions of life, and with insight and craftsmanship attests to the continuity of Black creativity.

For more than half a century, Brown has also made a significant impact in the development of American literature as a pioneer in Black American criticism and as a respected authority of Black culture. He is one of the principal architects of Black criticism. His critical essays and books are seminal works that give an insider's perspective of literature by and about Blacks. His understanding of how social attitudes can affect and often distort life and character informs his writing in *The Negro in American Fiction* (1937), a detailed survey of the treatment of Black characters. One of Brown's earliest and most stunning contributions to critical thought is his assertion that politics and polemics have everything to do with the way an oppressed group is portrayed. Brown brings into the liturgy of criticism the singular truth that the treatment of an oppressed group in literature parallels its treatment in life, and predictably, the greater the incidence of oppression, the greater the degree of misrepresentation, exploitation, and justification in the literature. Of great influence on later critics, *The Negro in American Fiction* remains the foundation upon which much criticism of Black life and character rests.

Brown's examination of Blacks as creators in *Negro Poetry and*

Drama (1937) and his unpublished study of Afro-American theater, written as a part of the Carnegie-Myrdal research project, bring criticism to a new level of maturity. As Brown surveys the poetry of Dunbar, McKay, Cullen, Hughes, and others, as well as the drama by O'Neill, Connelly, and Green, he evaluates each, not only as a reflection of experience, but also as a way of intensifying experience. He expects that the poet or playwright will have his work bear the accumulated weight of his aesthetic tradition and, in so doing, will utilize his artistry to the fullest.

Above all, Brown's critical approach is characterized by a sagacious use of synthesis. Brown recognizes the various cultural elements that have come together to create a society where, despite years of fractionalism caused by racism, discrimination, segregation, caste, and brutalization, Blacks and whites share a culture that inextricably binds them together. Thus, he necessarily brings to his criticism a knowledge of the many literary and aesthetic forces that shape the literature.

Sterling Brown is also a guardian of the images, values, history, and ethos of Black people. Stressing the importance of ethnic memory and the ethical stance, he affirms the folk tradition as the wellspring of original, imaginative, and traditional values. During the 1930s and 1940s, his studies of the folk experience and culture were the fullest and most perceptive of any in the field. An acknowledged authority in Black music, he has written essays on the blues, ballads, spirituals, work songs, and jazz. Brown's essay, "The Blues as Folk Poetry" (1930), is a pioneer work that analyzes and interprets blues lyrics. "Blues, Ballads and Social Songs" (1940), "Stray Notes on Jazz" (1946), "The Blues" (1952), "Negro Folk Expressions: Spirituals, Seculars, Ballads and Work Songs" (1953) are among the other articles in which Brown brings a thorough interpretation and literary analysis to folk forms. Brown's work in this area initiated a tradition that has been continued by such critics as Amiri Baraka and Albert Murray.

From 1936 to 1939 Sterling Brown was national editor of Negro affairs for the Federal Writers' Project, and under his direction the project produced the first extensive studies of the nation's Black communities. Two of the more outstanding ones are *The Negro in Virginia* (1940) and *Washington City and Capital* (1937). His involvement in the FWP is, however, only one index to his continuing interest in documenting the participation of Blacks in American society. Brown has written an article concerning the role of Blacks in "Athletics and Arts" (1951). He has addressed the proverbial question, "What does the Negro want?'' in a 1945 essay entitled ''Count Us In,'' and he has interpreted the American caste and class system in an essay, ''The American Race Problem as Reflected in American Literature'' (1939). Also in 1941, Sterling Brown, along with Ulysses Lee and Arthur P. Davis, edited the landmark anthology, *The Negro Caravan*. Then seen as an essential gathering of essays and literature about Black life, it remains today the most comprehensive and valuable resource of its kind.

Finally, Brown, associated with Howard University for more than fifty years, has spent the better part of his energy interpreting and disseminating knowledge of Black cultural achievements. His love for teaching has been matched only by his success at inspiring in his students a sense of personal discovery and commitment. A forerunner, Brown has prepared the way for the resurgence of interest in Black literature and studies witnessed during the last two decades. Before many scholars recognized Black studies as a legitimate field, Brown taught the first courses in Black literature at Howard University and, as a visiting professor, lectured on Black literature and culture at Atlanta, Minnesota, Vassar, and New York University. Brown has read his poetry and spoken to college audiences all over the country; his keen knowledge of his subject and skillful reading of his poetry have attracted a large following.

Brown's influence reaches beyond the boundaries of the United States. Leopold Sedar Senghor, one of the architects of Negritude, calls Brown ''an original militant of Negritude, a precursor of our movement.''[4] Senghor, who became aware of Brown's poetry and criticism in the 1920s and 1930s through the pages of *Opportunity* and *Crisis*, attributes to Brown, McKay, Cullen, Hughes, and other writers of the Negro Renaissance the inspiration for the cultural movement whose concepts fostered identity among Blacks in Africa and the diaspora. In addition, Brown's poetry has been translated into Spanish, French, German, and Russian and has been read in literary circles throughout the world.

However, one of the great paradoxes of American literature is that Sterling Brown, who has done as much as any one man to identify the foundations of the Black aesthetic tradition, has been so little studied. Brown's significance as a poet, critic, and scholar of Black life and culture has yet to be systematically documented and evaluated. During the last twenty years, only a few critics have begun to give Brown the critical attention his work merits.

The most extensive examination of Brown's poetry to date has been done by French scholar Jean Wagner, in *Black Poets of the United States*. This important study examines the poetry of Dunbar, McKay, Toomer, Cullen, Johnson, Hughes, and Brown. It became more available to critics and students of American literature in 1973 when Kenneth Douglas translated the book originally published in French (1950). The strength of the volume results from Wagner's comprehensive and thorough scholarship. He gives Brown's poetry, some of which was never before published, a close critical analysis and focuses on its important thematic patterns.

However, it is Stephen Henderson, in his book *Understanding the New Black Poetry* (1974), who suggests an ingenious approach to the study of Brown's poetry. Henderson critically analyzes Black poetry using Black music and speech as referents to explain and appreciate its original and innovative forms. He recognizes the distinctive forms that Brown has adopted from the folk and has reshaped into his own poetry. As he sees Brown and other Black poets absorbing their themes, forms, and feeling from the oral culture, he suggests that the meaning of the poetry can be best revealed by discussing it in terms of theme, structure, and "saturation"—"fidelity to the observed or intuited truth of the Black experience in the United States."[5] Though his critical comments on Brown's poetry are brief, they are provocative and often revelatory.

Two other writers have contributed to a rediscovery of Brown's poetry. In 1974 Charles H. Rowell published an important article on Brown's use of folk elements which appeared in *Studies in the Literary Imagination*. In "Sterling A. Brown and the Afro-American Folk Tradition," Rowell says that Brown, among others, has attempted to build "a self-conscious art upon folk art."[6] A year later, Sterling Stuckey, in a critical introduction to the reprint of *Southern Road*, went back roughly forty years to reconstruct Brown's literary standing. Stuckey gives terse illuminating interpretation of little-known poems like "Cabaret" and isolates those qualities in Brown's poetry that ensure its continued appeal. Perhaps more than any of the above mentioned critics, Stuckey succeeds in convincing the reader that he is closely in tune with the poet's nature and spirit. He writes:

In spite of all, whatever his setbacks, whatever his triumphs, Sterling Brown has maintained through it all possession of his soul and kept the faith with his fellows, living and dead. He is an artist in the truest sense: the complete man, he has attempted to master the art of living. One is reminded, when thinking of him, of Lionel Trilling's reference to certain "men who live their visions . . . who *are* what they write."[7]

Stuckey's introduction came forty years after Alain Locke had hailed Brown as a new, important poet of folk-life in Nancy Cunard's *Negro Anthology*. Since that time, scholarship on Brown has not kept pace with his growing influence. Fortunately, however, with the publication of *The Collected Poems of Sterling A. Brown* in 1980, scholarship on Brown has taken a decided leap. Michael S. Harper, who selected the poems, writes that "this collection secures [Brown's] rightful place at the center of American letters."[8] Since 1980, Robert G. O'Meally, Kimberly W. Benston, and Henry Louis Gates, Jr., are among the critics who have given his poetry serious study.

However, very little critical attention has been given to Brown's criticism. His critical surveys and articles were first studied in a dissertation written by Ila Jacquith Blue at the University of Michigan (1959). In the study entitled "A Study of Literary Criticism By Some Negro Writers, 1900–1955," she discusses some central problems of literary theory, including the nature and function of art, the function of criticism, and critical approaches to the genres. She generally succeeds in presenting Brown's critical judgments against the contemporary background of American criticism. Beyond this study there are only cursory comments about his criticism, although it is generally known that Brown has made a significant impact on the development of Black American literature. Critic Darwin T. Turner writes: "No other critic has inspired as much admiration and respect from his students and successors in the field. In every stream of creative Black literature Sterling Brown is the source to which critics return."[9] While Turner claims that Brown "is the literary historian who wrote the Bible for the study of Afro-American literature,"[10] Eugenia Collier says that Brown's early works of criticism laid "the foundations for critical concepts yet to come,"[11] and Arthur P. Davis and Jay Saunders Redding, distinguished critics of American literature, write that Brown has "done more than any other one person to influence and direct the course of Negro American writing."[12] Yet despite this acclaim, his critical work remains in need of a full assessment.

Brown's achievement and influence in the field of American literature and culture are significant. He is truly the bridge whose influence spans the modern development of Black literature. Brown has linked the early stirrings of expression with present literary development, affirming the breadth of the Black creative experience in America. He has made the necessary connections between oral folk culture and self-conscious literature, identifying in his own poetry and the writings of others their debt to the folk. Brown has also managed to eliminate the much touted gulf between the particular racial experience and the universal experience because he knows the two are one.

NOTES

1. These lines from a traditional spiritual appear on the frontispiece of *Southern Road*, Brown's first volume of poems. Though spirituals were not collected until the Civil War, these songs have roots in the eighteenth and early nineteenth centuries.

2. Amiri Baraka, "Sterling Brown: A Repository of Information and Inspiration," *Sterling A. Brown: A UMUM Tribute*, ed. Black History Museum Committee, 2d ed. (Philadelphia: Black History Museum UMUM Publishers, 1976), p. 49; hereafter this source will be identified as *Sterling A. Brown: A UMUM Tribute*.

3. Interview with Sterling A. Brown by Steven Jones at the poet's home, Washington, D.C., May 10, 1973, IAH transcript, p. 7. This and the following quotations are made with the permission of Sterling A. Brown and the Institute for the Arts and the Humanities, Howard University, Washington, D.C.

4. Leopold Sedar Senghor, "An African Perspective On Sterling Brown," *Sterling A. Brown: A UMUM Tribute*, p. 14.

5. Stephen Henderson, *Understanding the New Black Poetry: Black Speech and Black Music as Poetic References* (New York: William Morrow & Co., Inc., 1973), p. 10.

6. Charles H. Rowell, "Sterling A. Brown and the Afro-American Folk Tradition," *Studies in the Literary Imagination*, 7 (Fall 1974): 132.

7. Sterling Stuckey, "Introduction," *Southern Road*, by Sterling A. Brown (Boston: Beacon Press, 1974), p. xxx.

8. Sterling A. Brown, *The Collected Poems of Sterling A. Brown* (New York: Harper & Row, 1980), p. xi.

9. Darwin T. Turner, "Afro-American Literary Critics: An Introduction," *The Black Aesthetic*, ed. Addison Gayle, Jr. (New York: Doubleday, 1971), p. 71.

10. Darwin T. Turner, "For Sterling Brown: A Remembrance," *Sterling A. Brown: A UMUM Tribute*, p. 23.

11. Eugenia Collier, "Prologue: Early Critical Works," *Sterling A. Brown: A UMUM Tribute*, p. 24.

12. Arthur P. Davis and Saunders Redding, eds., *Cavalcade: Negro American Writing From 1760 to the Present* (Boston: Houghton Mifflin Company, 1971), p. 400.

2

THE LITERARY UPBRINGING OF STERLING A. BROWN

For the better part of his life, Sterling A. Brown has testified to the continuity of the Black man's creative response to American culture. Through his work and his life he has demonstrated not only that a vital Black culture exists but also that it exists as an integral part of American culture. Brown is one of a group of Black writers and critics, including Alain Locke, Richard Wright, Ralph Ellison, Gwendolyn Brooks, and Amiri Baraka, who have viewed the culture of Black America as an integrated cultural tradition. As he was nurtured in the forms of Western culture, he cultivated an appreciation for the writings of Chaucer, Shakespeare, Milton, Synge, Whitman, Sandburg, Robinson, Frost, and others. However, he also came to appreciate what Richard Wright called "The Forms of Things Unknown"—the anonymous folk utterances, spirituals, blues, work songs, and folklore created and passed on by Blacks in the United States.[1] Brown recognized in the development of these folk expressions the emergence of a culture. He attributed its strength and vitality to the merging of diverse cultural elements, a process that effectively created more than the sum of the combining parts. For Brown, like his colleague Alain Locke, the very elements that make Black expressions uniquely expressive of Black life make them at the same time "deeply representative" of American life.[2]

Essentially, Brown's genius is his ability to synthesize these diverse elements that make up American culture into one creative response. As his long life nearly coincides with the development of modern Black American literature, his creative method and aesthetic philosophy have reached backward, then forward, to make meaningful the complex set of values, sensibilities, and forces that define the Black cultural experience. Cognizant of the vagaries of American society in which, for any number of racial and ethnic groups, one culture is learned and the other lived, Brown has synthesized what he could of American and European cultures, has explored his own indigenous culture, and has rejected the negativism that certain segments of the society have attached to Blackness.

This gift for synthesizing, for bringing together and reconciling diverse elements, marks his personal and professional life. Born into the Black middle class of Washington, D.C., he does not accept the narrow interpretation of culture, meaning "cultivation" or "sophistication," that LeRoi Jones (Amiri Baraka) has attributed to the group.[3] Without denying who he is, Brown rejects the divisiveness of color consciousness, which was far too evident during the first four decades of the twentieth century. He also rejects the hysteria of middle class apologists and the vapidness of a newly arrived at respectability. Educated at Williams College and Harvard University, Brown says that he received his finest education from the semi-literate farmers and migrant workers of the rural South. It is significant also that, though he is the son of a Howard University minister and professor, he does not confine his referents to the boundaries of a preacher's home; his referents include the blues moans and jazz of the barrel house and the speech of the "low-down" folk.

For Brown, the process of reconciling the contradictions of his own social group and the complexities of American society has borne fruit. He has cultivated the faculty of racial memory and acquired a broad understanding of letters and life. An account of Sterling Brown's life, though interesting in its own right, is significant for the revelation of this process.

Preferring the role of raconteur to that of autobiographer, Brown has not published an account of his life. However, in May 1973 he participated in a series of interviews which constitute the only extended commentary of his early life.[4] His vivid recollections, told in a style that is earthy, humorous, often pithy, and sometimes profane, put him squarely in the tradition of Mark Twain, an association he acknowledges freely, calling himself "the best liar at Howard University."[5] True to this tradition, Brown fills his account with numerous anecdotes and the personalities of people living and dead. As he reflects on his childhood, his comments are tinged with a proud awareness of the cultural tradition that is a part of his "upbringing." His family, his contact with several exceptional teachers, and his acquaintance with prominent intellectual and political leaders of the Black race are remembered in such a way as to make his early experiences not only humanly interesting but also important for an understanding of the development of the mature sensibility evident in his writings.

Born on May 1, 1901, in a house at Sixth and Fairmount in Washington, D.C., Sterling A. Brown was the last of six children and the only son born to Reverend Sterling Nelson Brown and Adelaide Allen Brown. He grew up on the campus of Howard University where his father had taught in the School of Religion since 1892.

The year Brown was born, Rev. Sterling N. Brown became the pastor of the newly organized Lincoln Temple Congregational Church, that would later be known for its progressive and intelligent leadership. This was the high point of Sterling Nelson Brown's ministerial career which had begun during his years as a student at Fisk University. In an autobiographical account entitled *My Own Life Notes*, Rev. Sterling N. Brown sketches the events of his life. Born into slavery in Roane County, Tennessee, in 1858, Sterling Nelson Brown was one of thirteen children. After emancipation, his father and mother, "their best days behind them," provided for their children by raising crops on a small tenant farm. His father also operated his own blacksmith's shop. However, despite their efforts, the family was in a steady battle with poverty.

Because of his family's meager resources, the young Sterling Nelson had to postpone his education several times. In 1872, when the crops failed and his father took ill, he was forced to stop his schooling and find work to help support the family. In his autobiography he tells how, at the age of thirteen, he sought work on the Cincinnati Southern Railroad gang. He writes vividly about this experience:

The very sight of the rough men, rude tents and huts terrified me, but the needs of a sick father and almost starving family nerved me to go ahead and not falter. I called upon the superintendent, who was stern and indifferent and hardly gave me time to speak before he shouted out: "What do you want here, boy? We have no work for you to do."[6]

Though he considered giving up and returning home that very moment, he prevailed upon the superintendent to give him a chance. Finally, the work boss relented and commanded him to "get a shovel and go at it."[7] However, despite a plucky attempt to keep up with the workmen on the gang, the boy was no match for the railroad men. Just before quitting time the next day, the boss told the boy to pick up his pay, after admonishing him, "This is no place for you."[8] Depressed in spirit, he made his way home with a small piece of bacon bought with his wages.

Soon after that, Sterling Nelson Brown got work as a molder in a brickyard and saved enough money to buy a small farm for his parents. With the remaining few dollars, he entered Fisk in 1875 and for several years taught school in the surrounding counties to earn money to continue his studies. Prior to graduating from Fisk in 1885, he served as a preacher in various churches throughout the South. Though quick to emphasize that he was "not a minister but only a teacher," from a very early age he was dedicated to the idea of winning others to the Christian faith.[9] In 1885 Sterling Nelson Brown graduated from Oberlin Theological Seminary and began a forty-year career dedicated to that same idea.

When Reverend Brown came to Washington in 1889, the city was reputed to have "the most distinguished and brilliant assemblage of Negroes in the world."[10] He found himself in the company of the race's most noted leaders: Frederick Douglass, author and civil rights crusader; John M. Langston, former congressman from Virginia during Reconstruction and acting president of Howard University; Senator B. K. Bruce; and Congressman John K. Lynch, both formerly of Mississippi. In fact, Lincoln Temple was often the center of important conferences and debates on race questions. Several debates between Booker T. Washington and W.E.B. Du Bois took place in his church. In 1903, a conference on "How to Solve the Race Problem" was held there. Many of the militant members of the conference later joined forces with liberal movements which culminated in the founding of the NAACP in 1910.[11]

Rev. Sterling N. Brown and other Black leaders were "attracted by the period's visions of reform" and worked arduously so that Blacks would have nothing "short of a full man's chance to be and do their best." [12] After the close of the First World War, in an article entitled "The Negro's Question Mark," he sounds a note similar to the clarion call of Alain Locke's "The New Negro" written six years later:

The dawning of a new day has come and with it is born new hopes. These are giving rise to new views and larger visions. Old things are done away with and there is the embodiment of a new man to deal with. This is true in civic, political and religious life. The time has fully come for the good people of America to get right on the question of racial cooperation. The day of theorizing and antagonism must be relegated to the rear. The call is for a true type of Christian heroism that holds to the right and stands four square on the eternal principle of justice for all, the Negro to be included. Fifty years in the school-room and in the exercise of some degree of freedom together with the world awakening have brought to my people a clearer self appraisement and they are thinking in terms never before dreamed of. It is useless to talk of ever satisfying them short of a full man's chance to be and do their best. The Negroes of America are not anxious to make the greatest possible Black man, as such, but rather the best possible man, and when such a man is made he wants every opportunity which a man deserves for life, liberty and the pursuits of happiness. Upon this they rightly take their stand and from this comes a hopeful enthusiasm so essential to real development. [13]

Reverend Brown's involvement and vision presented to his son, Sterling Allen, an image of moral courage. Growing up with his father's accounts of his early years in Tennessee, his struggle for an education, and his career as a teacher and minister, Brown was impressed by his father's purposefulness and forthrightness. Though Brown's fun-loving nature rejected his father's penchant toward sobriety and reserve, Rev. Brown's standards of integrity and spiritual strength made an indelible mark on his character. [14]

There was yet another, more personal side to Brown's father, one that the poet captures in the poem "After Winter":

He snuggles his fingers
In the blacker loam
The lean months are done with,
The fat to come.

His eyes are set
On a brushwood-fire
But his heart is soaring
Higher and higher.

Though he stands ragged
An old scarecrow,
This is the way
His swift thoughts go.

Butter beans fo' Clara
Sugar corn fo' Grace
An' fo' de little feller
Runnin' space.[15]

In these poetic reminiscences of days with his father on a farm near
Laurel, Maryland, Brown portrays him as hopeful, loving, and unmistakably earthy. The depth of feeling in the poem may serve to suggest
the extent of the father's impression on his only son.

Equally impressive to the young boy were stories told about his
grandfather, "Handy." So nicknamed because of his skill as a carpen-
ter, blacksmith, wheelwright, and general handy man, he was "a strong,
able bodied" man. The following description is given of him in Reverend Brown's autobiography:

He had interesting characteristics, and though quiet in conduct and modest as
a blushing woman, he would never consent to be whipped by a master. He
was manly to the core and would fight like a tiger when attacked. He had the
distinction of whipping every overseer who tried his hand on him and was sold
several times for one reason that he would not take a flogging without fighting back.[16]

Certainly this description fired Brown's imagination, and his grandfather's manly courage became flesh many times over in the heroes of
his ballads.

For the small boy growing up at Howard University, considered by
many the capstone of higher education for Blacks, there was no dearth
of outstanding figures whom he could emulate. Teaching at Howard
then was Kelly Miller, whom Brown remembers as "a very shrewd
and very perceptive" interpreter of the racial situation.[17] Also Alain

Locke, later spokesman for the New Negro Renaissance, came to Howard in 1912 after being in Europe for several years as a Rhodes scholar. Brown recalls Locke as "very European, dapper . . . a man of tremendous intellect and genius, a very slight man with a very great big brain. . . . "[18] And among others, Brown admired Montgomery Gregory, organizer and director of the Howard Players from 1911 to 1924. Also, Brown relates with a good deal of enthusiasm his first meeting with W.E.B. Du Bois, editor of *Crisis*, and one of the leading voices in Black advancement during the period. He says that when Du Bois found out that he was the son of Rev. Sterling N. Brown, Du Bois embraced him. Brown also remembers his part in the mammoth "Star of Ethiopia Pageant," which Du Bois produced annually for several years using hundreds of school children from Dunbar and Armstrong high schools. As Brown relives the seriocomic clash of the Ethiopians from Dunbar and the Armstrong Arabs and mimicks the shrill voice of Du Bois, "And Ethiopia shall stretch out her wings . . . ," it is clear that the drama and the message were not lost on young Sterling.

However, the person who perhaps most encouraged Brown's admiration for literature and the cultural heritage of Black people was his mother. Adelaide Allen, born and raised in Tennessee, was also a graduate of Fisk University. She was valedictorian of her class and read a poem at the dedication of Livingstone Hall, one of the first buildings erected at the University. Her cousin, Georgia Gordon, was one of the original Jubilee Singers of Fisk who introduced the spirituals to the world. The heritage of Fisk University and the Negro spirituals was dear to her.

Brown remembers that she first introduced him to poetry.

My mother read . . . Longfellow; she read Burns; and she read Dunbar—grew up on Dunbar—" 'Lias! 'Lias! Bless de Lawd!'" "The Party" and "Lay me down beneaf de willers in de grass. . . . " We lived on Eleventh Street then above Lincoln Temple Church, and I remember even now her stopping her sweeping . . . now standing over that broom and reading poetry to me, and she was a good reader, great sense of rhythm.[19]

Her facility as a reader of poetry was inherited by her son, as was her love for books. "I grew up in a house of books," he said, "I have many of them."[20] Included in the family library were *The Narrative of the Life of Frederick Douglass*, W.E.B. Du Bois' *Souls of Black Folk*, the biographies of Charles Sumner and William Lloyd Garrison by Archibald H. Grimke, the books and speeches of Rev. Francis J. Grimke, and the pioneer histories of Black life written by Carter G. Woodson. The impact of these books on Brown was great. In addition to being inspiring documents of racial struggle and advancement, they were also written by men who were close friends of Brown's father. These men were outstanding examples and sources of pride. In them Brown saw firsthand and up close Black men using the power of the written word for the betterment of their people. Indeed, the love of books that his parents shared became his most precious inheritance.

Growing up in racially segregated Washington, D.C., Brown was insulated, for a while, from a city that "marked [him] as inferior." [21] He attended Lucretia Mott School, named for the famous abolitionist and feminist; it, like most public facilities, was segregated. Brown recalls that many of the schools in Washington's Black community were named after outstanding people in Black history—Thaddeus Stevens, Benjamin Banneker, Henry Highland Garnet, Paul Laurence Dunbar. Knowledge of these people was part of Sterling's "upbringing." At Mott he had a teacher by the name of Katie Lewis. She was a "beautiful reader of poetry" and further encouraged his appreciation for poetry. By the time he got to Dunbar High School, Brown's experience had been far more influenced by his associations in Black schools and his father's church than by the specter of segregation in theaters, dining halls, museums, and most public facilities with the exception of public transportation.

Years later, reflecting on the historical and social ramifications of a situation that forced Black children and teachers into what were euphemistically called "separate but equal" facilities, Brown says:

First rate graduates of certain colleges if they were white could get better jobs. They could go into business; they could go into banking; they could go into industry. Our "talented tenth," in DuBois' words, had to go into very few fields—law, medicine, teaching. So, at Dunbar High School, we had a number of Phi Beta Kappas (as teachers). Now, I haven't worked out any statistical survey . . . , but I think there were more Phi Beta Kappa Black teachers at Dunbar and Armstrong and Cordoza than there would be in the white schools. [22]

A reporter for *New Yorker* magazine bears out Sterling Brown's theory and says that the school's success results from "a combination of its student's social class and a peculiar set of historical circumstances that existed in the early years of its development."

These circumstances were what produced Dunbar's faculty—the best that any all-black high school has ever had. As almost every early Dunbar graduate likes to boast, all the teachers had B.A.s, M.A.s, or Ph.D.s, and many were members of Phi Beta Kappa. Why was this so? First of all, the federal government paid black teachers in Washington the same salaries as white teachers—possibly the only place in the South where such parity existed. That policy alone might have been enough to attract highly qualified teachers. But without another special circumstance there might have been no such teachers to attract. Many of the exceptional black teachers who came to Dunbar had turned to teaching only because there was not much else for them to do. In the early years of Dunbar's history, black college graduates—however well-trained, however brilliant—were seldom hired by white institutions in any serious intellectual capacity. Those who were not lucky enough to be lawyers or doctors—and who did not wish to be postal clerks, low-level government workers, soldiers, Pullman porters, or manual laborers—found that teaching was the most distinguished career open to them. And those who resorted to teaching either joined the faculty of a black university like Howard or headed for Dunbar High School.[23]

Certainly, Dunbar High School could boast a distinguished, accomplished teaching staff. Two of Brown's teachers, Angelina W. Grimke and Jessie Fauset, were creative artists in their own right. Angelina Grimke, author of a play, short stories, and numerous poems, was one of Brown's English teachers. Jessie Fauset, remembered for her novels portraying the Black middle class, taught French and Latin at Dunbar for many years. Brown recalls that she was "brilliant" and "a little impatient with stupid kids."[24] In history, Brown had Haley Douglass, the grandson of Frederick Douglass, and another man named Neville Thomas, president of the Washington branch of the NAACP. In one interview Brown tells an ancedote about Neville Thomas which illustrates the race consciousness that prevaded the school.

He was tough. He was teaching us ancient history, but we knew a way, if we hadn't studied, to get by him, and that was to start talking about race discrimination. . . . He would ask us about the Peloponnesian War, and we would say, "Yes, Mr.Thomas. But we want to tell you we went into Hecht's store last evening, and they wouldn't let us eat at the diner. . . . " Then he would give us a long lecture. He was a great NAACP man. He was a great teacher. He might have gotten away from Rome, but he taught us a lot about what it meant to be a Negro in the United States.[25]

The quality of the educational experience at Dunbar was borne out in many of its graduates who achieved distinction later in life. Percy Barnes, professor of chemistry at Howard University; William H. Hastie, former governor of the United States Virgin Islands and U.S. Circuit Judge; and Charles Drew, who gained national repute as chief researcher in blood plasma, all attended Dunbar during Brown's years there. Brown also knew and admired Jean Toomer, a former student at M Street High School, who later became one of the most gifted writers to surface in the 1920s. Two other distinguished alumni of Dunbar High School—Mercer Cook, educator and son of the famous musician, Will Marion Cook, and W. Montaque Cobb—remember Sterling Brown from high school days as "Dutch." They recall that he had achieved the singular honor of making captain of the Cadet Corps in his junior year and major in his senior year. According to Mercer Cook, " 'Dutch' not only led the Corps but also organized the debating society, won the scholastic honors, and won the unquestioned leadership of the student body, and most important, the friendship, admiration and respect of all his peers."[26]

For Brown, his experiences in the Washington public schools were sources of pride. The influence of his parents, teachers, and acquaintances indelibly marked his sense of identity and his outlook. Thus, he left Dunbar High School fortified for the anonymity he would face as a student at Williams College in Williamstown, Massachusetts.

At the age of seventeen, Brown entered Williams College on an academic scholarship. For many years it had been customary that Williams would award a scholarship to Dunbar's top student. Brown was annoyed by the obvious tokenism of the tradition, yet he admitted that, at the time, it was considered "a distinction." Brown was among a handful of Blacks who attended Williams; they were kept apart from the rest of the student body because the officials believed "they would be happier together." Actually, separation was nothing new for Brown. Until coming to Williams, the only white boy with whom he had associated closely was the son of the druggist who did business in his neighborhood. While the subtle racial affronts and the separation were often demeaning to him, the hardest fact to accept was the realization that he "was nobody up there," not "even a token."[27]

Brown tells a story that illustrates the extent of the Blacks' isolation at Williams. When he came to Williams, the first thing he did was buy a phonograph and whatever jazz was available, including Mamie Smith's recording of "Crazy Blues."

I would play this record in my room, but my buddies who were ahead of me in school didn't want my playing it, so they would not come over until after midnight, and they would come over and make these . . . window things [blinds] come down and then put a towel over it, you see, and play the "Crazy Blues."[28]

Brown makes the point that they wanted to hear the music but did not want the white students in the neighboring room to know that they were listening to (what was then considered) barrel house music. Though he considered their actions phony, Brown admits that he and his Black classmates were troubled by an acute double consciousness that existed among the Black students scattered throughout the academic diaspora.

Therefore, whether by design or choice, Brown's activities revolved around a nucleus of Black students at Williams. Allison Davis, the late John Dewey Professor at the University of Chicago; Carter Marshall, who taught medicine at Yale University and Howard; Ralph Scott, who later worked in government and in school administration in Washington, D.C.; and Mortimer Weaver, who taught at Howard, made up the handful of Blacks with whom Brown associated at Williams. Brown, Davis, and Scott would "go for long walks and decide the race problem; we decided the problem of women which was a serious thing here." He added, "This was a monastic institution and the opportunities for, let us say, conversation with the fair sex were limited."[29] However, Brown occupied his time serving on the debating team, waiting tables in Berkshire Hall, pledging Omega Psi Phi, and playing tennis for the Common Club Tennis Team. Brown and Allison Davis teamed up for an imposing doubles combination and won national competitions. He also made Phi Beta Kappa in 1921.

At Williams, Brown learned to think critically about literature. Probably the teacher who most influenced him was George Dutton.

Describing Dutton as a "sarcastic, sharp-witted man who didn't suffer fools gladly," Brown remembers that Dutton was an unconventional professor interested in critical realism, modern fiction, and American literature (then considered a less than respectable area).[30] On one occasion, Dutton was discussing Joseph Conrad and related an incident that had special meaning for Brown. Joseph Conrad was being lionized in England—H. G. Wells and Galsworthy and other notable writers and critics were present to honor the Polish novelist.

Conrad was sitting over in the corner, quiet, not participating. Dutton said he was brooding and probably thinking about his native Poland and the plight of his people. He's there in London [lionized], but he's still not of it. He's lost. Dutton looked right at me and I had a feeling then—and this is over fifty years—I still have the feeling that he was talking to me. Now, don't let the lionizing fool you . . . you've got a job to do.[31]

Dutton taught Brown the writers of the Romantic Movement and the modern novel. Though Dutton taught the British novel, he encouraged Brown to read Flaubert's *Madame Bovary*, Dostoevski's *The Brothers Karamazov*, and the novels of Sinclair Lewis and Henry James. Exposed to the critical realism of George Dutton, Brown discovered an approach to literature that he could embrace.

When Brown graduated from Williams in 1922, he had already begun to write poetry. As a graduate student at Harvard University, he discovered a book that opened new vistas in his understanding and appreciation of poetry. The book, *Modern American Poetry*, by Louis Untermeyer, struck Brown as a bold manifesto proclaiming the new direction poetry would take in the future. He was affected by the editor's contagious enthusiasm as he hailed the vigorous new poets who ushered in a respect for the use of everyday speech, freedom of choice in subject matter, and an unembarrassed celebration of American culture. Untermeyer wrote in his introduction:

Suddenly the "new" poetry burst upon us with unexpected vigor and extraordinary variety. . . . For three years the skies continued to discharge such strange and divergent phenomena as Vachael Lindsay's *General William Booth Enters into Heaven* (1913), James Oppenheim's *Songs For the New Age* (1914), the first anthology of *The Imagists Poems* (1914), *Challenge* (1914), Amy Lowell's *Sword Blades and Poppy Seed* (1914), Lindsay's *The Congo and Other Poems* (1914), Robert Frost's *North of Boston* (1914), Edgar Lee Master's *Spoon*

River Anthology (1915), Carl Sandburg's *Chicago Poems* (1916). By 1917, the "new" poetry was ranked as "America's first national art"; its success was sweeping its sales unprecedented. People who never before had read verse turned to it and found they could not only read but relish it. . . . The new work spoke to them in their own language. And it did more: it spoke to them of what they had scarcely ever heard expressed; it was not only closer to their soil but nearer to their souls.[32]

Brown read the work of the Imagists. He approved of their insistence on using the language of common speech and employing the exact word, in lieu of the merely decorative word. He upheld their right to freedom in choice of subject and later vigorously exercised that freedom in his own poetry. Although Brown did not restrict his verse form to the *vers libre* of Amy Lowell's and Hilda Doolittle's lines, he was impressed by the Imagists' resourcefulness in creating new rhythms. Brown saw the Imagists attempting to present the image exactly, clearly, and with considerable concentration.[33] Brown later would bring a similar power of concentration to bear on a portrait of a Virginia farm woman. The poem is cited here in part:

> The winter of her year has come to her,
> This wizened woman, spare of frame, but great
> Of heart, erect and undefeated yet.
>
> Grief has been hers, before this wintry time.
> Death has paid calls, unmannered, uninvited;
> Low mounds have swollen in the fenced off corner,
> Over brown children, marked by white-washed stones.
> She has seen hopes that promised a fine harvest
> Burnt by the drought; or bitten by the hoarfrost;
> Or washed up and drowned by the unlooked for rains.
> And as a warning blast of her own winter,
> Death, the harsh overseer, shouted to her man,
> Who answering slowly went over the hill.
>
> She, puffing on a jagged slow-burning pipe,
> By the low hearthfire, knows her winter now.
> But she has strength and steadfast hardihood.
> Deep-rooted is she, even as the oaks,
> Hardy as perennials about her door.
> The circle of the seasons brings no fear,

Folks all gits used to what dey sees so often;
And she has helps that throng her glowing fire
Mixed with the smoke hugging her grizzled head.[34]

For example, demonstrated in the lines, "Low mounds have swollen in the fenced off corner,/Over brown children, marked by white-washed stones" is Brown's commitment to the precise wording and the presentation of the clear, crisp image attributed to Imagist poetry. According to Glenn Hughes, the Imagists took the highest traditions of all great literature—"hardness of outline, clarity of image, brevity, suggestiveness, freedom from metrical laws"[35] and turned them into "vivid patches of life."[36] Brown saw value in their literary tenets. However, more than any single statement of principle defended by the Imagists, Brown identified with their militant spirit. The Imagists took poetry out of the domain of conservative critics and academic reactionaries, who were stranded without timeworn standards to guide them, and brought poetry into an arena of controversy. For Brown, the Imagists' efforts constituted one of the healthier signs that poetry was ridding itself of the effete and taking on muscle. Above all, the Imagists stimulated new verse forms and a vitality of expression in a period when interest had waned for poetry.

However, more than any popular poets of the period, Edwin Arlington Robinson and Robert Frost had the greatest influence on Brown's literary outlook. Edwin A. Robinson, Brown said, "took up the undistinguished, the failures and showed the extraordinary in ordinary lives."[37] Robinson's sympathetic portraits of the tragic, ironical, and pathetic lives of people in a small fishing village in Maine intrigued the young Black poet. Portraits such as the frustrated dreamer Miniver Cheevy and the enigmatic Richard Cory confirmed Brown's intuition that the drama of life was everywhere present in the lives of ordinary people. Brown also admired Robinson's technical skill. With a virtuoso hand, Robinson achieved a fresh, natural, vigorous verse using traditional forms, a feat that Brown would later attempt in his own poetry. Robinson's influence on Brown is reflected in such poems as "Maumee Ruth," "Southern Cop," and "Georgie Grimes." In the latter poem, Brown has used a tightly controlled rhymed stanza to convey the essence of a fear-ridden man who has just killed his woman.

Georgie Grimes, with a red suitcase,
    Sloshes onward through the rain,

Georgie Grimes, with a fear behind him,
   Will not come back again.

Georgie remembers hot words, lies,
   The knife, and a pool of blood,
And suddenly her staring eyes,
   With their light gone out for good.

Georgie mutters over and over,
   Stumbling through the soggy clay,
"No livin' woman got de right
   To do no man dat way."[38]

The poem in its directness and economy bears comparison with Robinson's "Richard Cory," a brilliantly executed poem that searchingly portrays a regal gentleman who "put a bullet through his head."[39] Robinson, "as a psychological portrait painter," generally influenced Brown's explorations in folk portraiture. The memorable figures of Ma Rainey, Sam Smiley, and the magnificent Sporting Beasley "manifest that searching for truth, the probing analysis" that distinguished much of the work of Edwin Arlington Robinson.[40] In Robinson, Brown also recognized that a welding of the traditional and the original, the oral and the literary, often produced striking effects. And this recognition prompted Brown's experimentation which resulted in poems like "Memphis Blues" and "Southern Road," two of his finest efforts.

In Robert Frost, another New England poet, Brown found a poet concerned with the lives of the people. Recording as he wrote the language, customs, and temperament of the people of New Hampshire, Frost was able to reveal their spirit. For Brown, the people of "The Death of the Hired Man," "Birches," and "The Mending Wall," to name a few, were drawn with a penetrating realism which exposed a complex system of human emotions: one man's insistence upon his dignity and independence, the dogged adherence of another man to the custom of mending the wall despite the challenge of another who questions the efficacy of good fences, and the vitality of the human spirit which encourages a man grown "weary of consideration" to be transported by the memory that he, too, was once a swinger of birches.

Fifty years after Brown first read the poetry of Robert Frost, he acknowledges his debt to Frost in a speech given at Williams College in 1973.

Now I'm going to close with a poem from a man who taught at Dartmouth. He comes from this neighborhood, and he wrote about New Hampshire and North Boston, a man who has meant a great deal to me. Langston Hughes has meant much to me, Richard Wright, Claude McKay, Ralph Ellison, but I have learned also from people like Robert Frost.

This poem is called "In Dive's Dive." I met Robert Frost once and quoted this to him, and he said that I was the only person he knew that knew this poem and respected it. I loved it. He asked me did I play poker, and I told him no, and he said that he didn't play good poker either. We talked about poker and there was a whole slough of new poets there. He and I were the old poets talking about "In Dives' Dive."[41]

Brown was enthusiastic about the poem. He saw Frost alluding to the Biblical character Dives, who captured the imagination of one of the writers of the spirituals—"Rich man Dives, he lived so well, when he died he found a home in hell." He saw Frost hooking the allusion up with the modern day equivalent of a den of iniquity and compressing these ideas into a stunning epigram that talks about much more than a poker game.[42]

Like Frost, Brown was late in years, and, as he surveyed his life, he found a string of losses. But like Frost, "he is not laying any blame on anybody." Explicating the poem, Brown said, "I, Frost, an American individual, will take my chances. I'm not a good poker player, but I'm not complaining. It does not matter to me who runs the dive. . . . I'm going to play my hand out with the cards that come." For Brown the poem is "a strong statement of a man's belief in America and himself."[43]

As Brown identified with the gambler's stoicism, he also intuitively understood the stoical mood that pervades much of Frost's poetry— "at once wise and sad, the happy sad blend of the drinking song."[44] There are no tears in this writer; there are only revelations. The passionless acknowledgement of death's victory over a young sawmill worker in "Out, Out—," the portrait of a tormented husband who silently grieves the loss of his first born in "Home Burial," the revelation in "An Old Man's Winter Night" that one condition of old age is loneliness—all wed Frost to stoicism. Brown later infused into poems like "Southern Road," "Memphis Blues," and "Strange Legacies," what James Weldon Johnson called "that not much known characteristic, Negro stoicism."[45] The quality that allows the gambler to "take a look at another five" is essentially the quality of Brown's rural folk who, serene in the face of adversity, say, "Guess we'll give it one mo' try."

Frost and Robinson passed on to the younger poet something of their art. Brown later identified himself with Robinson's dramatic technique by creating a series of personalities who became the subject matter of his poetry. Brown's vision, like Robinson's, was essentially tragic.[46] In the manner of Frost, he rooted his portraits in realism. Not a photographic realist, Brown preferred to show the essential truth of life, in Frost's words "to strip it to form."[47]

Brown saw the poetry of Frost and Robinson standing in sharp contrast to much of late nineteenth century poetry. He said that with these poets, "you got a view of life that was so far from a pastoral view. This was hardship. This was tragedy; but it was not the gentle kind of, I think, condescending attitude to the people that you would find in James Whitcomb Riley, or as far as our people were concerned . . . in Dunbar (in Dunbar's portraits)."[48] According to Brown, the "harsh edges to this life" were softened in the sentimental idylls and cheerful, homely philosophies that were the stock in trade of writers such as Riley and Eugene Field.

The new trend in regionalism Brown applauded; as Frost and Robinson had brought their cherished sections of New England life, Edgar Lee Masters in *Spoon River Anthology* vivified a small Midwestern town. In this exceptional work, Brown found regionalism and realism working nicely to reveal the frank, often brutal, truths of life in this section. The folk of the town were examined under a searching light with their hypocrisies, their triumphs, and their defeats in full view. For Brown, Masters testified in these epitaphs to the rich material that was available to the writer who sought to explore fully the lives of ordinary people. Masters writes:

Life all around me here in the village:
tragedy, comedy, valor and truth, courage,
constancy, heroism, failure—all in the loom,
and oh, what patterns![49]

No doubt, Masters' choice of subject matter met with the young poet's approval, for Brown a few years later explored in much the same way the depths and complexity of rural Black folk. However, while Masters' outlook was pessimistic, Brown salvaged from despair what he could of hope. While not indulging in boundless optimism, Brown demonstrated an unshakeable faith in his race and believed in his people's ability to advance even under the most trying circumstances.

Brown's interest in delving into the depths of human experience and character necessitated a close look at language. In an interview he said, "The poets that struck me were those who were poets of the people and poets of direct—not florid . . . American speech."[50] His fascination with language, which he said began when as a child he was exposed to the "primitive raciness" of his schoolmates' speech, developed into a mature appreciation of the power of the racy, vigorous, individualized speech that was so much a fixture of the "new poetry."

However, Brown realized that what the new poets were doing with language was not new. More than a hundred years before, William Wordsworth announced in the preface to the second edition of the *Lyrical Ballads* (1800) that he had adopted for selected poems the "plainer and more emphatic language spoken by humble, rustic folk." Wordsworth attempted to capture the language of men who "convey their feelings and notions in simple and unelaborated expressions, a language he considered more permanent, and far more philosophical, than that which is frequently substituted for it by poets. . . . "[51] Though Brown was aware of Coleridge's charge that Wordsworth's claim lay wide of his actual mark and that Wordsworth was a far better philosophical poet than a dramatic one, Brown saw Wordsworth exploring, with varying degrees of success, the potentialities of common speech.[52] Brown was also aware of the efforts of the Irish Literary Movement, particularly such writers as Dublin born playwright, John M. Synge, who took "a dialect that had been debased by English authors and got to the genuine quality of folk speech."[53]

As Synge spoke the language of the Aran Islander, Brown saw the American poet, Carl Sandburg, using the rough, coarse, slangy speech of Chicago laborers. According to Louis Untermeyer, "In Sandburg, industrial America has its voice: *Chicago Poems* (1916), *Cornhuskers* (1918), *Smoke and Steel* (1920) vibrate with the immense purring of dynamos, the swishing rhythms of threshing arms, the gossip and laughter of construction gangs, the gigantic and tireless energy of the modern machine."[54] As Brown was to later point out in *Negro Poetry and Drama*, Sandburg "included snapshots of Negroes caught at work and play'' and showed ''his great interest in Negro folk music'' in his *American Song Bag*.[55]

Brown was also aware of the new atmosphere that supported freedom of thinking and experimentation. Vachel Lindsay, perhaps the most influential white poet on Black life at that time, experimented with integrating poetic forms with musical cadences and attempted to capture the syncopated jazz and ragtime rhythms in his popular collection *Congo and Other Poems* (1914). Citing specifically the poem ''Congo,'' Brown would read its lines with vigor. He admitted that he enjoyed the rhythm. Lindsay was breaking up the meter in a way that was provocative. However, because Lindsay set out to write, as the subtitle would suggest, ''A Study of the Negro Race,'' Brown believed that Lindsay failed directly in proportion to his lofty intentions to treat the subject adequately, and he tagged Lindsay's attempt ''phony.'' Though Brown challenged what he considered to be a superficial and condescending treatment of Black themes, he was impressed with ''the marvelous ragtime fling'' Lindsay got into his poems, with Lindsay's interest in breaking up the rhythm, and with his free handling of new material.[56]

In fact, the poets who most appealed to Brown during this period (when he was himself crystallizing his poetic approach) were those who used freedom as their banner: freedom to choose new materials; freedom from stilted, florid poetic diction, freedom to experiment with language, form, and subject matter in new, unconventional ways; and freedom from the kind of provincialism and Puritanism that Van Wyck Brooks said in *America's Coming of Age* (1915) has stymied the growth of literature and art in America. Consequently, several of the literary attitudes and poetic techniques that were characteristic of the works of Robinson, Frost, Masters, Sandburg, and Lindsay were incorporated into Brown's own poetic approach. He shared with them their interest in the poetic potential of the American idiom and their interest in the underprivileged. He accepted with equal enthusiasm Whitman's mandate to find new words, new potentialities of speech and ''a better, fresher, busier sphere.''[57] He found increasing pleasure in discovering the power and vitality of language, especially the language of the common man. He also shared with them their expansive and democratic approach to people by exploring and appreciating the dramatic and epic nature of ordinary life.

Along with these American poets, the late nineteenth-century English poet, Alfred Edward Housman, also had a significant impact on Brown's development as a poet. A. E. Housman was essentially a poet of dramatic situation. Generally in his poems he allowed his characters to convey the essence of the mood, emotion, story, idea, attitude, or meaning intended by the poem. Similarly, Brown later adopted a dramatic framework for many of his poems. Specifically, Housman's "When Smoke Stood Up From Ludlow" and Brown's "Old Man Buzzard" offer a good opportunity for comparison. In Housman's poem published in *A Shropshire Lad*, the poet creates a clever dramatic framework in which a blackbird flutes a prophetic warning about the inevitability of death to a young farmer plowing in the field. In "Old Man Buzzard," which appeared in *Southern Road*, Brown adopts a similar theme and framework to his purpose. The buzzard admonishes the farmer Fred, who toils in the fields like the young yeoman, that with no respect to persons "Death comes a-orderin'/Folks aroun'." Yet in the final stanza Fred, unlike Housman's man, does not allow the thoughts of mortality to cloud his vision and sounds a note of acceptance. Though markedly different in idiom—the stiff British idiom has been replaced by the idiom of the Black folk tale—and in tone— Housman's romantic sentimentality gives way to Brown's realism— Brown's close reading of Housman is apparent. Also, as the above poems would suggest, several of the themes that would later figure prominently in Brown's poetry were handled by Housman. As Cleanth Brooks observed, "Two of Housman's constant themes are courage and stoic endurance, and these are themes which are almost obsessive for several of our best contemporary writers."[58] Brooks named William Faulkner and Ernest Hemingway as two such writers. It would be safe to say that for Sterling Brown these themes also became central to his poetic expression. In a sense, the theme of courage forges a kinship between Housman's young soldiers recruited to die for the Queen and the tragic young men in Brown's poems who find themselves in an undeclared war with lynch mobs, convict camp guards, and "Southern cops." Like Housman, Brown will come to celebrate courage, strength, and manliness in his poems.

However, for this analogy to be useful, knowing what Brown rejected in Housman is as significant as knowing what he emulated. Brown rejected the poetic diction of Housman's Victorian period. Also, Brown was not to be confined by the same "narrow ambit of interests" which Cleanth Brooks attributes to Housman.[59] Brown's gallery of characters was full and his scope wide. It is necessary, furthermore, to separate Brown from Housman's characteristic fault of slipping into sentimentality. As Cleanth Brooks suggests, Housman had problems in maintaining integrity of tone. He was not always successful in achieving "an intense sympathetic response" without making a direct appeal for the reader's sympathy.[60] In contrast, one of Brown's characteristic strengths, according to Louis Untermeyer, is his detachment which allows him "to expostulate without ranting, or even raising his voice, and laugh without adopting the comic attitude too often expected of the Negro as entertainer. . . . He does not paint himself blacker than he is, nor does he slouch in grotesque or falsely sentimental verse to win the applause of a white audience. . . . "[61] Finally Brown's outlook cannot be subsumed under the rubric of pessimism which has been Housman's lot. Brown absorbed the folk's tragic sense of life that required a full facing of its realities and a strength to endure. Nevertheless, despite the differences that separate the poetic approaches of Housman and Brown, the influence of the elder poet on Brown is evident.

Thus, undoubtedly, Brown's interest in language and the common man was encouraged by these poets. It made inevitable the exploration of his own folk tradition that led to the achievement, with the publication of *Southern Road*, of a portrayal of folk life that exhibited a genuine and deep understanding of folk thought and feeling unmatched by any other New Negro Renaissance writer. By the time Brown graduated from Harvard in 1923, he had already accepted an approach to poetry that needed only the inspiration of a catalyst to set his creativity into motion.

After graduating from Harvard, Brown became convinced that he wanted to teach. Though he was discouraged by several friends who thought he could put his talents to better use, he was so sure of the importance of teaching that he even influenced other Williams men to go into the profession. At the suggestion of both his father and historian Carter G. Woodson, Brown went to Virginia Seminary in Lynchburg, where he taught English for the next three years. There Brown became intensely interested in writing. For the first fime, he said, "I found something to write about. I found a world of great interest and it was a world of people and the poetry of the time—the poetry that I was reading—was a people's poetry."[62]

The Black people of the rural communities surrounding Lynchburg, as steeped in the traditions of the spirituals, the blues, the aphorisms, the old lies, and the superstitions of folk life as they were in the purplish red clay of the foothills of the Blue Ridge mountains, taught the young professor something of folk humor, irony, fortitude, and shrewdness. In turn, Brown's honest, uncondescending friendship with several of these people brought him into the inner circle of their community. They told him the humorous stories that were kept like fine, aged wines until the right time. With equal ease, they boasted about their first generation "Seminary" students and lambasted the village scoundrels. They took special pleasure in introducing the young professor to "white lightning" and "life everlasting," indigenous products of the region.

Among those people Brown met while at Virginia Seminary, two stand out: Mrs. Bibby and Calvin "Big Boy" Davis, both of whom figure significantly in his later poetry. Mrs. Bibby, the mother of one of his students, typified in many ways the tough-mindedness and strength Brown admired in these people. Brown later portrayed her in two contrasting poems, "Virginia Portrait" and "Sister Lou," included in *Southern Road* (1932). In something of a portrait in its own right, Brown told an anecdote that is marked by the presence of this small, spry "Indian looking woman." One evening about eight or ten of the neighbors had gathered in her kitchen to talk with the young professor who visited regularly. Smoking her clay pipe, which she lit by picking up coals from the fireplace, Mrs. Bibby sat silently listening to them talk about Brother Moore, the village "ne're do well."

Brother Moore was a no good, trifling, shiftless guy as ever was, but everybody there would say "but he mean good." Brother Moore's hog would get out and get into somebody's corn field, "well—you know, but he mean good" and so . . . you build that up until finally my little friend, Mrs. Bibby, takes this pipe out of her mouth and spat at the fireplace . . . and said "well he may mean good but he do so doggone po'."[63]

She cut quickly through the sentimentality to the keen perception— "but, he do so doggone po'." To the young teacher with his sensibility tuned away from romantic sentimentality toward the truer notes of realism and irony, her response struck just the right chord. On the many occasions that Brown was in her home, he became aware of her "quiet nonchalance," her "courtly dignity of speech and carriage," "her strength and steadfast hardihood,'' and her grief-tempered faith. Her disappointments when the crops were ruined by drought or by unexpected frost, her grief over her children who predeceased her, her simple joys are all captured in a pair of remarkably drawn portraits of a woman who was "illiterate, and somehow very wise."

Brown recalls that a group of his students brought Calvin "Big Boy Davis" to his classroom. This was the first of many times the wandering guitar player would come to his classroom and to the school parties to play his spirituals and "gut bucket" blues for the few coins that would keep him going. Brown remembers his friend as a "wonderful guy, head taller than I, huge shoulders. . . . I learned a great deal from him, learned the best John Henry, I'd ever heard."[64] In the poem "When de Saints Go Ma'ching Home," Brown reconstructs one of Big Boy's memorable performances. The poet limns his portrait: "His face a brown study beneath his torn brimmed hat,/His broad shoulders slouching, his old box strung/Around his neck."[65] The poem's dedication reads: "In Memories of Days Before He Was Chased Out of Town for Vagrancy," recalling Big Boy's up and down career as a roustabout. In the poem "Odyssey of Big Boy," Brown gives a freer picture of Big Boy; though many of the experiences are not those of the wandering guitar player, the poem vividly suggests the lore of the roustabout as he jumps the freight from one town to another, as he goes from one menial job to the next with little to relish except the sweet gals on his knees and thoughts of immortality. Big Boy was also the prototype for "Long Gone," symbolizing the wanderlust of Black men who by compulsion and necessity spent most of their life on the road.

In Brown's subsequent teaching posts at Lincoln University in Missouri (1926–1928) and at Fisk University (1928–1929), he found himself wandering to the hotels and the shoeshine parlors in Jefferson City, to the Black business establishments in Nashville, Tennessee, and to the rural communities in the Black belt of the South. Also, one of his students at Lincoln University, Nathaniel A. Sweets, remembers that "there were those who considered 'Prof' Brown a bit 'tetched' to be spending so much time with 'those weird characters' who frequented 'The Foot,' an area that bordered the campus."[66] On the back roads of "The Foot," Brown conversed with Revelations, a self-appointed prophet of doom. He also spent long hours listening to the tales told by a waiter named "Slim" in the Jefferson City Hotel. He later wrote a series of humorous poems with this master yarn spinner as the central figure.

When Brown arrived at Fisk University, where President Thomas Elsa Jones was intent on faculty building, there was an assemblage of brilliant and accomplished teachers, among them: Black sociologist Charles S. Johnson; Horace Mann Bond, distinguished scholar in education and history; musicologist John Work; Edith St. Elmo Brady, first Black Ph.D. in Chemistry; and Aaron Douglas, outstanding artist.[67] However, as Lewis W. Jones, one of Brown's Fisk colleagues recalls, Brown was just as likely to be exchanging lies at Gillie's Barbershop as engaging in get-togethers with the faculty. Brown describes Gillie (Will Gilchrist) as "the best liar I ever ran across."[68] Jones writes: "His [Gillie's] commentaries on life and people were always related with a straight face. He never showed any emotion, however much his audience would crack up, laughing until their eyes watered. He and Sterling became friends, and on Sterling's recommendation other Fisk faculty members became Gillie's customers and audience."[69]

These were the people whose language and outlook held a certain fascination for Brown. More than fifty years later, Brown said:

I was interested in how a person . . . could say so much without using too many words. The blues line, "You gotta hanful of gimme and a mouth full of much obliged," that to me said plenty—"Sun's gonna shine in my back do' some day," "My girl's got a heart like a rock tossed in the sea," "my gal's got teeth like Klondike Gold/Everytime she smiles, I lose my loving soul," or, in the spirituals, "Don't know what my mother wanna' stay here/For this ol' world ain been no friend to her"—lines like that are just the lines of the guy in the street. . . . They had a richness that to me was a very attractive kind of thing and what it revealed was what I hadn't found too much of. I didn't see it in *Porgy and Bess*. I didn't see it in the comic stereotypes that the *Cosmopolitan* and *Redbook* were so full of; I didn't see it in Roark Bradford. I saw something—in this—I saw a very tonic shrewdness; I saw an ability to take it. . . . I saw fortitude; I saw an irony and the humor . . . a double edged humor built up of irony and shrewd observation.[70]

Brown listened well to these people; many of them were the parents and relatives of his students, and he found in them a tragic sense of life, an outlook that he later explored and absorbed into his poetry. Brown also found an unbeatable spirit that enabled them to accept and endure life. These people Brown attempted to portray. Like Jean

Toomer's Georgia, the South opened up Sterling Brown. His experiences there convinced him of the possibility of poetry that would speak the language of his people, as it revealed their souls.

Appropriately, too, it was in the South, where his love for books and language had been wedded with a sharpened sensitivity to the ways of folk life, that he met Daisy Turnbull, his wife of more than fifty years. On one of his several trips to Roanoke to play tennis with his friend Authur Downing, he met her. He was attracted to the auburn-haired beauty with "brave eyes." She was attracted to the young, agile tennis player who wore his cool urbanity as naturally as his tweed coat and amber-colored pipe. When asked about their courtship, Brown said, in predictable fashion: "I just about bought the railroad, the Norfolk and Western Railroad. Of course, I bought the Southern, too, because I had a girl up in Baltimore . . . bought a lot of railroads then." [71]

Daisy Turnbull graduated from Virginia Seminary and College before Brown went there to teach. She taught school for one year after graduating and then went to Philadelphia where she worked as a secretary. When her sister became seriously ill, she came back to Roanoke to take care of her young children. It was then that she met Sterling Brown. They were married in December of 1927. Daisy went with her husband to Lincoln University in Missouri and to Fisk University in Tennessee.

Daisy Turnbull Brown helped Brown live his vision. On the occasion of their fiftieth wedding anniversary, she recited superbly Housman's poem "Loveliest of trees, the cherry now." Then, "three-score years and ten," she had seen many springs with the blooming of the cherry trees and knew they would not come again. The sensitivity and depth that she brought to the reading convinced those who heard her that she was somehow more than the proverbial woman behind the great man.

Daisy Turnbull Brown had grown up in the house her grandparents had built after Emancipation. She had grown up hearing the tales her grandmother told of their harrowing experience as slaves to a prominent family in Roanoke. Of very fair complexion, she had also grown aware of the ironies of the color line. Some whose complexions were as fair as hers had chosen to cross over to the quasi-freedom of the white world. For Daisy Brown, however, that option was unacceptable because she had learned too well her family's history and its heritage of slavery.

Her background, though, explains only in part the quiet strength that was a mainstay in her relationship with Brown for more than half a century. Daisy Brown believed implicitly in those values that Brown espoused. She was the first to applaud her husband's rejection of the typically bourgeois stance with its contempt for the lower classes and its evasion of "life." She shared Brown's enthusiasm for people, his infectious humor, and his keen poetic sense that made her at once his sharpest critic and most devoted admirer. Because she recognized her husband's tendency to be highly critical of his work and his tendency to abandon work that did not reach his near-perfectionist standards, she was greatly responsible for encouraging Brown to complete the books and articles that appeared in the 1930s and 1940s, Brown's most productive period.

By 1927 Brown received his first attention as a promising poet. Though a couple of years before he had won second prize for an essay on Roland Hayes submitted to an *Opportunity* contest, it was not until 1927 that he tested the waters with the prize-winning poem "When De Saints Go Ma'ching Home." In that same year Countee Cullen included six of his unpublished poems in the anthology, *Caroling Dusk*. During this period several of the poems that would later be published in *Southern Road* were printed in such magazines as *The Crisis*, *Opportunity*, *Contempo*, and *Ebony and Topaz*. Brown had reached a significant level in his development as a poet. He now knew what he wanted his poetry to be.

I wanted what Milton said about poetry. I wanted it too be simple, sensuous and impassioned, and I still stand by that. A lot of critics . . . don't think that there's a critical position behind what Langston and I were doing. . . . What I wanted was a simple, sensuous poetry. By sensuous, I mean that it makes you see; it makes you feel; it makes you hear. Your senses are pulled in—in other words, the experience is rendered. . . . I wanted it to be impassioned; that is, I wanted to have a feeling there that was communicated to the reader. I didn't want to yell; I wanted to make him yell, but I wanted to use a kind of language that would make him yell. . . . I wanted to communicate, and I found a language that was pithy, economical, metaphoric, imaginative, and, . . . capable of expressing all ranges of human emotions.[72]

In Brown's search for an expressive language and its accompanying literary tradition, his attention was naturally drawn to Paul Laurence Dunbar, the popular poet of his parents' generation. From his childhood he had cherished his mother's reading of such favorites as "Candle-Lighting Time," "Little Brown Baby," "Turning the Children in Bed," and "In the Morning." The warmth and good cheer of the hearthside and an aura of pastoral contentment combined with snatches of humor and catchy rhythms made the poems truly memorable. Later, as a student of poetry, Brown closely considered Dunbar's qualities and found that he was not only the first American Black to "feel the Negro life aesthetically and express it lyrically," as William Dean Howells had claimed two decades before, but also the first American poet "to handle Negro folk life with any degree of fullness."[73]

This was not unqualified praise, however, for Brown saw Dunbar's poetry as limited in several important areas. Dunbar's forced mimicking of the plantation tradition conventions popularized by Irwin Russell, Joel Chandler Harris, and Thomas Nelson Page resulted in "unworthy perpetuation of plantation sentiments" in such poems as "Parted" and "Corn Song." For Brown, Dunbar's giving poetic voice to such sentiments as the weary slaves gratefully singing to the delight of a kindly master, freedmen giving back their freedom, or slaves, separated by the auction block, blithely believing in God's purpose, at best perpetuated "a cruel misreading of history."[74] Dunbar ignored the hardships of Black life; the insults, inequities, peonage, brutalities, and lynching present in peasant life were conspicuously absent from his pastoral poetry. Brown was convinced that any poet intent upon showing a true picture of folk life would not allow these omissions. Also, Brown found Dunbar's tone of conciliation with its concomitant insistence on "forgetting and forgiving" evasive and backward glancing.

Aside from stock situations and characterizations, Brown regretted that Dunbar rarely used his poetic talent to capture the "wit and beauty possible to folk speech." Rather, Dunbar was content to copy the pat phrases and unfortunate misspelling of conventionalized dialect poetry. Though, as Brown noted, Dunbar regretted that the world had turned from his "deeper notes to praise a jingle in a broken tongue," this recognition was not enough to prompt him to explore fully the potentialities of dialect.

However, Brown was clearly impressed by the achievement of this young poet whose life was poignantly short. Brown considered many of Dunbar's poems in standard English to be of high quality; their lyricism, skillful rhythms, and accomplished poetic vocabulary put Dunbar in the forefront of poets of his period. Yet, in spite of these achievements, Brown judged that his standard poetry does not retain the "freshness, humor and life" of his dialect poetry. Brown clearly saw Dunbar's career marked by tensions that his short career did not allow time to resolve.

In all, Brown learned from Dunbar's tensions and unfulfilled promise. He would attempt a dialect capable of more than humor and pathos, he would dare to reveal the harsher as well as the gentler sides of folk life to achieve a full picture, and he would replace Dunbar's untenable models with surer models from the folk tradition.

Brown's formative years as a poet roughly coincided with the meteoric existence of the "Harlem phrase" of the New Negro Renaissance, which began about 1923 and plummuted to an end with the coming of the Great Depression of 1929. Though often not included in the group of writers who are usually mentioned in connection with the New Negro Renaissance, Brown shared in and was influenced by this unprecedented outpouring of the creative energies of Black writers. Novelists Wallace Thurman and George Schuyler broached the tabooed subject of intra-racial color consciousness. Jessie Fauset and Nella Larsen attempted the portrayal of the small but growing Black middle class, while Rudolph Fisher portrayed the emigrants from the rural South and their sometimes traumatic adjustment to city life. Claude McKay, the gifted West Indian poet, frankly revealed the deep gnawing hatred and the desperate urge to challenge the oppressor that had been masked in conventional poetry by Black writers. "He," in Alain Locke's words, "pulled the psychological cloak off the Negro and revealed even to the Negro himself, those facts disguised till then by his shrewd protective mimicry or pressed down under the dramatic mask of living up to what was expected of him."[75] New York bred Countee Cullen, whom Brown later called the "most precocious" of the New Negro Renaissance poets, brought a high degree of technical skill and fluent lyricism to his poetry.[76] In his first and what is considered best volume, *Color* (1925), Cullen brought these gifts together in the poem "Heritage," which "is a statement of the atavism that was a cardinal creed of New Negro poetry."[77] Brown's friend from childhood, Jean Toomer, in the most strikingly original single volume of the period, *Cane*, made the faces of his characters flow into his reader's mind and the pine scented landscape of Georgia come alive with mysterious beauty. In his work the New Negro poet took on an illusive yet pervasive soul.

The best known New Negro poet, Langston Hughes, did not attempt to explore the depths of the human psyche like Toomer; he was content to discover the "flow and rhythm of Black life." The "most experimental and versatile author of the Renaissance," Hughes wrote poetry that had the greatest appeal to Brown because in many ways they were fellow travelers taking the same literary paths. Hughes, like Brown, was concerned with the Black masses. He made heroes of washer women, elevator boys, porters, tenants, ruined girls, and "longheaded jazzers." Though Jean Wagner in *Black Poets of the United States* forces a difference between Hughes and Brown by suggesting that Brown handles the folk who have roots and "ties to the earth" while Hughes handles the rootless masses, this distinction is immaterial. Both poets approached their subject objectively and dramatically. Hughes, the urban poet, wrote about the lonely piano player crooning in the night:

> I got the Weary Blues
> And I can't be satisfied.
> Got the Weary Blues
> And can't be satisfied—
> I ain't happy no mo'
> And I wish that I had died.[78]

Brown was handling the same levels of life in "Ma Rainey" or "Tin Roof Blues."

Hughes, called the poet laureate of Harlem, never tired of exploring its color and vibrancy. In his first two volumes of poetry, *The Weary Blues* (1926) and *Fine Clothes to the Jew* (1927), such poems as "Lenox Avenue Midnight," "Jazzonia," "Minnie Sings Her Blues," "To a Black Dancer in the Little Savoy," "Harlem Night Club," together recreated the jazzy, blues-tinged, frenzied, exotic world of Harlem nights.

On the other hand, Harlem did not hold the same charm for Brown. According to Wagner, Brown, "hostile to the rowdy atmosphere of the city where popular traditions are commercialized and prostituted," was instinctively drawn to the South. Brown also did not share Hughes' atavistic yearning for Africa or his romantic fascination with color and blackness. Instead of the rainbows of colors Hughes lavished on his palette, Brown's portraits were studies in brown.

More important, however, Brown shared Hughes' faith in the inexhaustible resources to be mined in folk music and speech. Their poetry was experimental; they sought to combine the musical forms of the blues, work songs, ballads, and spirituals with poetic expression in such a way as to preserve the originality of the former and achieve the complexity of the latter. They also shared a much needed humor, an ability not to take the world or themselves too seriously. Whatever the primary interest and the extent of the literary gifts of these Renaissance writers, they shared a concern for a deeper and franker self-revelation than had been possible in the waning period of conciliation and supraracial sensitivity.

In *Negro Poetry and Drama*, which appeared in 1937, Sterling Brown suggests the forces that worked together to bring about the growth of the New Negro and the unusual outpouring of writing that reflected it.

The extensive migrations from the South, quickened by the devastations of the bollweevil, the growing resentment at injustice, and the demand of northern industries; the advance of the Negro in labor, wealth and education; the World War with its new experiences in camp and battle; the Garvey movement with its exploitation of "race," all of these contributed to the growth of the "New Negro. . . . "

The New Negro was marked by self-respect (which admittedly at times, became self-preening) and by self reliance. He asked for less charity and more justice.[79]

Brown also suggests that Black writers, like others of their generation, were caught up in a wave of self-determination and self-reliance.

According to cultural historian Nathan Huggins, the war had also made Black people aware of their global identity and had enhanced their self-concept as they compared themselves to disillusioned white men who searched for "valid authentic experience."[80] A growing racial awareness among Blacks prompted self-discovery, discovery of the ancestral past in Africa, and folk and cultural roots reaching back into colonial times. As Black writers found in Africa and in their folk tradition sources of pride, they also discovered within themselves a new kind of militancy that voiced their race's increasing resentment of social injustice. As Alain Locke pointed out in *The New Negro* (1925), "the definitive presentation of the artistic and social goals of the New Negro movement," the old attitudes of self-pity and apology, were replaced by a franker acceptance of the Black man's position vis-à-vis American society.

> The intelligent Negro of today is resolved not to make discrimination an extenuation for his shortcomings in performance, individual or collective; he is trying to hold himself at par, neither inflated by sentimental allowances nor depreciated by current social discounts. For this he must know himself and be known for precisely what he is, and for that reason he welcomes the new scientific rather than the old sentimental interest.[81]

According to critic Abraham Chapman,

> The Negro Renaissance can be seen as the first major cultural culmination of the inner resources and strength of the American Negro, the refusal to be kept down, the rejection of the myriad connotations of negativeness that the propagandists of white supremacy tried to attach to the reality of being Black, the conflict within Negro life against the barren policies of accommodation, and the refusal of the Negro intellectuals and writers to be locked out of their "rightful" place as creators of American culture.[82]

Black writers and intellectuals joined other American artists in a search for new forms and values in American literature. As Huggins pointed out, it was no mere coincidence that both Alain Locke and Van Wyck Brooks saw the literature by Americans turning the corner away from imitativeness toward cultural maturity.[83] The vanguard of New Negro poets shared with the poets of the larger "new poetry" movement a reaction against sentimentality, didacticism, optimism, and romantic escape. As they learned to shun stilted poetic diction in favor of a fresher, more original language, they achieved greater technical skills and humanized their poetry.[84]

This spirit of liberation and innovation reached Brown on the college campuses of Southern schools. While at Virginia Seminary, Brown read McKay's *Harlem Shadows* (1922). In McKay's poetry Brown recognized a spirit of rebellion that was sincere and courageous. He was impressed by McKay's sensitive treatment of his native Jamaica and his skillful handling of standard English and the conventional poetic forms. However, Jean Toomer's *Cane* (1923) and Langston Hughes' *The Weary Blues* (1926) spoke to Brown as McKay's book could not. In Toomer's tour de force, Brown found language that was innovative and free, an irreverence for traditional poetic forms, an absence of cloying sentimentality, and a pervasive sense of racial memory which Brown cherished above all else. For Brown, Jean Toomer, who sought to "catch the plaintive soul, leaving, soon gone," had acknowledged the folk gift and at the same time had created out of its energy a work of remarkable dignity and originality.

When Brown left Fisk University in 1929 to take a teaching position at Howard University, the Harlem inspired Renaissance had of necessity burned itself out; yet it had so sparked Brown's imagination that three years later, when his own volume of poetry would appear, the mark of that era would be on his writing.

NOTES

1. Richard Wright, "The Literature of the Negro in the United States," *Black Expression: Essays By and About Black Americans in the Creative Arts*, ed. Addison Gayle, Jr. (New York: Weybright and Talley, 1969), p. 210; hereafter, this collection of essays will be cited as *Black Expression*.

2. Alain Locke, "The Negro Spirituals," *Black Expression*, p. 47.

3. LeRoi Jones, "The Myth of a 'Negro Literature,' " *Black Expression*, p. 192.

4. These interviews were conducted by Steven Jones. The first interview with Sterling A. Brown was conducted at his home in Washington, D.C., on May 4, 1973. The second interview was held at Founders Library, Howard University, Washington, D.C., on May 10, 1973, and the third interview was held at Sterling Brown's home. Transcripts of these interviews are available at the Institute for the Arts and Humanities at Howard University.

5. Sterling A. Brown, "A Son's Return: 'Oh Didn't He Ramble,' " *Kujichagulia* (Williams' Black Student Union Newspaper), November 1973, pp. 4–6.

6. Sterling Nelson Brown, *My Own Life Notes* (Washington, D.C.: Hamilton Printing Co., 1924), pp. 9–10. A copy of this autobiography is available in the Moorland-Spingarn Research Center at Howard University.

7. Ibid., p. 10.

8. Ibid.

9. Ibid., p. 12.

10. Sterling A. Brown, "The Negro in Washington," *Washington: City and Capital* (Washington, D.C.: Government Printing Office, 1937), p. 78.

11. Ibid., p. 80.

12. S. N. Brown, *My Own Life Notes*, p. 47.

13. Ibid.

14. "Sterling A. Brown: A Biographical Sketch," *Sterling A. Brown: A UMUM Tribute*, p. 4.

15. Sterling A. Brown, *Southern Road* (New York: Harcourt Brace and Co., 1932), p. 79.

16. S. N. Brown, *My Own Life Notes*, p. 7.

17. IAH transcript of a speech given by Sterling A. Brown, May 18, 1973, p. 4.

18. Ibid.

19. Interview with Sterling A. Brown by Steven Jones at poet's home, Washington, D.C., May 14, 1973, IAH transcript, p. 9.

20. Ibid., pp. 9–10.

21. Ibid., p. 4.

22. Ibid., pp. 4–5.

23. Jervis Anderson, "Our Far-flung Correspondents: A Very Special Monument," *New Yorker*, 20 (March 1978), pp. 106–7.

24. Interview with Sterling A. Brown by Steven Jones at poet's home, Washington, D.C., May 14, 1973, IAH transcript, p. 11.

25. Ibid., pp. 11–12.

26. Mercer Cook, May 1, 1979, speech at Sterling A. Brown Day, Museum of African Art, Washington, D.C.

27. Interview with Sterling A. Brown by Steven Jones at poet's home, Washington, D.C., May 14, 1973, IAH transcript, p. 19.

28. Interview with Sterling A. Brown by Steven Jones at poet's home, Washington, D.C., May 4, 1973, IAH transcript, p. 29.

29. Brown, "A Son's Return," p. 5.

30. Ibid.

31. Interview with Sterling A. Brown by Steven Jones at the poet's home, Washington, D.C., May 14, 1973, IAH transcript, p. 18.

32. Louis Untermeyer, ed., *Modern American Poetry: A Critical Anthology* (New York: Harcourt Brace and Co., 1921), pp. 13–14; hereafter cited as *Modern American Poetry*.

33. Stanley K. Coffman, Jr., *Imagism: A Chapter for the History of Modern Poetry* (Norman: University of Oklahoma Press, 1951), pp. 28–29.

34. Brown, *Southern Road*, pp. 27–28.

35. Glenn Hughes, *Imagism and the Imagists: A Study in Modern Poetry* (Stanford, California: Stanford University Press, 1931), p. 4.

36. Ibid., p. 21.

37. Brown, "A Son's Return," p. 6.

38. Brown, *Southern Road*, p. 22.

39. Edwin Arlington Robinson, "Richard Cory," in *Modern American Poetry*, ed. Untermeyer, p. 150.

40. Untermeyer, ed. *Modern American Poetry*, p. 142.

41. Brown, "A Son's Return," p. 6.

42. Robert Frost, *The Complete Poems of Robert Frost* (New York: Holt, Rinehart and Winston, 1964) (1949), p. 409.

43. Sterling A. Brown, "A Son's Return: 'Oh Didn't He Ramble,' " *Kujichagulia*, November 1973, p. 6.

44. Frost, *Complete Poems*, p. vi.

45. James Weldon Johnson, "Introduction," Sterling A. Brown, *Southern Road*, p. xv.

46. Mark Van Doren, *Edwin Arlington Robinson* (New York: Literary Guild of America, 1927), pp. 33–34.

47. Untermeyer, ed., *Modern American Poetry*, p. 217.

48. Interview with Sterling A. Brown by Steven Jones and Stephen Henderson at Howard University, Washington, D.C., May 10, 1973, IAH transcript, p. 2.

49. Edgar Lee Masters, *Spoon River Anthology* (New York: Macmillan, 1916), p. 89.

50. Interview with Sterling A. Brown by Steven Jones and Stephen Henderson at Howard University, Washington, D.C., May 10, 1973, IAH transcript, p. 1.

51. William Wordsworth, *The Complete Poetical Works of Wordsworth*, ed. Andrew J. George (Boston: Houghton Mifflin Co., 1932), p. 791.

52. Samuel T. Coleridge, *Biographi Literaria* (Chapter 1), *The Best of Coleridge*, ed. Earl Leslie Griggs (New York: Roland Press Company, 1934), p. 158; Richard Harter Fogle, *The Idea of Coleridge's Criticism* (Berkeley: University of California Press, 1962), p. 78.

53. Transcript of a speech given by Sterling A. Brown on May 18, 1972, as part of Afro-American Studies Department Program, p. 9. This transcript was made by the Institute for Arts and the Humanities.

54. Untermeyer, ed., *Modern American Poetry*, p. 17.

55. Sterling A. Brown, *Negro Poetry and Drama* (Washington, D.C.: Associates in Negro Folk Education, 1937), p. 93.

56. Sterling A. Brown, IAH transcript of speech given for Afro-American Studies Department, Howard University, May 18, 1972, p. 8.

57. Untermeyer, ed. *Modern American Poetry*, p. 8.

58. Cleanth Brooks, "Alfred Edward Housman," *A. E. Housman: A Collection of Critical Essays* (Englewood Cliffs, N.J.: Prentice Hall, Inc., 1968), p. 63.

59. Ibid., p. 66.

60. Ibid.

61. Louis Untermeyer, "New Light From an Old Mine," *Opportunity*, 10 (August 1932): 250.

62. Transcript of speech given by Sterling A. Brown, May 18, 1972, IAH transcript, p. 7.

63. Interview with Sterling A. Brown by Steven Jones and Stephen Henderson, Howard University, Washington, D.C., May 10, 1973, IAH transcript, pp. 16–17.

64. Transcript of speech by Sterling A. Brown, May 18, 1973, IAH transcript, p. 12.

65. Brown, *Southern Road*, p. 18.

66. Nathaniel A. Sweets, "Prof. Brown at Lincoln University: The Roaring Twenties," *Sterling A. Brown: A UMUM Tribute*, p. 47.

67. Lewis W. Jones, "Sterling A. Brown (The Fisk Year—1928–29)," *Sterling A. Brown: A UMUM Tribute*, p. 51.

68. Interview with Sterling A. Brown by Steven Jones and Stephen Henderson at Howard University, Washington, D.C., May 10, 1973, IAH transcript, p. 29.

69. Jones, "Sterling A. Brown," *Sterling A. Brown: A UMUM Tribute*, p. 52.

70. Interview with Sterling A. Brown by Steven Jones and Stephen Henderson at Howard University, Washington, D.C., May 10, 1973, IAH transcript, p. 10.

71. Ibid., p. 20.

72. Ibid., p. 7.

73. Brown, *Negro Poetry and Drama*, p. 32.

74. Ibid., p. 33.

75. Alain Locke, "Sterling Brown: The New Negro Folk-Poet," *Negro: An Anthology*, ed. Nancy Cunard (New York: Frederick Ungar Publishing Co., 1970) (1934), p. 92.

76. Brown, *Negro Poetry and Drama*, p. 69.

77. Ibid., p. 71.

78. Langston Hughes, *The Weary Blues* (New York: Knopf, 1926), pp. 23–24.

79. Brown, *Negro Poetry and Drama*, p. 60.

80. Nathan Irvin Huggins, *Harlem Renaissance* (New York: Oxford University Press, 1971), pp. 6–7.

81. Alain Locke, ed., *The New Negro* (New York: Albert & Charles Boni, Inc., 1925; reprint ed., New York: Atheneum, 1970), p. 8.

82. Abraham Chapman, "The Harlem Renaissance in Literary History," *CLA Journal*, 11 (1967): 44.

83. Huggins, *Harlem Renaissance*, p. 6.

84. Brown, *Negro Poetry and Drama*, p. 60.

3

THE HOWARD YEARS: THE INTELLECTUAL MILIEU AND BROWN'S LEGACY

Coming to Howard University to teach in 1929, Brown continued a tradition begun by his father forty years before. Though Rev. Sterling N. Brown had not wanted his son to teach at Howard University immediately after graduating from Harvard, he wanted to see him teach at Howard eventually. However, Brown's father was ill when he returned to Washington and did not live long enough to see him become a member of the faculty. Yet from the early 1890s when Sterling N. Brown became a professor of theology at the School of Religion until his son's retirement from the English Department in 1969, the name Sterling Brown was "a standing ground in the catalog." [1]

During Brown's early years at Howard, the school under the leadership of Mordecai W. Johnson was truly becoming "the capstone of Negro education." Besides phenomenal growth in the school's financial and physical resources, Howard University attracted a host of brilliant minds. When Brown joined the faculty, Alain Locke, the first Black American Rhodes Scholar and the intellectual leader of the New Negro Renaissance, was professor of philosophy; Ernest Everett Just, internationally known scientist, was professor of biology; and Kelly Miller was the distinguished professor of sociology. Brown joined the English Department while Charles Eaton Burch, a Daniel Defoe scholar, was the chairman and Benjamin Brawley, its most widely known member. Though a member of the English Department, Brown felt a greater affinity with men like Ralph Bunche in political science, E. Franklin Frazier in sociology, Abram L. Harris in economics, Charles H. Thompson in education, and Rayford W. Logan in history. All these men joined the Howard faculty in the 1930s. As Brown later describes them, they made up ''a group of young faculty insurgents determined to develop Howard into a first-class college.''[2] With these men Brown discussed the hated specter of segregation that continued to make two cities of Washington, D.C., tokenism, the struggling civil rights organizations, local politics, lynching, the Scottsboro case, fascism, the war, McCarthyism, and the promise of integration. It was also in this circle that Brown was able to cultivate a view of literature that issued from a deep understanding of the historical, sociological, economic, and political dimensions of American society. In the essay section of *The Negro Caravan*, Brown credits Bunche, Harris, Frazier, and others with shedding light on the reality of the American experience lived by Blacks.

No reader with an open mind could review the work of these scholars and retain the stereotyped concepts of Negro life and character. Whether dealing with the shadow of the plantation lying darkly over Negro sharecroppers, or the hardships of families congested in northern slums, or the frustrated lives of Negro youth from Natchez to Harlem, or the struggle of Negro labors against unemployment and prejudice, or the pitiful inadequacies of schools for Negroes in the South, or the chicanery of white voting officials, all of these have added enormously to the new realism about Negro life of which America is becoming aware and must become even more aware. These men have won respect in the world of scholarship. They are social analysts rather than solvers of a race problem.[3]

Brown's genial, vivacious personality also often made him the center of a larger social group that was made up of Howard professors and Washington professional people. In 1949 Brown became a member of the Gourmets Club, founded that year by Alfred Edgar Smith. About once every month or two, Brown joined with W. Montaque Cobb, distinguished professor of anatomy in the Howard Medical School; Arthur P. Davis, fellow professor in the English department; physicians C. Herbert Marshal and Frank Horne; and others. The twelve-member group usually met in the home of Otto McClarrin. Journalist McClarrin writes that through Brown he met such people as ''E. Simms

Campbell, the famous cartoonist, and his wife; John Hammond, the millionaire who 'discovered' Count Basie, Billie Holliday, Teddy Wilson, Lionel Hampton and so many other jazz greats . . . ; those fascinating jazz pianists Willie 'The Lion' Smith, Eubie Blake, Meade Lux Lewis, Duke Ellington and most members of his orchestra, actors like Oscar Brown, Jr., and Roscoe Lee Browne; the jazz violinist Eddie South, the African drummer James Hawthorne Bey, Ralph Bunche, Alain Locke, Lillian Smith, author of that controversial novel of 1944 *Strange Fruit*, Jimmy Witherspoon, T-Bone Walker, Frederic Ramsey, Jr., and too many lesser known artists and intellectuals to list here.''[4]

Sterling Brown's long association with Howard University paralleled Mordecai W. Johnson's thirty-four-year tenure as president of the University (1926–1960). In an interview, Brown remembers the often controversial president as a man of courage ''who fought for freedom of speech.''[5] Though attacked as a radical and accused of teaching communism at Howard, Mordecai Johnson took militant stands against segregation and exploitation of Blacks in this country and did not relinquish his right to raise questions concerning injustice to ''the weaker and the disadvantaged people of the earth.''[6]

Though, as Brown recalls, Dr. Johnson and he did not always agree on issues,[7] there were occasions when Brown admitted, ''I would have gone to jail for him. . . . ''[8] One such occasion was during the height of the McCarthy period when the Federal Bureau of Investigation investigated Dr. Johnson and several members of the Howard University faculty. Brown relates, with characteristic humor, the events of those days and his own appearance before an FBI official. Asked by the man whether he was a Communist, Brown replied: ''Listen son, any Negro who has been to the seventh grade and is against lynching is a Communist. I have been to the eighth grade and am against a hell of a lot more than lynching.''[9] Although twenty or more Howard University professors were interrogated by the Federal Bureau of Investigation for alleged subversive activities, there were no repercussions from the administration. Brown said, ''Among our people it was a credit . . . a badge that you were a radical.''

Brown, like others at Howard, was aware that avowed radicalism and an insistence upon academic freedom among the faculty and administration could mean the limiting or total withdrawal of support for the University by the federal government. However, historian Michael R. Winston, writes that for the leadership at Howard, there was no retreat from principles.

When many more prestigious universities wavered on the question of academic freedom in the face of the McCarthy era hysteria, Dr. Johnson held Howard firm as a bastion of free inquiry and expression. The values for which Howard has stood since its founding could not be preserved by equivocation or discreet self-censorship.[10]

Mordecai Johnson's stance to preserve academic freedom was vindicated. McCarthy hysteria and government investigation did not undermine the University's viability. For Brown, Johnson's leadership was marked by courage, a quality that had long attracted his admiration.

Sixteen years after joining the Howard faculty, Sterling Brown was appointed to a teaching position in the English Department at Vassar College. A symbol of the breaking down of racial barriers in previously all-white faculties at prestigious institutions, the appointment made national headlines. Brown had taught at Vassar for three terms prior to this appointment and had been well received. Stephen Henderson writes that, while at Vassar, Brown "immersed himself in the total life of the institution; he lectured on jazz, wrote articles for the Vassar literary magazine, and gave informal talks on democracy and folk literature."[11] Before going to Vassar, Brown had received national recognition as an author, as the editor on Negro affairs in the Federal Writers' Project, as a Guggenheim Fellow for 1937–38, a Julius Rosenwald Fellow 1942, a member of the Carnegie-Mydral Study, a member of the Committee on Negro Studies of the American Council of Learned Societies, and as an editor for the *Encyclopedia Britannica*. With his appointment to Vassar, Brown was viewed by his colleagues at Howard as having reached a logical plateau for his scholarship.

To understand the significance that Brown's colleagues brought to his achievement, one must understand the history of Black scholars in the caste-ridden academic system in the United States during the first four decades of this century. Many of these men and women had come to live with the blatant, dual standards and isolation imposed by segregation, the continuous questioning of Black intellectual capacity, the centuries of stereotyped attitudes and condescension on the part of whites and had resigned themselves to the fact that their efforts would be constricted by the boundaries of segregation.[12] In an article entitled "Through the Back Door," Michael R. Winston discusses the dilemma of Black scholars who desired the "superior research advantages" of wealthy white institutions but were "condemned to work in institutions on the whole unsympathetic to their work."[13] However, the changing political and economic status of Blacks after 1945 had the positive effect of increasing opportunities for Black scholars.

With the doors of white institutions cracked a little, several of the top Black scholars were invited to join all-white faculties at prestigious schools. Brown was among the first. Allison Davis, Brown's close friend, left Dillard University for the University of Chicago. Howard economist Abram L. Harris also went to Chicago. And the noted young historian, John Hope Franklin, left Howard for Brooklyn.[14] However, Brown decided to remain at Howard. Though he spent several summer sessions away from Washington—University of Minnesota, summer, 1945; New York University, summers, 1949 and 1950; University of Illinois (Chicago Circle Campus) summers, 1967 and 1968—Brown continued to teach at Howard until his retirement in 1969. Some years later he explains his decision: "I was born on the Howard campus. I am devoted to Howard. These are my people and if I had anything to give, they would need it more."[15]

And Sterling Brown did give. As he recalled he taught "everything." He taught freshman English, American literature, Shakespeare, the Romantic movement, Victorian literature, "Great Issues," and a course called "Introduction to World Literature," later known as English 143. Brown also taught pioneer courses in Afro-American literature. Arthur P. Davis, co-editor of *The Negro Caravan* and longtime friend, credits him with planting the seeds of interest in Afro-American literature and with sustaining this interest through the 1940s and 1950s. He writes:

Three of the outstanding seed-planters in Afro-American literature were professors at Howard: Benjamin G. Brawley, Alain LeRoy Locke and Sterling A. Brown. Under Professor Brown, courses in Negro literature were taught at Howard when very, very few black and no white schools had such courses. In addition, Brown's own publications and his strong belief in the importance of

Afro-American letters helped to keep alive that literature in the lean years between the end of the New Negro Renaissance (c. 1940) and the 60's—years
in which the interest in Black writings created by the Renaissance had drasti-
cally decreased.[16]

Reflecting on his long career as a teacher at Howard University,
Sterling Brown said, "My legacy is my students."[17] With a career
that spans more than forty years, Brown has naturally had an impact
on thousands of students; yet his influence can be graphically seen in
the life's work of several of his most outstanding students. Perhaps
one of Brown's brightest students, Ulysses Lee, received a B.A. from
Howard and a Ph.D. from the University of Chicago. When Lee was
a young professor at Lincoln University in Pennsylvania, Brown invited him to be one of the editors of the anthology *The Negro Caravan*. Brown had been impressed by Lee's thorough scholarship while
a student at Howard and as an assistant editor in Negro Affairs in the
Federal Writers' Project. Lee's major work, *U.S. Army in World War
II, the Employment of Negro Troops*, also demonstrates the high level
of scholarship that Brown had recognized.

Eugenia Collier, a teacher and critic of American literature, credits
Brown with starting her "on a pathway of life long commitment, life
long discovery and life long service." She recalls that when she was
"the most callow and wide-eyed member" of Sterling Brown's soph-
omore World Literature class, he "demystified the entire range of
Western culture" when he said, to the delight of his students, "Achilles
wasn't right bright."[18] A few years later as a graduate student at Columbia, she hungered for the naturalness and relevance Brown brought
to his classroom and decided that she would fill the void by beginning
her own quest for her roots by writing a master's thesis on Brown's
poetry. She dedicated her two-volume anthology *Afro-American Writing: Prose and Poetry* to Brown and wrote in *Sterling A. Brown; A
UMUM Tribute*, "Whatever contribution I make to Black people . . .
derives ultimately from the wisdom, the art, and the humanity of Sterling Brown."[19]

Writer, spokesman for the Black Arts Movement, and music critic
Amiri Baraka recalls the informal jazz seminars that Brown taught at
Howard in 1952. Called LeRoi Jones in those days, he, poet A. B.
Spellman, and others met in the lounge of Cook Hall where Brown,
drawing on his vast knowledge of Black music and an enviable collec-

tion of blues and jazz recordings, made Black American music "historical." [20] As Baraka remembers, the most significant revelation that he carried away from these sessions was that Black music could be analyzed historically. [21] As Brown explained it to them, the evolution of Black music was related to social as well as economic factors; its singers and musicians created the forms, style, and nuances. Its development could be traced from the earliest hollers on isolated plantations through the secular sorrow songs called blues to the brassy blast or mellow sound of jazz bands. Moreover, its development reflected the responses and reactions of Blacks to American society.

What Baraka absorbed from Brown's analysis of Black music acted as a catalyst in his own theorizing on the subject. A little more than ten years later in *Blues People*, Baraka reflects Brown's idea of the interrelatedness of music and life in his own theoretical framework. Baraka postulates "that if music of the Negro in America, in all its permutations, is subjected to a socio-anthropological as well as musical scrutiny, something about the essential nature of the Negro's existence in this country ought to be revealed, as well as something about the essential nature of this country, i.e., society as a whole." [22]

With Jones' publication of *Blues People*, Brown, relinquishing his role of teacher for that of critic, saw in his former student's interpretation a regrettable misunderstanding of the debt modern jazz artists owe to the early pioneers. In this connection Brown said:

I think there's an impatience on the part of young Negro writers who misinterpret early jazz music, who see it as a vestige of slavery—when it was not that. It had its own strength, its own dignity; it had its own protest. I don't think we ought to give it up as easily as we do. I think we've taken the stereotypes that they've given about the jazz artists. I miss that in LeRoi Jones' *Blues People*. I miss a continuity of understanding. He says this is an important thing, but he doesn't really go into the blues or the early jazz people, and I don't think you have to set up [John] Coltrane [the late modern saxophonist] against Louis [Armstrong], you know, to degrade one. I think you've got to understand Louis' grinning and all the rest and see that as part of an approach that they had to take at that time. The music is not grinning. What he does with his horn is a very important thing. [23]

As Brown had shared with Baraka his fluid interpretation of the history of Black music, he brought to his criticism the same objectivity that had demanded the respect of his students. His role as an influential teacher of Baraka and as a sharp critic was not, then, inconsistent with his overall approach. For Brown, according to another student, Michael R. Winston, "never imposed a matrix on how to think about a problem" but emphasized critical thinking. Winston also recalls that Brown brought to the classroom "a catholicity of interest," a store of "hard-won insights," and a keen, "restless intelligence." Winston says that Brown was the fulfillment of his idea of a college professor. He was penetrating with his questions, and he utilized "a background" approach that necessitated a broad, expansive knowledge of many areas of learning. "Clearly one of the best read scholars at Howard, Brown read in the natural sciences, the social sciences, German literature, French literature, and the novel." Winston adds, "the most striking think about him intellectually is the intensity of his intelligence."[24]

Brown had a different impact on each student. To Kenneth B. Clark, the author of *Dark Ghetto* and "the psychologist whose theories lie behind the 1954 Supreme Court school desegregation decision," Brown opened his eyes to "the awe, the wonder, the fascination of human creativity."[25] To actor Ossie Davis, Brown was the rock in the weary land of academia[26] who was a scholar but "was also homey, Negro, grits, and gravy."[27]

Brown's reputation as a teacher also reached outside the campus. He worked with many scholars in Black literature and culture who were not students at Howard University. Robert Bone, author of *The Negro Novel in America*, consulted Brown during the writing of the book. Jean Wagner, the French scholar who has done the most definitive study to date of Black poetry written in the first half of the twentieth century, made many trips to Washington to talk with and learn from Brown. Brown's deep interest in the literature of oppressed groups attracted Rosey E. Pool, author of *Beyond the Blues* and the teacher of the young Jewish girl who wrote *The Diary of Anne Frank*. On one occasion she talked with him about the five years she spent in a Nazi concentration camp. Brown gave guidance and criticism to Roger Rosenblatt during the writing of his book, *Black Fiction*. Jerre Mangione also met with Brown on several occasions while doing his study of the Federal Writers' Project that resulted in *The Dream and the Deal*. Benjamin A. Botkin and Alan Lomax worked closely with Brown on folklore projects as a part of the Federal Writers' Project. Lomax writes, "I saw Sterling (not in classrooms) but standing up for the right of his people's culture in governmental and scholarly circles."[28] Lomax cites

Brown's work in the Writers' Project and in the American Council of Learned Societies. On numerous occasions, Brown, with a rare intellect, passion, and humor, passed on his knowledge.

Though Sterling and Daisy had no children of their own, they raised an adopted son, John L. Dennis. They also welcomed many "spiritual" sons and daughters into their home. Poet Michael Harper, historian Sterling Stuckey, critic Stephen Henderson, photographer Roy Lewis, historian Michael Winston, and teacher Eloise Spicer are among those who forged a close relationship with the Browns.

Several scholars who have benefited from his generous gifts of time and inspiration have dedicated books to him. Among them are Thomas Sowell, *Black Education: Myths and Tragedies*; Sterling Stuckey, *The Spell of Africa, The Development of Black Nationalist Theory*; Ronald Fair, *World of Nothing* (a novel), Richard Long and Eugenia Collier, *Afro-American Literature, an Anthology of Prose and Poetry*; Don L. Lee, *Dynamite Voices*; and Jean Wagner, *Black Poets of the United States*. Jean Fagan Yellin, Bernard Bell, and Sherley Williams also acknowledge their indebtedness to Brown in their individual studies of American literature.

Writers and scholars visiting Washington, D.C., made the Brown home a "priority stop" on their trip. Dudley Randall, publisher of Broadside Press, remembered an April night in 1973 when Gwendolyn Brooks, Mari Evans, Carl Carter, Connie Carter, Hoyt Fuller, Don Lee (Haki Madhubuti), and he were invited there after attending a Gwendolyn Brooks seminar at Howard. Randall writes that they "sat at the feet of the venerated poet while he showed us his rare books and entertained us with anecdotes (lies, he called them) of W.E.B. Du Bois, Walter White and other outstanding men he had known." [29] Randall points out the significance of the night when three generations of poets were present at Brown's announcement that Broadside Press could publish his book-length collection of ballads entitled *The Last Ride of Wild Bill* (1975). Randall knew that the availability of Brown's work would help to ensure "that a new generation will acclaim his poetry."

When Brown retired in 1969 after a brilliant forty-year career as a teacher at Howard University, there was, ironically no special note made of his departure. However, according to several sources close to Brown, this oversight was in keeping with the years of benign neglect by the administration in general and the English Department in particular that Brown had come to expect. Brown himself says that there was not much enthusiasm at Howard for the type of thing he was doing. Brown recalled that the University was not even willing to support his work on *The Negro Caravan*.

Surprisingly, it was only in the sixties that Brown read his poems at Howard University though he had been asked to read on many campuses across the country. This may be explained to some degree by a reluctance on the part of some conservative faculty members to appreciate a professor who knew the blues, jazz, and barrel house songs and felt as equally at home with Leadbelly as he did with Ralph Bunche. Yet, as Michael R. Winston states, "Non-conformity cost him more than he realized." [30] Though he went back to Harvard in 1931 to begin work on the doctoral degree, Brown never bothered to complete it. Brown resisted routine; he was reluctant to fit himself into a rigid schedule. His resistance to routine led him to abandon a project in which he was commissioned to write a centennial history of Howard University with Rayford Logan. Also, for most of his life, he had been highly critical of superficial respectability in literature as well as life; this criticism carried over to academia where he saw the doctorate symbolizing, in some cases, intellectual snobbishness instead of intellectual competence. In addition, Brown's temperament was not well suited for the isolation and the myopia often required of the researcher. Brown's catholicity of interests led him to do the quick study, distilling in epigrammatic terms ideas that may have taken extensive work to treat exhaustively. However, Brown's decision not to get the final degree cost him some ambivalence on the matter and seemingly resulted in his chronic sensitivity whenever anyone affixed the title "Dr." before his name.

The five or six years before his retirement were troubled ones for Brown. The stress caused by what he perceived to be years of neglect had begun to surface. Inclined to lulls of depression, Brown craved attention. Sterling Stuckey, who introduced the second edition of *Southern Road*, believes that his need was satisfied to some degree by his audiences at poetry readings.

Each time, whatever the age group or racial compositon of the audience, his reading was singularly successful, which buoyed his spirits, for he had in fact wondered perhaps more than he ever let us know how the younger generation would relate to his poetry. It was evident that despite his great gifts as a poet, he was troubled by a not inconsiderable lack of recognition.[31]

However, the turbulent years of 1968 and 1969 finally brought him greater recognition from the students. "Howard students said that they wanted a black university, and they wanted it named after Sterling A. Brown." Stephen Henderson writes that Howard and other institutions also began to honor the poet, critic, and teacher who had been in their midst but somewhat ahead of their time.

With the changing intellectual climate brought on by the ferment of the '60s, institutions have begun to catch up with him. As a result, Howard University awarded him an honorary doctorate in 1971. Honored at the same time was his fellow Washingtonian, Duke Ellington. Brown takes pride in the event, for he has spent his entire life defending black cultural achievements, the literature, the folklore and the music. . . . Moreover, the last years at Howard had been turbulent, often times bitter for one who symbolized for the students a link with the progressive elements of their history—the advocacy tradition of Du Bois and Delany and the disarming self-sufficiency of the common man himself.[32]

During these years Sterling Brown was the respected advisor to NAG (Nonviolent Action Group), Howard's version of SNCC. Stokely Carmichael, Courtland Cox, Charlie Cobb, and Mike Thadwell were among the students who sought guidance from the "Prof."[33] The students would crowd into his basement lined with shelves of books and phonograph records where they would have rousing discussions on Marxism, Pan-Africanism, civil rights, Malcolm, Martin Luther King, non-violence vs. direct action. Sometimes the discussion would give way to an impromptu poetry reading in which Brown would read "Slim Greer," "Old Lem," "Southern Cop," "Remembering Nat Turner," "Crispus Attucks McKoy," or "The Ballad of Joe Meek." Brown recalls that Stokely Carmichael was an enthusiastic fan of "The Ballad of Joe Meek." Undoubtedly, Carmichael was impressed by the hero, who goes through a metamorphosis as radical as the philosophical one he and Charles Hamilton called for in *Black Power*.

Sometimes, too, Brown found himself going against the currents of popular thought. He believed the hairstyles, dashkikis, and the term "black" were merely "the flicker and not the flame" of the movement.[34] "I'm a Negro," Brown would say. "I'm proud to be called a Negro. W.E.B. Du Bois was a Negro. Paul Robeson was a Negro. Ralph Bunche was a Negro," he said emphatically, closing the case. Genevieve Ekaete, one of his students, believes that Brown "suffered from the currents of change."[35] Both Sterling and Daisy Brown, very light-skinned Negroes, were often viewed askance during a period in which the dominant slogan was "black is beautiful". Daisy Brown, who was no stranger to the inanities of color prejudice, related an incident to Ms. Ekaete that Brown could only describe as "grotesque." In 1970, at a night in honor of her husband, she was not allowed at first into the room where he was to read his poems. To compound the ironies, Brown, who had arrived a few minutes before she had, was barred from the room until one of the organizers saw what was happening and ushered him to his seat. According to Daisy, she was not allowed into the room until "the tall and black and bearded" Courtland Cox rescued her and put his arms around her. "Thank God for you, Courtland," she said as he escorted her to her seat.

However, once inside the room, the Browns met the stares and hostile glares of those who apparently would advance the race by their self-righteous chauvinism. Daisy relates the hurt and humiliation she felt as she heard the whispered queries, "Is she black?" She states: "I've been black if you want to use the term . . . 70 years and more. And to have these kids say that. It hurt. I can't help if my skin is white, but it hurt." Fortunately Ossie Davis was there that night and, sensing how uncomfortable they were, came over and hugged them. And Daisy said "Thank God for Ossie."[36]

Brown, cutting through the absurdity, said, "Any glorification of black that brings about cruelty is bad."[37] Those who learned at his knee found it difficult to accept uncritically easy generalizations whether they were scathing indictments of the race or equally dangerous idealizations. Brown's wisdom and wit were magnets to the young minds who recognized the quality of his judgment and the greatness of his spirit. Otto McClarrin, who entered Howard in 1936, said, "[Brown] helped me tear down the ghetto walls that restricted me intellectually."[38]

Despite the welcomed attention he received from his students during this period, there still remained in his mind the nagging realization that he was "a writer of few books." Brown was disturbed not only that his poetry was not known critically outside of small circle of admirers, but also that he may not get to complete the volumes of poetry that would assure his position as a significant American poet. At that point in Brown's life he felt a strong sense of failure that precipitated periods of depression. There was a period, though, when Brown was at "the height of his powers."[39]

Indisputedly, 1929 to 1945 was Brown's most productive period as a writer. During this period he contributed poetry, reviews, and essays to *Opportunity, New Republic, The Nation, Journal of Negro Education, Phylon, Crisis,* and numerous other publications. His essays covered a wide range of interests including American theater, folk expressions, music, athletics, oral history, and social customs. Perhaps Brown's most influential essay of the period was "Negro Characters as Seen by White Authors" (1933) in which he first brought attention to the misrepresentation of Black character and life in American literature. Four books were published in the short span of six years: *Southern Road* (1932), *The Negro in Washington* (1936), *The Negro in American Fiction* (1937), and *Negro Poetry and Drama* (1937). In 1941 *The Negro Caravan,* a much needed anthology of writings by and about Black Americans, appeared. Brown coedited this book with Arthur P. Davis and Ulysses Lee.

In reviewing this period, however, one is acutely aware of the many books that were in Brown's head but were never completed or published. The book *No Hiding Place,* which was to appear in 1937, remained unpublished until 1980 when it appeared in *The Collected Poems of Sterling A. Brown,* selected by Michael S. Harper. When Brown submitted his second manuscript to Harcourt, Brace and Company it was rejected. According to historian Sterling Stuckey, who was instrumental in getting *Southern Road* reprinted in 1976: "The rejection of the manuscript, said to be on a level with *Southern Road,* remains something of a mystery. There is reason to believe, however, that more than possible sales considerations figured into the decision."[40] Brown himself speculated that the poems in *No Hiding Place,* with their emphasis on social themes, may have been considered "troublesome" in a period marked by social upheaval and slow economic recovery. Those in decision-making positions may have been made uncomfortable by the more than metaphoric significance of *No Hiding Place.* There could be no hiding from the realities of peonage, lynching, and racism that Old Lem, a kind of spokesman emeritus for the volume, conveys. He had watched men's lives destroyed by the fear and cowardice of other men, men who must "come by tens." His insight, "They burn us when we dogs/They burn us when we men." is jarring. Yet poems like "Old

Lem'' did get a hearing. "Break of Day," "Remembering Nat Turner," and "Southern Cop" carried Brown's unmistakable message of growing impatience with things as usual.

In 1942 Brown was on leave with a Rosenwald Fellowship to write a book "A Negro Looks at the South." The book was to have been published by Doubleday, Doren and Company.[41] As a part of his research, he set out to draw "a fair sampling of current talk among American Negroes from a store of conversations harvested up and down the Atlantic Seaboard, from Massachusetts to Mississippi, but mainly in the Deep South." A few of these conversations, "some recorded on the spot at interviews " and others "bootlegged" into his notebooks, are preserved in "Out of Their Mouths," a piece that appeared in *Survey Graphic* (October 1942). In it Brown allowed the people to speak for themselves. "The People Yes . . . Yes Indeed," the Sandburg line with Sterling-Brownian emphasis, introduces the first section of these conversations and adequately conveys the enthusiasm with which Brown has continued to view the common man.

Whether Brown found his people "in army camps or juke joints or dorms or offices or commissaries or cabins or Jim Crow coaches or bus stations," he got them to do the talking, and then he listened intently.[42] They groused about the war, cursed the South's ubiquitous caste system, and revealed their individual philosophies of resistance and reconciliation. They also talked about Southern traditions in tones that were ironic, paradoxical, and sometimes humorous. For example, Brown related a conversation that reveals the problem of etiquette in a caste system:

Little red-haired girl (Negro): Ethel and I got on the elevator in the department store. You know Ethel is lighter than I am, and her hair is straighter. A white man got on, looked at me, and especially my hair. I was looking at him out of the corner of my eyes. He wasn't sure, and finally took off his hat. We burst out laughing. Right away he put his hat back on his head.[43]

In explaining his interviewing technique, Brown maintained an affinity between Chaucer and himself. "I'm like Chaucer," Brown said; "Chaucer got in with everybody—crooks, priests, nonpriests." Like Chaucer, Brown would spur his interviewee on. "Someone would tell Chaucer a bunch of lies and Chaucer would say, 'And I said his opinion was good.' Now, It's an awful opinion and Chaucer was a wise man. To keep this cat talking, he said, 'and I said his opinion was good.' " Brown admitted, "That is me . . . I am a yes-man."[44] Brown also found Chaucer's advice—to "rehearse, as nigh as ever he can every word"—useful as he attempted to capture the essence of their speech in his sketches. Though the book "A Look at the South" was never completed, it appears that, as in the glimpses given in "Out of Their Mouths," Brown would have drawn heavily on the cultural and social thinking of the common folk and would have used their language as his divining rod for authenticity.

Shortly thereafter, Brown wrote a perceptive article entitled "Count Us In," which appeared in *What the Negro Wants* (1945). It draws heavily on Brown's firsthand observations of the South. As the title suggests, Brown deals with the enigmatic paradox of the physical presence of Blacks in the South and their political and social invisibility, which was enforced by a knotty system of rules, codes, and customs designed to keep Blacks out of the democracy and "in their place." The largest part of the article deals with the equally paradoxical situation of the Black soldier in World War II; "expected to be a man doing a man-size job," he must be something less than a man in civilian life.[45] The violent aversion to change on the part of a number of Southern whites, the survival of the equally dangerous system of patronage, and the oddities of segregation receive a searching analysis in this article.

Of all his unpublished works of the period, Brown's study of the "Negro in American Culture" is the most outstanding. As a member on the staff of the Carnegie-Myrdal project, he wrote an exhaustive study of Black theater which was used in preparation of Gunnar Myrdal's *An American Dilemma*. In this study, Brown traces Black theater—from the earliest dramatizations of Black characters by White actors in blackface, through the minstrel and musical shows and pioneer actors' attempts on the legitimate stage, to problem plays and plays of social realism. His critical and interpretive skills reached a high level in this study. With an encyclopedic knowledge of a then virgin field and careful and extensive research, Brown highlighted those plays that established a trend or signaled a turning point in this history of the treatment of Black life and character on the American stage. Brown demonstrated in this work that his forte is baring the essence of an image and fitting it into the continuum of literary development.

Regrettably, Brown did not do the cultural history that was squarely within his talents, nor has he published a volume of poetry that matches in quality his first book. Yet one cannot ignore the significance of those contributions that Brown has made to Black literature and culture.

NOTES

1. Interview with Sterling A. Brown by Steven Jones and Stephen Henderson at Howard University, Washington, D.C., May 10, 1973, IAH transcript p. 30.
2. Sterling Brown, "Ralph Bunche, Statesman," *The Reporter*, 1 (December 1949), p. 4.
3. Sterling A. Brown, Arthur P. Davis, and Ulysses Lee. eds., *The Negro Caravan* (New York: Dryden Press, 1941), p. 831.
4. Otto McClarrin, "Sterling Brown as a Superior Person," *Sterling A. Brown: A UMUM Tribute*, pp. 41–42.
5. Interview with Sterling A. Brown by James Early and Ethelbert Miller at Howard University, Washington, D.C., May 19, 1978.
6. Michael R. Winston, "Introduction," *Education for Freedom*, pp. 10–11. Also see Mordecai Johnson, "Negro Problem of National and World Significance," *Education for Freedom*, p. 26. (Washington, D.C.: Moorland-Spingarn Research Center, Howard University, 1976).
7. Speaking of Mordecai Johnson's leadership in a May 19, 1978, interview at Howard University, Brown said that he was in Dr. Johnson's "bad graces." Brown described Dr. Johnson as a tyrannical leader whose inability to take criticism and any difference of opinion made those who would refute him *persona non gratis* in his eyes.
8. Interview with Sterling Brown by James Early and Ethelbert Miller at Howard University, Washington, D.C., May 19, 1978.
9. Ibid.
10. Winston, "Introduction," *Education for Freedom*, p. 11.
11. Stephen Henderson, "Sterling Brown," *Ebony* (October 1976): 130.
12. Michael R. Winston, "Through the Back Door: Academic Racism and the Negro Scholar in Historical Perspective," *Daedalus*, 100 (Summer 1971): 687–707.
13. Ibid., p. 703.
14. Ibid., p. 708.
15. Henderson, "Sterling Brown," *Ebony*, p. 130.
16. Arthur P. Davis, "History of English 248–249," Institute of the Arts and Humanities, Howard University, 1977.
17. Genevieve Ekaete, "Sterling Brown: A Living Legend," *New Directions: The Howard University Magazine* (Winter 1974): 5.

18. Eugenia Collier, "Prologue: Early Critical Works," *Sterling A. Brown: A UMUM Tribute*, p. 24.

19. Ibid.

20. His collection included the blues of Blind Lemon Jefferson, Big Bill Broonzy, and LeRoy Carr; the pioneer recordings of Mamie Smith and Victoria Spivey; and the even then classic "race records" by Bessie Smith, Sarah Martin, and Ida Cox. Jazz greats were also generously represented in the collection: Fletcher Henderson, Jelly Roll Morton, Louis Armstrong, Fats Waller, and Duke Ellington.

21. Interview with Amiri Baraka, Lincoln University, Pennsylvania, May 15, 1979.

22. LeRoi Jones, *Blues People: Negro Music in White America* (New York: William Morrow and Company, 1963), pp. ix–x.

23. Hollie West, "The Teacher . . . Sterling Brown, The Mentor of Thousands . . . ," *The Washington Post*, November 16, 1969, p. F3.

24. Interview with Michael R. Winston, Moorland-Spingarn Research Center at Howard University, March 7, 1979.

25. West, "Sterling Brown," *The Washington Post*, p. F1.

26. Ossie Davis in a speech at the Museum of African Art, Washington, D.C., May 1, 1979. This day was proclaimed Sterling A. Brown Day by the mayor of Washington, Marion Barry.

27. West, "Sterling Brown," *The Washington Post*, p. F1.

28. Alan Lomax, "Sterling A. Brown: A Unique Intellectual," *Sterling A. Brown: A UMUM Tribute*, p. 33.

29. Dudley Randall, "Sterling Brown as Seen by Publisher Dudley Randall," *Sterling A. Brown: A UMUM Tribute*, pp. 45–46.

30. Interview with Michael R. Winston, Moorland-Spingarn Research Center at Howard University, March 7, 1979.

31. Stuckey, "Introduction," *Southern Road*, p. xv.

32. Henderson, "Sterling A. Brown," *Ebony*, p. 129.

33. James G. Spady, "To Have Lived in the Days of the 'Senegambian,' " *Sterling A. Brown: A UMUM Tribute*, p. 35.

34. Genevieve Ekaete, "Professor and Poet Sterling Allen Brown: Saying Yes to His People," *The Washington Post*, March 23, 1974, p. B5.

35. Ibid.

36. Ibid.

37. Ibid.

38. McClarrin, "Sterling Brown as a Superior Person," p. 38.

39. Henderson, "Sterling A. Brown," *Ebony*, p. 130.

40. Stuckey, "Introduction," *Southern Road*, p. xxxii.

41. Donald Jones, "Sterling Brown Defends 'Zoot Suits,' Wearers," *Sepia Socialite* (October 29, 1942): 3.

42. Sterling Brown, "Out of Their Mouths," *Survey Graphic*, 31 (November 1942): 480.

43. Ibid., p. 481.

44. Ekaete, "Sterling Brown," p. B8.

45. Sterling Brown, "Count Us In," in *What the Negro Wants*, ed. Rayford W. Logan (Chapel Hill: University of North Carolina Press, 1945), p. 319.

4
STERLING A. BROWN AND THE FEDERAL WRITERS' PROJECT

From 1936 to 1940 Brown focused his attention on the Federal Writers' Project. It was the only period in his career that was not devoted primarily to teaching. Brown brought to his position as editor of Negro affairs a ranging knowledge of literature, criticism, and American folklore with which he tied an enthusiastic interest in American history and culture. In a period in which economic woes had turned ethnic and racial groups against each other and in which the knowledge of the past and present cultural and sociological situation of Blacks was still very much in the dark ages of myth and propaganda, Brown's energy and talents would be sorely tested.

When Sterling Brown was appointed the Project's national editor of Negro affairs in 1936, he accepted one of the few significant positions given to Blacks under the New Deal. Brown's appointment was, in large measure, a result of the insistence of several Black leaders such as Walter White, Ralph Bunche, John P. Davis, William Hastie, Robert Weaver and others, and the organizations they represented, "that a Black person knowledgeable in literary criticism and history be appointed at the national level to look out for Black affairs."[1] Jerre Mangione, in explaining the genesis of Brown's appointment, writes that FWP director Henry G. Alsberg, "alert and sympathetic to the desire of the New Deal administration to make WPA jobs available to Negroes, . . . encouraged Negro studies and tried to persuade his state directors to hire as many qualified Black writers and researchers as possible. . . . "[2] Sterling Brown's appointment, therefore, as Mangione suggests, was Alberg's way of emphasizing the Project's intentions to include Blacks in fairer proportions on the employment rolls as well as to assure the inclusion of Black subjects in the American Guide Series.

Originally Alsberg and his editorial assistant George W. Cronyn had planned to include a separate section entitled ''Negro Culture in America'' in a five-volume American Guide. To this end, they met with James Weldon Johnson and Alain Locke at Howard University to plan this section. However, they eventually dropped this idea in favor of including an essay on Black history and lore in each state guidebook when Bunche, John Davis and Alfred E. Smith, an advisor for Negro matters in WPA, persuaded Brown to accept the appointment as editor of Negro affairs.[3]

Certainly, Brown, then associate professor of English at Howard University, was an excellent choice, for no one was more qualified than he or more sensitive than he to the need for truthful, objective studies of life and culture of Black Americans. When he took the position, Brown had already published his first volume of poetry, *Southern Road*, in 1932 and a second book of poems *No Hiding Place* was being considered for publication. He had published the *Outline for the Study of the Poetry of American Negroes* (1931) which was used with the *Book of American Negro Poetry*, edited by James Weldon Johnson. Also Brown had done extensive research in American fiction, poetry, and drama which formed the basis for the critical studies, *The Negro in American Fiction* and *Negro Poetry and Drama*, both published in 1937. And for a decade preceding his appointment, his poems, reviews and essays appeared in such magazines as *The Crisis*, *Esquire*, *Folk-Say*, *The Nation*, *The Journal of Negro Education*, *The Journal of Negro History*, *The New Masses*, *The New Republic*, and *Opportunity*.

Brown was, therefore, well qualified to fill this position which offered him a singular opportunity to deal first hand with producing a portrait that sketched the Black American as a participant and not a problem. For the next four years, the following statement would represent the ideological thrust of Brown's program:

The Negro has too seldom been revealed as an integral part of American life. Many Negro historians have attempted to counter the neglect, but the result has been over-emphasis and "separateness." Where white historians find few or no Negroes and too little important participation, Negro historians find many and too much. This racial bias is understandable but it does not produce the accurate picture of the Negro in American social history.[4]

Through the vehicles of the state guidebooks and special collateral studies, Brown and his staff aimed to counter the neglect and distortions that were characteristic of material on Blacks. Understanding how false Black images had been fashioned in the literature and on the American stage and perpetuated because of their popularity, Brown was convinced that they should not be a part of the picture of Blacks fixed for posterity in FWP books.

Therefore, Brown saw his appointment as proof that the FWP intended to give fair treatment to qualified Black writers as well as Black subject matter. He discovered quickly, however, that he was powerless to ensure the hiring of qualified Blacks outside his immediate staff and that attaining a fair treatment of Black material was fraught with difficulty.[5]

In any assessment of Brown's accomplishments and failures as editor of Negro affairs, three points must be considered if any understanding of Brown's position is to be grasped. First, Brown was appointed to serve in an advisory and editorial capacity. Though he aggressively pursued the aims of FWP, in regards to Blacks, he had to rely on the clout of the central office director to bring pressure to bear on state directors. Second, Brown, like other Project workers, was enmeshed in an agency which, in additon to being young and frequently unsure of its aims, carried with it the bureaucratic tangle, the delays and the political pressures characteristic of older agencies. In the preface of *Washington: City and Capital*, the first major guidebook published by the FWP, the editors pointed out that the young, inexperienced agency had undertaken "one of the largest and most difficult editorial tasks" ever attempted in the country.[6]

Third, and clearly the most challenging obstacle, Brown's work, especially with the state guides, was hampered by partisanship. A number of FWP workers, feeling obligated to present their states as important nationally, engaged in "some local chest thumping" at the government's expense.[7] It was just such chest-thumping that too frequently deteriorated into attitudes of prejudice, masking as sovereign attitudes, which plagued Brown and unfortunately found their way into the copy of guidebooks. Brown who insisted on integrity and truth in guide material was often confronted by the flagrant use of stereotypes of glaring misconceptions concerning disease, mortality, crime, and illiteracy among Blacks. When there were not shrieking charges of reverse chauvinism and infringement upon states rights, there was the equally disheartening silence from those who regarded their Black population as not worth the bother. Whether or not Brown saw himself as the guardian figure of Black images and culture, these assaults thrust him into the role.

With a small editorial staff, including two research assistants from Howard University, Ulysses Lee and Eugene Holmes, Brown coordinated all the Writers' Project's studies by and about Blacks. He reviewed copy prepared by Project writers for inclusion in state guides and suggested revisions. He coordinated an extensive gathering of ex-slave narratives begun in 1934, under the auspices of the Federal Emergency Relief Administration. When Brown inherited the project, research teams were operating in eighteen states. Believing this history of the American Black to be essentially "a story untold," Brown encouraged studies of Black history and folklore in several states. He also was in charge of an inventory of historical manuscripts concerning Black Americans, done as a part of the WPA Historical Records Survey. An enormous volume of material required Brown's attention.

During the summer of 1938, for example, Brown himself was collecting materials on the manuscript titled "Portrait of the Negro as American," and editing guidebook material, ex-slave narratives, a study on the underground railroad and special local studies on the Negro in Virginia, Louisiana, Little Rock, Florida, New York, Philadelphia, South Carolina and Georgia.[8]

Brown's responsibilities also included monitoring the number of Blacks employed in the Project. In a report prepared by his office in February, 1937, the estimated number of Blacks employed was 106, representing only about two percent of the total number of workers enrolled in the Project. For the duration of the Writers' Project, "the number ranged widely between eighty and one hundred fifty, depending on the assumption and conclusion of special projects, and the whims of state directors."[9] Unfortunately, the directors operated for the most part autonomously, especially in their hiring of Blacks despite the urging of the national office to increase the number of Blacks employed.

Brown reported that on some projects all the Black employees had been removed. His frustration is obvious as he singled out the case of Mississippi where "two of the four Negroes were dropped, one 'left' to 'haul cotton,' and the fourth was transferred."[10] The situation in Mississippi generally held throughout the Southern states. Blacks were not used on the projects, with the exception of those working in special projects like those which resulted in the studies, *The Negro in Virginia* and *Survey of Negroes in Little Rock and North Little Rock*.

However, despite the regional biases and neglect that often blocked the hiring of Blacks, several Black writers, some young and unknown others with established reputations, joined state projects during Brown's tenure as Editor on Negro affairs. Twenty-seven year old Richard Wright joined the Writers' Project in 1936. While working for the Project, Wright achieved distinction as a gifted writer of fiction. Before leaving the Writers' Project in 1938, Wright had worked on both the Chicago and New York City projects and had contributed guide material to the Illinois and New York City guidebooks. Margaret Walker, a promising young poet, put her age up to join the Project and became the youngest member of the Illinois group. Another writer, Ralph Ellison, who would later write the classic fictional study of a Black man's invisibility, joined the New York City Project in 1938 and worked steadily on it for the next four years. His work assignments led him to information concerning the history, folklore and culture of Black people which was destined to inform his later fictional works. Frank Yerby, Katherine Dunham, Willard Motley, Ellen Tarry, Roi Ottley, and Ted Poston were among other Black writers whose careers were launched while working on the Writers' Project.

Another group of Black writers received valuable exposure in special Writers' Project anthologies. In the book, *American Stuff*, "a collection of short stories, poems, and Americana by fifty Project writers,"[11] Richard Wright's sketch, "The Ethics of Living Jim Crow" was clearly the most outstanding piece of writing in the volume. Poems by Sterling Brown and Claude McKay also appeared in this collection. Several magazines, including *The New Republic*, *New Masses*, and *Poetry* magazine, devoted large sections or entire issues to WPA writers. Notably, the short stories of Richard Wright and poems by Margaret Walker, Frank Davis, and Sterling Brown appeared in these publications. These appearances were not only important for the national exposure they gave to individual writers but also were significant because they chronicled their writers' responses to the rising tide of socialism, unionism and labor coalitions among the races, crime, poverty, racial violence, disenfranchisement, and other pressing issues of the times.

A few Black writers, such as Arna Bontemps, Zora Neale Hurston, and Claude McKay, were established writers before coming to work on the Project and were able to use this opportunity to increase their creative projectivity. Zora Neale Hurston, while a member of the Florida Project, published *Their Eyes Were Watching God* (1937), *Tell My Horse* (1938), and *Moses, Man of the Mountain* (1939). Arna Bontemps published *Drums at Dusk* (1939) while a supervisor on the Illinois Project. And Claude McKay gathered material for his last book *Harlem: Negro Metropolis* (1940) while a member of the New York Project.[12]

Besides these field workers in state projects, Brown had contact with many consultants on Black affairs throughout the country. A partial list includes: Mary McLeod Bethune in Florida, Monroe Work and Frederick D. Patterson in Alabama, Horace Mann Bond and Allison Davis in Louisiana, Charles S. Johnson, Thomas Talley and John Work in Tennessee, N. P. Tillman and Rayford Logan in Georgia, and Arthur P. Davis and Anne Spencer in Virginia. Brown was certain that these people were essential if the rich material about Blacks was to be brought to light. Brown was equally certain that "for anything like a fair representation of the Negro in the Federal Writers' Project more Negro workers (were) urgently needed."[13]

In actuality, however, the largest part of what was written about Blacks in the FWP was written by whites. For instance, the gathering of ex-slave narratives was largely the work of white interviewers. Concerned that these interviews achieve a high level of authenticity and honesty in their presentation of this material, Brown and Alsberg sent a detailed set of suggestions to each state where workers were involved in collecting ex-slave narratives. Specific guidelines suggested the proper interviewing procedures and techniques designed to record the material accurately without excessive intrusion and distortion by the interviewer. Brown was especially concerned that the dialect recorded be appropriate and untampered with.

I should like to recommend that the stories be told in the language of the ex-slave, without excessive editorializing and "artistic" introduction on the part of the interviewer. The contrast between the directness of the ex-slave speech and the roundabout and, at times, pompous comments of the interviewer is frequently glaring.[14]

Brown's long-standing acquaintance with folk speech had convinced him that there was nothing degraded about it. On the contrary, he recognized in the dialect a musicality and often an ironic turn of phrase worth preserving. Brown also felt strongly that readers were repelled by the excessive use of misspellings, commas, and apostrophes by several interviewers all in the name of recording the speech peculiarities of a group. With simplicity as the method of approach, Brown recommended "that truth to idiom be paramount, and exact truth to pronunciation secondary."[15]

Working with the Project's folklore editor, Benjamin Botkin, Brown also restructured the interviewer's questionnaire to include questions that revealed attitudes and issues rarely viewed from an ex-slave's perspective. In a March, 1972 interview with historian Gladys-Marie Fry, Brown told her that the questionnaire was redesigned to include such neglected topics as the freedman's attitudes toward Reconstruction, voting, holding office, and the influence of secret organizations.[16]

However, because of the strong influence exerted by state editors in determining the shape of slave narrative material, Brown's efforts at the national level could not ensure a consistently high standard of authenticity. For example, in the South Carolina project, interviewers had real difficulty recording "gullah" dialect of Blacks living in the coastal regions. This problem was compounded by the tendency of several old story tellers to deceive their interviewers by telling fanciful tales about slavery that stretched the truth. The question as to whether a group of Black interviewers could have interpreted and presented the ex-slaves more authentically is, at this point, academic, for the director of the Project in South Carolina, Miss Mable Montgomery, refused to hire Blacks as interviewers, believing that whites were more "discriminating."[17]

On the contrary, Brown believed that the tendency of some writers to proclaim confidently that they had captured the essence of "the Negro Type" led to the imbalances and distortions that too frequently appeared in ex-slave narratives and guidebook materials. In his comments on material dealing with survivals among Georgia coastal Blacks, later published as *Drums and Shadows* (1940), by the Georgia Writers' Project, Brown indicated that the book suffered from a "lack of balance." The thrust of his criticism was aimed at interviewers and writers who were mesmerized by the quaint and the eccentric. In a report written more than six months before the book was actually published, Brown wrote:

> By concentrating on the primitive aspects of a few people interviewed, a whole section and a large number of people who have many more things of equal and greater importance in their lives, are really done injustice. To concentrate on Daddy Grace's and Father Divine's services to the exclusion of so many more preachers who may not be as spectacular and eccentric—although quite as emotional—is an example of this lack of balance.[18]

For Brown, what had promised to be an earnest study of the customs and beliefs of Georgia Coastal Blacks resulted in "a quest for eccentricities."[19] Extensive rewriting and editing, excessive irregularities in recording dialect, and biases of both interviewer and the informant seriously undermined the overall quality of these narratives.[20]

Unfortunately, the treatment of Black subjects in some guidebook material, especially that written in projects in Southern states, was often far less successful than that presented in ex-slave narrative write-ups. Sometimes Blacks were often summarily absent from guidebook copy. In a controversy that centered around the historical essay done by the Alabama project, Brown and Cronyn, took issue with the fact that Booker T. Washington was given only passing notice in the essay. The state director, Miss Myrtle Miles, reasoned that Washington, "was not a native Alabamian" and should not be given preferential treatment simply because he was a national figure. Brown and Cronyn saw Miss Miles' stance as a direct slight to the memory of Washington and an indication of her prejudicial attitudes against him and the "other million" Blacks in Alabama's population.[21]

Booker T. Washington's treatment in Alabama state guide copy is emblematic of the persistent patterns of neglect and silence that characterized the treatment of Blacks in state copy. In the city and tour descriptions of several Southern states, no mention was made of heavily populated Black areas such as Beaufort, Tallahassee, Biloxi, Portsmouth, and Blackwell, Arkansas.[22] Entire Black communities in the six New England states went unnoticed in state guides that were written before Brown became editor. For example, in *Massachusetts: A*

Guide to Its Places and People, the question of Black people was settled with only passing reference to Phillis Wheatley, Frederick Douglass, and Crispus Attucks.[23] The omissions were often blatant. Miami FWP workers predictably left out of their history copy such colorful public transportation regulations as "Nigger, don't let the sun set on you here." Missouri workers decided that photos of rural shanties occupied by Black families in Independence were better left out. And the New Jersey project found it expedient to omit the fact that illiteracy among Blacks was much lower than that among whites.[24]

Invariably, when Blacks were mentioned in much of the early copy, the reliance upon stereotypes, misconceptions, and inexcusable ignorance evoked myths instead of men. Blacks in Georgia had "only affectionate regard" for their masters; in Dover, Delaware, they "whistle melodiously" while they work;[25] and in Alabama they were "economically and spiritually better off" in the three of four decades before the Civil War than they were in the twenty years after the war.[26]

Brown saw the latter statement made in connection with the Alabama project's essay on "Negro Life in Alabama" as an inexcusable apology for slavery. He heartily rejected the project's intent to cast the Negro in the light of a long-cherished plantation tradition. Needless to say, any suggestions and criticisms that he made to the Alabama staff met with resistance. What resulted was a pitched battle of letters that lasted several months. Predictably, Brown's criticisms and revised essay made him the target of personal attacks. Calling Brown's criticism "biased," the state director argued that the facts as Brown presented them "could not possibly be received by our fellow citizens of good judgment with approval." She added, "I believe, Alabamians understand the Alabama Negro and the general Negro situation in Alabama better than a critic whose life has been spent in another section of the country however studious he may be."[27] She rejected out of hand Brown's essay as representing the viewpoint of "a Yankee" even though it relied upon the studies of Howard Odum and Arthur Raper, white scholars of the University of North Carolina. However, because Brown received the support of Alsberg and Cronyn in the Washington office, his corrections stood.

Sterling Brown engaged in another skirmish with the director of the South Carolina project over the write-up on the Negro section of Beaufort Guide. Brown objected to certain passages in the section because they lacked genuineness which he felt was sacrificed for popularity.

He, therefore, rewrote the section. Upon receiving the revision, the director Mabel Montgomery charged that Brown had written a "sociological discourse carrying a northern slant." In a letter addressed to Henry Alsberg, she said that "Beaufort is tired of being portrayed from a northern view point which is obvious in Professor Brown's treatment." In her estimation, the changes suggested by Brown would have the effect of undermining the "color and charm" of the article and would deprive Beaufort residents of the "picturesque" treatment which pleased them immensely.[28] Brown, in answering Miss Montgomery, was convinced that the "half-truths" prevalent in the original article were not enough, however picturesque and pleasing they were to Beaufort whites. Yet, despite these efforts, Brown's criticisms were largely ignored.

Perhaps no other project frustrated Brown's efforts at copy editing more than the Mississippi project. In a May, 1938 letter to Alsberg, Brown went on record as having previously criticized and objected to "the complete omissions, as well as distortions, and anti-Negro propaganda," that appeared in the published guidebook, *Mississippi: A Guide to the Magnolia State*. Brown objected to the way Blacks were summarily stereotyped and patronized in a section entitled "Negro Folkways." By way of introduction, the narrator of the book confidently tossed off aspects of the personality of the Mississippi folk Negro.

Those who know him well enough to understand something of his psychology, his character, and his needs, and like him well enough to accept his deficiencies, find him to be wise but credulous—a superstitious paradox. He seems to see all things, hear all things, believe all things. But ask him a question and he will have neither seen, heard, nor believed. He counsels himself and walks his way alone.[29]

Generally, however, the response to criticisms sent out from his office was, in Brown's words, "all that could be desired." "Dogmatic generalizations and expressions of prejudice" occurred less and less frequently and enlightened and sympathetic treatment was given to Black subjects in such states as Louisiana, Ohio, and Georgia. Though "Brown arrived too late to prevent the gross neglect of the American Negro in the six New England state guidebooks," he persuaded most state editors to include material on Black Americans in their guidebooks.[30] He especially urged the adequate treatment of Blacks living in towns and cities where their numbers were large, and wrote a comprehensive set of suggestions to assist state directors in handling this portion of the population. Recognizing that Blacks frequently belonged to the "backyard problem" of cities, he, nonetheless, argued that "if our publications are to be true guides to American life, the Negro cannot be so completely relegated to the background."[31]

The coverage given to Blacks in the guidebooks, though admittedly sketchy, reflected the impact of Black life and culture on American society and the complex, often paradoxical attitudes that pervade race relations. Also suggested in the guides was the developing sympathetic relation of the New Deal toward American Blacks. "The New Deal social and economic legislation represented a change from the racism and exclusionism of the old order. It was fitting and necessary that the FWP should describe the important contribution of . . . Negroes to American life."[32]

Brown applauded the New Deal's concern that Black participation be fairly represented and pushed for a more extensive investigation of Black history and culture than could be accomplished in the limited scope of the guidebooks. To this end, he initiated field projects in several states where researchers delved into historical records, newspapers, books and journals, collected folklore and ex-slave narratives, and conducted numerous interviews in an attempt to piece together the grossly neglected story of the Black American. Of the special projects initiated at Brown's suggestion, the one conducted in Virginia resulted in the most outstanding publication. *The Negro in Virginia*, the collective effort of fifteen Black writers and researchers, was published in 1940 and immediately became the model for other studies of its kind.

Under the supervision of Roscoe E. Lewis, who wrote the first and final drafts of the work, the project worked for more than three years to make the book a reality. All along Brown supported the efforts of this project with many practical suggestions and criticisms. He also sent Ulysses Lee of his staff to Hampton for several weeks to work with Lewis on the book. In the "Preface" of the book, Lewis noted that it was appropriate that the first WPA book on the Negro be produced in Virginia: "for here the first African natives were brought and held in enforced servitude, and here, also, more than two centuries later, freedom for some 5,000,000 of their descendants was assured on the surrender grounds at Appomattox."[33] As Brown had envisioned, *The Ne-*

gro in Virginia, a rich, dramatic, often inspiring chronicle of the race's progress in that state, essentially told the story of the Black man in America.

One year after its publication, Brown, Arthur P. Davis and Ulysses Lee, wrote about the book's importance in the anthology *The Negro Caravan*.

The significance of *The Negro in Virginia* is that it is an instance of a governmental cultural agency's sponsorship of a serious history of a minority group. It has been praised as one of the finest productions of the Federal Writers' Project. It is the first state history of the Negro ever published. Not the work of a professional historian, its approach through anecdote, interview, and documents makes for good social history.[34]

As Lewis stated the project's aim to tell impartially of the "springs that watered" and "the droughts that withered" the roots of Black families nurtured in Virginia, he echoed Brown's long-held aspiration to see the story of American Blacks told impartially, truthfully, and, therefore, powerfully.

Perhaps, the second most significant work to come out of the Special Black studies projects, *The Negro in New York: An Informal Social History, 1626–1940*, was published many years after the end of the Writers' Project. Jerre Mangione, in *The Dream and the Deal*, tells the interesting story of the disposition of the enormous amount of material researched and collected by the New York City project and the intervening quarter of a century that passed before the book's publication. According to Mangione, Roi Ottley, who supervised the project's Black writers, boldly appropriated this material at what he thought was the end of the project.

Ottley kept the material only long enough to draw from it the information needed for his book, *New World A-Coming*. In 1940, about a year after he had left the Project, he delivered all the Project papers in his possession to the keepers of the Schomburg Collection of Negro Literature and History in the New York City Public Library. The curator accepted the material for safe keeping without asking any questions that might embarrass Ottley, apparently aware that, with the firing of Henry Alsberg from the Project in 1939 and the resignation of Sterling Brown in the following year, the Writers' Program, as it was now called, had no further interest in Negro studies.[35]

Shortly before resigning from the Writers' Project, Brown wrote these comments about the New York book he assumed was close to publication: " 'Negroes of New York' (as it was then referred to) should be an extremely valuable work, one of the most significant of the publications of the project." [36] Aware of the potentially great attraction of the book, Brown strongly suggested to Ottley that the book should be shored up on all sides. He wrote, "Since the book is on one of America's controversial subjects, all care should be taken to make it one hundred proof." [37] Finding occasional inaccuracies in interpretation and bibliographical references, Brown suggested that they be rechecked for accuracy and logic. He urged balance in the presentation of personalities and events in such a way as to prevent colorful figures from dwarfing more significant social movements. He also urged a consistency in tone to avoid distracting leaps "from extreme Harlemese to the academic."

Though Brown admittedly made these comments to make a good book better, "The Negro in New York," as finally published, fell short of the book "unimpeachable in accuracy, interpretation, and style" which Brown had envisioned. However, to the book's credit, northern racial attitudes were presented in raw truth. The harshness and beauty of life in New York for thousands of Blacks were exposed without bias. And in that, Brown believed the book achieved significantly.

Besides being involved in reviewing and editing the work coming out of these special state-wide studies, Brown and his staff were engaged in writing a book of national scope titled "The Portrait of the Negro as American" and collecting material to be used in a documentary study of the Underground Railroad. Working with Brown on these projects was Glaucia B. Roberts. Joining his staff in June, 1936, she was chiefly responsible for all editorial work done in the office during the year (1937–1938) Brown spent on the Guggenheim fellowship. In January, 1940, Brown was still attempting to bring these projects to completion. "The Portrait of the Negro as American" was to be a "composite portrait of the American Negro, set squarely against the background of America, . . . an essay in social history and biography, not an exercise in race glorification." Obviously enthusiastic, Brown promised that the project would result in something not attempted before. The book would include dramatic scenes from Black history such as "Jim Beckwourth ruling over the Creeks with big lies and big deeds, John Chavis teaching the classics to slaveholders' sons, Denmark Vesey plotting at Charleston, Harriet Tubman leading the slaves out of 'Egypt,' Frederick Douglass being mobbed in Illinois, Madison Washington leading the 'meeting' on the *Creole*.'' The Black soldiers who fought at Boston Common, Bunker Hill, San Juan Hill, and in the trenches in France and "newsworthies" like Joe Louis, Father Divine, Bojangles Robinson, and the Scottsboro boys would join the countless other Americans of color in forming this "mosaic of Negro life in America."[38] However, this work and the other studies started by his office, remain unfinished histories. With Brown's resignation from the Project a few months later, the manuscripts became the property of the archives of the Library of Congress, leaving the composite portrait of American Blacks incomplete.

The full-scale study in the Underground Railroad was also never completed. However, Sterling Brown was able to rescue from oblivion many little known facts concerning "one of the most dramatic chapters in the saga of democracy" by including them in "Saving the Cargo: Sidelights on the Underground Railroad." In this piece published in 1941, he writes:

Too many historians seemed anxious to dismiss the abolitionist as "fanatics" and "hotheads," and to establish slavery as a kindly guardianship for wards who were "naturally docile." To these historians, the Underground Railroad with its thousands of passengers was an uncomfortable rebuttal, to be thrust out of sight. But the truth—of countless fugitives taking the long chance, trudging through the night toward the North Star, hidden by friendly whites and Negroes in attics and closets, barns and hayracks, passing back by "grapevine telegraph" messages of successful ruses, of the safe roads and the hazardous, and the good news of final arrival at Rochester, Syracuse, Buffalo, Boston, or better still "under the paw of the British Lion" in Canada—this truth could not forever be hidden.[39]

In this article Brown tells of the heroism of unsung heroes as well as the spirited abolitionism of Harriet Tubman, Henry Highland Garnet, and Samuel Ringgold Ward. The dramatic accounts of rescues and escapes and tales of the menacing presence of slave-catchers and the betrayal of "Judases ready to sell their brothers for a price" rounded out his brief but important "sidelights." Like those who banded together to ensure the safe passage of slaves to freedom, Brown became an agent ensuring the passage of a significant body of historical information about

Blacks in this country. For he believed, "To forget men and women of this mettle is to do injustice to the story of American democracy."[40]

However, as it happened, Brown made his single most enduring contribution to the Writers' Project in the early days of his association. As an editor on the national staff, Brown was involved in writing the massive guidebook, *Washington: City and Capital*. To this volume, which was published in 1937, Brown contributed the essay, "The Negro in Washington." At once an assessment and indictment of the plight of Blacks in Washington, the essay was Brown's master stroke of social criticism.

In recounting the story of Black life in the nation's capital—the blight of the slave yards ensconced in the seat of justice, the notorious alley system and the crime, squalor, and disease that laced it, the network of self-help organizations, and the separate and unequal participation of Blacks in the workings of Washingtonian "democracy," Brown was able to suggest the city's duplicity. He began his essay with the subtle statement of irony by the Irish poet Thomas Moore who had visited the capital when it was still young. Moore's lines brought into sharp contrast two societies, one slave and one free, and the medley of "manacles and rights" that characterized them.[41] Continuing this theme, Brown traced the incongruous co-existence of the ideal of freedom and justice and the often disappointing reality of Black life in the District. He wrote about Blacks' zeal for education which was fired by the knowledge of a tradition of overcoming insuperable odds, he cited their political apathy resulting from decades of disenfranchisement, and he noted their seething rage, the result of a heritage of frustration and despair, which threatened to erupt in riots and racial violence.[42] "In this border city, Southern in so many respects, there is a denial of democracy, at times hypocritical and at times flagrant."[43] And more important, Brown, with the controlled, perceptive view of an insider, a Black Washingtonian, presented for the first time the vibrant portrait of a people whose very presence represented a challenge to Washington's democracy.

Brown's essay sent shock waves through the seats of government. In April, 1939, Representative Frank Keefe, a Republican from Wisconsin, charged the central office with allowing "the influence of communistically inspired agitators" to insert "insidious propaganda" into the Washington Guide.[44] This was not the first time that a Project publication had been labeled Communist propaganda. Sterling Brown, who had the final responsibility for the essay, found himself the object of FBI scrutiny for the next five years.[45]

The so-called "insidious propaganda" that Brown allowed in the guide was a report that George Washington Parke Custis, foster son of President Washington and father-in-law of Robert E. Lee, had left a tract in Arlington to his Black daughter, Maria Syphax. Through Keefe labeled this material libelous and "stimulating racial intolerance," Brown considered his charges as "badges of honor." Ulysses Lee, who had assisted Brown with much of the original research was amazed that so much was being made of this issue, especially since the Custis family had not objected to the material mentioned in the essay. He was also surprised to find the files missing when he returned to the public library at which he had done his original research. Unfortunately, in the subsequent edition of the Washington guide, for all its brave facts and revelations, this episode was deleted.[46]

For Brown, the Federal Writers' Project was a practical experiment in flexing his critical muscles and in applying his developing aesthetic principles in the dynamic arena of government publications. Insisting on the validity of the Black cultural heritage, Brown used the Project to unearth, to what degree possible, the little known story of Black Americans. His efforts encouraged the first significant studies of Blacks and helped foster the preservation of ex-slave narratives and remnants of folklore, soon to be lost with the passing of aged cultural bearers. The value of these studies, according to Brown, rested on their ability to render the truth of Black life in such a way as to influence Black Americans to understand and appreciate the value of their contribution. Brown urged that, besides rendering a faithful portrayal of truth, these studies should reflect clarity and simplicity in style and a sympathetic, balanced approach.

In all his efforts as national editor of Negro affairs, Brown recognized the socio-historical forces that affected the way in which Black Americans were dealt with. Naturally, he expected resistance from certain groups who did not stand to benefit from a fair treatment of Blacks in either hiring practices or in written coverage in guidebook material. Brown was aware that some writers would continue to cast Blacks in neatly stereotyped grooves that served to justify and excuse the injustices of their cherished caste system. He also knew that certain interest groups would choose to ignore the presence of Blacks in urban areas and in the North, even though their numbers were large. However, his own critical approach eschewed futile gestures toward special group pleading or glorification, and his understanding of social forces in America permitted him no false optimism concerning the benefits of the Project to Blacks.

Despite Brown's valuable contribution, the Writers' Project achieved only a small part of what it held out to Black Americans. Though Brown attempted to make the Project an effective vehicle by which the participation of Blacks in American life could be presented on its own terms, his goals exceeded his grasp. Brown was a Black voice crying in the wilderness of the Depression years, and, as in the case of the proverbial prophet, the times were not yet able to accommodate his vision.

NOTES

1. Gladys-Marie Fry, *Night Riders in Black Folk History* (Knoxville: University of Tennessee Press, 1975), p. 20.

2. Jerre Mangione, *The Dream and the Deal: The Federal Writers' Project, 1935–1943* (Boston: Little, Brown and Company, 1972), pp. 257–58.

3. Monty Noam Penkower, *The Federal Writers' Project: A Study in Government Patronage of the Arts* (Urbana: University of Illinois Press, 1977), pp. 66 and 140.

4. Copy memo (Brown) to Munson, January 9, 1940, file, "Memos" Negro Studies, Federal Writers' Project, National Archives, pertaining to Record Group 69. Hereafter cited as Negro Studies. Records in the National Archives are indicated by the abbreviation NA followed by the record group (RG) number.

5. Penkower, *The Federal Writers' Project*, p. 140.

6. *Washington: City and Capital*, p. v.

7. Daniel M. Fox, "The Achievement of the Federal Writers' Project," *American Quarterly*, 13 (Spring 1961): 4.

8. Allen Francis Kifer, "The Negro Under the New Deal, 1933–1941" (Ph.D. dissertation, University of Wisconsin, 1961), Ann Arbor, Mich.: University Microfilms, Inc., 1971, p. 237. Memo (Brown) to Dr. (Benjamin A.) Botkin, June 11, 1938, file, "Memos," reports and miscellaneous records pertaining to Negro Studies, NA, RG 69.

9. Kifer, "The Negro Under the New Deal," p. 237.

10. Brown, "Report from the Editor on Negro Affairs," February 1937, file "Letters from State Directors," Negro Studies, NA, RG 69.

11. Mangione, *The Dream and the Deal*, p. 244.

12. Ibid., p. 257.

13. Brown, "Report from the Editor on Negro Affairs," Negro Studies, NA, RG 69.

14. Memo (Brown) to State Directors, n.d., file "General Letters," Negro Studies, NA, RG 69.

15. Ibid.

16. Fry, *Night Riders in Black Folk History*, p. 21.

17. Kifer, "The Negro Under the New Deal," p. 238.

18. Copy Memo (Brown) to Director of Georgia Project, August 16, 1939, file "General Letters," Negro Studies, NA, RG 69.

19. Ibid.

20. Fry, *Night Riders in Black Folk History*, pp. 22–23.

21. Copy George W. Cronyn to Myrtle Miles, November 5, 1936, file, "General Letters," Negro Studies, NA, RG 69.

22. Penkower, *The Federal Writers' Project*, pp. 140–41.

23. Federal Writers' Project, *Massachusetts: A Guide to Its Places and People* (Boston: Houghton-Mifflin Company, 1937), pp. 6ff.

24. Penkower, *The Federal Writers' Project*, p. 141.

25. Ibid., pp. 141–42.

26. Copy Myrtle Miles to Henry G. Alsberg, March 4, 1937, file, "Incoming Letters by State," Negro Studies, NA, RG 69.

27. Copy Myrtle Miles to George Cronyn, August 17, 1937, file, "Incoming Letters by State," Negro Studies, NA, RG 69.

28. Mabel Montgomery to Henry G. Alsberg, May 4, 1937, file, "Beaufort," Negro Studies, NA, RG 69.

29. Federal Writers' Project, *Mississippi: A Guide to the Magnolia State*, (New York: Viking Press, 1938), p. 22.

30. Mangione, *The Dream and the Deal*, p. 259.

31. Memo (Brown) to Henry G. Alsberg, June 8, 1937, file, "Memos," Negro Studies; Memo (Brown) to Alsberg, June 17, 1938, file, "Memos," Negro Studies, NA, RG 69.

32. Fox, "The Achievement of the Federal Writers' Project," p. 14.

33. Writers' Project of Virginia, FWP, *The Negro in Virginia* (New York: Hastings House, 1940), p. v.

34. Brown, Davis, and Lee, *The Negro Caravan*, p. 847.

35. Mangione, *The Dream and the Deal*, pp. 261–62.

36. Sterling A. Brown, "Editorial Report," April 11, 1940, file, "Memos," Negro Studies, NA, RG 69.

37. Ibid.

38. Memo (Brown) to Munson, January 9, 1940, file, "Memos," Negro Studies, NA, RG 69.

39. Sterling A. Brown, "Saving the Cargo: Sidelights on the Underground Railroad," *The Negro History Bulletin*, 4 (April 1941): 151.

40. Ibid., p. 154.
41. Brown, "The Negro in Washington," p. 68.
42. Penkower, *The Federal Writers' Project*, p. 204.
43. Brown, "The Negro in Washington," p. 90.
44. Penkower, *The Federal Writers' Project*, p. 203.
45. Ibid., pp. 204–5.
46. Ibid., p. 205.

5
THE INFLUENCES OF THE FOLK TRADITION

The single most pervasive influence on the literary career of Sterling A. Brown is the Black folk and cultural tradition. At many stages in his career as poet, teacher, and critic, he has rubbed shoulders with the people who are the source for a vital folklore, which has deeply influenced the way he thinks and writes about the Black man in American literature and culture. Brown has described himself as an "amateur" in his approach to folklore, distinguishing what he does from the scientific handling of the material used by the folklorist.[1] The tag is appropriate because Brown did not concern himself with such traditional folklore projects as mapping the spread of various folklore motifs over a specific geographical area from one generation to the next or systematically gathering histories of oral material in particular communities.[2] In his role as casual observer, Brown avoided the natural barriers of distrust and deception put up by some folk informants, who were intimidated by the collector with pen and pad or recording machine. He listened to the people when they were least self-conscious and recorded in his mind the subtle inflections, pauses, nuances, and gestures that annotated their speech and songs. In doing this, he became acquainted with the broad range of their emotional and social responses to life: their loves, resentments, hopes, despairs, joys, and sorrows. Thus, Brown has pursued the study of Black folk songs, folk tales, folk sayings, and folk speech for the sheer pleasure of revelation. The stuff of human social drama, the vigorous folk qualities, the vibrant speech and striking poetry, the patterns of spiritual struggle, the highly creative folk imagination, among others, have brought Brown time and again to this folk source, and he has not left unfulfilled.

During the 1940s and early 1950s Brown did his most extensive exploration of folklore and folk forms. However, even as he attempted a definition of folk culture, it was "breaking up." The isolation that had spawned it was being encroached upon, and the rural needs that it had served were giving way to the more modern demands and challenges of urban and industrialized centers. Viewing the prospects of folk culture, Brown gave this vivid picture of the changing cultural scene in 1953:

Where Negro met only with Negro in the black belt the old beliefs strengthened. But when mud traps give way to gravel roads, and black tops and even concrete highways with buses and jalopies and trucks lumbering over them, the world comes closer. The churches and schools, such as they are, struggle against some of the results of isolation, and the radio plays a part. Even in the backwoods, aerials are mounted on shanties that seem ready to collapse from the extra weight on the roof, or from a good burst of static against the walls. The phonograph is common, the television set is by no means unknown, and down at the four corners store, a jukebox gives out the latest jive. Rural folk closer to towns and cities may on Saturday jaunts even see an occasional movie, where a rootin'-tootin' western gangster film introduces them to the advancements of civilization. Newspapers, especially the Negro press, give the people a sense of belonging to a larger world. Letters from their boys in the army, located in all corners of the world, and the tales of the world, and the tales of the returning veterans, true Marco Polos, also prod the inert into curiosity. Brer Rabbit and Old Jack no longer are enough. Increasingly in the churches the spirituals lose favor to singout of the books or from broadsides, and city-born blues and jive take over the jook-joints.[3]

However, despite the encroachments and the demands of modern life, Brown saw the folk roots exhibiting "a stubborn vitality." For "even in the transplanting, a certain kind of isolation—class and racial"— remained, and the need of a transplanted people to define themselves also remained strong.[4]

Thoroughly familiar with the folk base of other cultures, Brown saw Black folk sharing with other folk groups the ability to limn their own portrait. Black folk shared and held in trust a common set of values, myths, and rituals which constituted, as George Kent suggests, their "definitions of existence." These "definitions of existence" were born and nurtured in some form of isolation—frequently geographical and in some cases psychological.[5] Black folk defined themselves despite and possibly in response to social, economic, and political conditions which were, more often than not, characterized by oppression, exploitation, denial, and persecution. They were able to preserve and pass on those values that were enduring and abiding.

Brown's approach to defining the folk was based on a revelation of them through the forms that they created. These forms express dramatically the folk character and scene. Like Brown, Ralph Ellison attributes to folk culture the power to portray a group's character. In this connection, Ellison articulates in an important interview appearing in *Shadow and Act* the value of folklore in answering the questions: "What are the specific *forms* of that humanity, and what in our background is worth preserving or abandoning." According to Ellison, folklore offers "the first drawings of any group's character" and "describes those boundaries of feeling, thought and action which that particular group has found to be the limitation of the human condition." "It's no accident," Ellison says, "that great literature . . . is erected on this humble base."[6] He further says that the Black folk tradition "teaches one to deflect racial provocation," "to master and contain pain," "to abhor as obscene any trading on one's own anguish for gain or sympathy, which springs not from a desire to deny the harshness of existence but from a will to deal with it as men at their best have always done."[7] Black folk "having retained their humanity before all of the conscious efforts made to dehumanize them," rely upon their own experience "for an accurate picture of the reality which they seek to change, and for a gauge of the values they would see manifest."[8] The power that Ellison attributes to the folk culture Brown could attest to because he had seen firsthand how the folk could wring out of a statement every drop of sentimentality and reveal frankly their weaknesses and their strengths, all the time testing their existence against reality. Brown also recognized how these same people, when the American society had locked them into a system of oppression and marshalled its forces to deny their humanity, had negated those forces in gestures of originality, vitality, and spirituality.

Yet, what is more significant, Brown brought to his study of folk culture a keen objectivity that ruled out an uncritical idealization of everything "folk." He read widely in Irish, English, German, and French folklore and literature. Relying on this solid basis of scholarship, Brown examined what Synge and Yeats had done with folklore in Irish literature and what Masefield, Hardy, and Galsworthy had done in English literature, and he saw Black folklore operating in much the same manner in American literature. His disciplined approach served to rescue folklore from bias and controversy and make it useful for the critic and creative writer.

From Brown's earliest exposure to the living folklore of neighboring Black settlements in Washington, D.C., and the rural communities in the South, he has taken the approach of the creative writer to this body of folklore. Speaking on the subject "The Approach of the Creative Artist" at the Conference on Character and State of Studies in Folklore in 1946, Brown said:

I became interested in folklore because of my desire to write poetry and prose fiction. I was first attracted by certain qualities that I thought the speech of the people had, and I wanted to get for my own writing a flavor, a color, a pungency of speech. Then later I came to something more important—I wanted to get an understanding of people, to acquire an accuracy in the portrayal of their lives.[9]

Brown was drawn to the wellspring of the tradition: the people themselves. On his travels in the South, on the plantations, in the camps, the fields and factories, Brown encountered people who responded to life in a manner that struck him as original and unpretentious. Living in a kind of isolation, sometimes "cut off from progress geographically"—like the sea-islanders, swamp dwellers, or the people on back-country plantations—or "socially isolated by segregation and lack of educational and economic advantages," these rural folk were left to their own resources to articulate the terms of their existence.[10] The sharecroppers, the convicts, the stevedores, the domestics, itinerant ministers, the roustabouts, the factory workers whom Brown met shared in common a set of customs, practices, values, beliefs, and ways of looking at the world that constituted their cultural heritage. It was their articulation of this heritage that was transmitted orally in the form of spirituals, blues, aphorisms, tales, rhymes, work songs, and ballads.

Staying close to the creators of the lore, Brown frequented the places where their wit and humor, tall tales and private jokes were allowed to flow freely. Through an intimate sharing with these people, Brown learned about folk character. Mrs. Bibby, "the wizened woman, spare of frame, but great of heart, erect, and undefeated," whom Brown met during his early years as a teacher, brought Brown into the circle of her wisdom. "Puffing on a jagged slow-burning pipe," she offered him and those others gathered around her hearth cogent messages of strength and dignity. For Brown, Mrs. Bibby exemplified the Christian faith that is the power behind the Black religious songs called spirituals. She helped Brown, the son of a minister, understand the joy of Christian fellowship that informs the spiritual lyrics. "I went down in the valley to pray. My soul got happy and I stayed all day."[11] As the "black and unknown bards" had found comfort and relief in true faith, Mrs. Bibby lived as if to support the claim, "I got a home in that rock, don't you see." "In God's bosom gonna be my pillow."[12] Mrs. Bibby is Brown's "Sis Lou." Comforting a dying friend, she promises:

> Jesus will find yo' bed fo' you
> Won't no servant evah bother wid yo' room.
> Jesus will lead you
> To a room wid windows
> Openin' on cherry trees an' plum trees
> Bloomin' everlastin'.
>
> An' dat will be yours
> Fo' keeps.
>
> Den take yo' time. . . .
> Honey, take yo' bressed time.[13]

Sustained by the heritage of the spirituals, Mrs. Bibby sees heaven as a refuge where the saints of God will meet.

> A—settin' down with Jesus
> Eatin' honey and drinkin' wine
> Marchin' round de throne
> Wid Peter, James and John[14]

As Mrs. Bibby's faith made real the existence of life after death, Revelations, the placard covered halfwit whom Brown met on the dust roads of a Missouri village, prophesied another truth.

> If a man's life goes
> Beyond the bone
> Man must go lonely
> And alone,
> Unhelped, unhindered
> On his own. . . . [15]

The ragged prophet, mumbling obscenities and oblivious to the laughter of the passersby, spoke in the manner of the old folk admonishing the uninitiated:

Life is short and full of blisters.

De quagmire don't hang out no signs.

De graveyard is de cheapes' boardin' house.[16]

Brown listened attentively as Revelations wheezed out the song, "You gotta walk that lonesome valley."[17] And long after Revelations had passed from this world, Brown carried with him the halfwit's text of the fundamental alienation and spiritual isolation of man.

Brown's meaningful contact with many rural Black people made him aware of the range of tones in Black expression, from the notes of fatalism in the warnings of Revelations to the side-splitting humor of master "liars" like Slim and Gilly. Gilly, a barber whom Brown had met in Nashville, and Slim, a loquacious Kansas City waiter who inspired the popular "Slim Greer" series, shared with Brown their consummate knowledge of the folk art of storytelling. They told their tales with a typically American exaggeration and bravado.

Another friend, Calvin "Big Boy" Davis, whom Brown had met at Virginia Seminary, shared with Brown his repetorie of blues, ballads, and barrel house songs. An imposing figure, standing "a head taller" than Brown's own six-foot-three frame, Big Boy passed on his considerable knowledge of railroad lore. Big Boy could make his guitar reproduce the sound of rolling train wheels; his guitar could ring like bells on a freight coming into the yard and sound "two longs and two shorts" like a train nearing the crossroads.[18] Big Boy was also a blues man. Picking out the blues on his guitar, singing "Trouble, trouble, deep down in muh soul," he helped Brown understand the weariness, the melancholy, the trouble in mind.[19] Several years after their meeting, Brown conceptualized the blues sentiment that Big Boy sang about.

One knows that when the river rises remorselessly above the highwater mark, when a loving man takes to the road and leaves the side of his good woman, when the train blows far down the track, or the steamboat heaves in sight around the bend, some singer a long ways from happiness lifts up his voice and tells the world of his trouble.[20]

In St. Louis in the immediate wake of a destructive cyclone, Brown remembered seeing a second-story bedroom with its front wall torn off, and an old woman sitting in a rocking chair, "moaning and chanting, weaving from the tragedy, her own blues."[21]

> The wind was howlin', buildin's begin to fall.
> I seen dat mean o' twister comin' jes lak a cannon ball.[22]

The victims of the "sorry tricks" of nature—the St. Louis cyclone, the Mississippi Valley floods, the ravages of the boll weevil—built their blues from the rubble and the ravaged fields. In the face of disaster, they sang to express their pain while also expressing their will to overcome. Crystallizing the concept in a superb definition, Ellison writes that the blues people kept the painful details of their experience alive, fingered its jagged grain, and transcended it "by squeezing from it a near-tragic, near-comic lyricism."[23]

Expressing their own personal catastrophe, blues singers often sang of careless or unrequited love. Blues singers such as Ma Rainey, Mamie Smith, Bessie Smith, Ida Cox, and Billie Holiday popularized blues that presented love with "shrewd" cynicism or irony or self-pity or sincere despair.[24] Women sang of their mistreating, two-timing, no-good men. Brown heard their discontent in:

> My man's got a heart like a rock cast in the sea[25]

> There are nineteen men living in my neighborhood
> Eighteen of them are fools and the other ain't no doggone good.[26]

He saw them taunting and masking their insecurity and lack of confidence.

> I ain't good lookin', ain't got no great long hair
> But I got ways, baby, that take me everywhere.[27]

He also intuitively understood their near tragic resignation.

> I hear my daddy call some other woman's name
> I know he don't mean me, but I'm gonna answer just the same.[28]

Traveling the roads of the South, Brown closely identified with the folk who longed for a far country, who needed to ramble and believed in "better times up the road." The poignancy of their longing for movement is captured in these blues lines:

> Soon as that freight makes up in the yard
> I'm gonna leave here, baby, if I have to ride the rods.
>
> Did you ever ride on the Mobile Central Line
> It's the road to ride to ease yo' troublin' mind.[29]

Crisscrossing the country, trains such as the Santa Fe, the Southern, the Yellow Dog, the CC. and St. Louis, the Coast Line, the N&W, the L&W, the C&D, the Rock Island, the Illinois Central Railroad Line, the Cannon Ball, and the Dixie Flyer—promised escape. The blues singers who sang their fame knew the frustration of the Black farmhand who, each harvesting season, found himself deeper in debt at the commissary; knew the violence of the turpentine camps and the meanness of the sheriff's men; and knew about cheating women and fly-by-night men. They also knew of dead-end jobs that stole a man's will to work. In a 1930 article, Brown quoted a young Black writer who understood as he did the fascination that trains held for Southern Blacks and the lure of the open road.

I have often thought that the Negro farmhand would lose heart once and for all, were it not for the daily encouragement he takes from the whistle of his favorite locomotives. Tied to his plow, under the red, burning sun, or aching with the loneliness of the sterile night, he can find all his desire for escape, all the courage he lacks in the face of the unknown, mingled with his inescapable hopelessness, in the deep-throated, prolonged blast of the express train, like a challenge to untravelled lands, a terrifying cry to his petty townships.[30]

For those who accepted the "challenge to untravelled lands," the roads usually led northward to the industrial centers of the South and North, to the big cities of the Midwest and East. Yet there, too, the creators and singers of the blues found a tough world where their dreams were often confined to tenements on streets with names like Market, Vine, Dearborn, State, Hasting, and Lomax Avenue.

If Brown was attracted by the lure of the railroad, he was also attracted to the folk's extravagant love of muscular heroes. Some were real like heavyweight fighter Jack Johnson, who challenged, "Heah ah is, big boy, yah see whah Ise at, come on in."[31] or Leadbelly who was "leadman on the hardest chain gangs of Texas and Louisiana" and survived to sing about "Jail House Blues."[32] Some were legendary like John Henry and Stackolee. The folk remembered the John Henry who pits his strength against the machine in one of America's best loved ballads. They also remembered the exploits of Stackolee, who reputedly kills a man over a Stetson hat, and when he goes to hell "challenges the devil to a duel—pitch fork versus forty-one revolver—and then takes over the lower world."[33] Notably, the folk's fascination with heroes and heroic episodes in legend and history runs as a dominant thread throughout Black literature.

In his travels, Brown discovered in the Black folk those qualities that the folk universally share: an ability to express themselves in language that is rich in imagery and metaphor, an awareness of nature born of necessity and a response to it born of familiarity, and the tendency to articulate their joys and pains simply, movingly, and relatively unself-consciously. In one of his earliest interpretations of the blues, Brown wrote: "Stoicism is here as well as self pity . . . rich humor as well as melancholy."[34]

As Brown absorbed the vibrations of folk life and acquainted himself with the tenacious, earthy, resilient folk character, he became suspicious of those writers who would confine Black character to a handful of cherished types. He could not ignore the complexity of folk character.

Both Uncle Remus and Leadbelly portray sides of the Negro folk, but to round out the portraiture Bessie Smith, Josh White, the Gospel Singing Two Keys, and such big old liars as those heard by E.C.L. Adams in Congaree swamps and by Zora Neale Hurston in Central Florida are also needed.[35]

In fact, the complexity of folk character became Brown's exacting measure of character portrayal. Brown also regarded the literature of the folk as the most convincing interpretation of Black folk life and character available to those who seek to know the truth about American Blacks. Writing in *The Negro Caravan*, he commented on the ability of folklore to dispel stereotypes:

> The record of the Negro author extends well over a century and a half. But Negro expression was not confined to the printed page, written under abolitionist sponsorship in the North. In the South, on cotton and tobacco plantations, in field and factory, along "slave row" and in the dark rooms adjoining the slave marts, in camp meetings and in secret brush arbors, the slaves were creating a fine body of folksong—such spirituals as "Swing Low, Sweet Chariot" and "Deep River," and such satires as "My Ole Mosser Promise Me." From these folk expressions of slavery to contemporary blues and worksongs, the folk Negro has revealed himself to be more than contented slave, comic buffoon, and wretched freedman.[36]

According to Brown, the spirituals had nothing of the contentment with slavery that seemed to be the cornerstone of writing by such interpreters of Black life as Irwin Russell, Thomas Nelson Page, and Joel Chandler Harris. Brown saw the interpretations of these men as limited and one-sided. Russell's jocular picture of life in the quarters, Page's fabrications concerning "the good old times" of slavery, and Harris' milquetoast treatment of folk animal tales were poor thirds, in Brown's opinion, to existing folk literature.[37]

> Negro folksongs, from the earliest down to those uncovered by Laurence Gellert, are invaluable to anyone seeking to know the American Negro. They constitute a very adept self-portraiture—each in humor, equally convincing in light heartedness and tragedy, they put to shame much of the interpretation of the Negro from without.[38]

Even those efforts by conscious artists within the race such as Phillis Wheatley, Jupiter Hammon, and Alberry Whitman, who stayed too close to accepted literary models of their day, pale in the light of existing expressions. Speaking of these poets in his survey of early Black poetry in *Negro Poetry and Drama*, Brown said that they were "frequently too self-conscious," and their poetry, too dependent on Western models, never achieved the depth of originality of folk expressions.[39]

Because folk literature was conceived and developed in the matrix of the folk circle, it was a product of folk acceptance. In the introduction to the "Folk Literature" section in *The Negro Caravan*, Brown gave a convincing view of how the folk pulled from a common storehouse in producing the spirituals. He explained that individuals "with poetic ingenuity, a rhyming gift, or a good memory" composed or remembered lines out of the folk storehouse and in conjunction with the group, and with its approval, shaped the stanzas. As these songs were passed from one generation to the next, the songs were changed, updated, and sometimes lost. However, the very group that produced them also helped to keep them alive.[40]

In folk art, the group and the creator functioned as one unit. For instance, a basic pattern in the folk communications, call and response, was designed to "synthesize speakers and listeners" in a kind of "perfected social interaction."[41] As the individual artist can only hope to create character and situation and recreate feelings and emotions that bring pleasure and insight to his audience, the folk artist, being so closely tied to group members, saw them not as a distant audience but as participants. His themes also were rendered in such a way as to apply broadly to the group, not specifically to individuals. As in some African communities, the folk artist based his messages on the synergic functioning of "I" and "We."

Such a community survives on the rhythm of "I am, because we are; and since we are, therefore, I am." What happens to one in some way affects the entire community, and what happens to the entire community necessarily affects all individuals within that community. Neither "I" nor "we" have meaning apart from the other.[42]

Ironically, the folk were aware that this pattern took on even deeper significance in the American society where individualism was a watchword of democracy, and racism, a reality. What finally emerged from the group circle was a portraiture of the folk—themselves, their concerns, their temperaments, and their group spirit, along with an art that did not suffer from self-consciousness or imitativeness.

The folk artists who created the blues, however, created in solitude, yet their blues messages intimately touched their listeners. In one of Brown's earliest interpretations of the blues entitled "The Blues as Folk Poetry," he brought attention to those qualities that allow the blues and other genuine folk expressions to stand with the best folk poetry.

Generally Brown found in the blues a sure-footed rhythm that hardly ever stumbles and a diction that rings with the authenticity of folk parlance.

> Ef I could holler lak a mountain jack,
> I'd go up on de mountain an' call my baby back.[43]

However, when the language and rhythmic quality fell short of this level, Brown attributed the faults to artlessness and commercialization and expected the discriminating audience "to be severely critical of clumsy inverted rhythms and strained figures as the one appearing in the 'Lonesome Desert Blues'."

> My mind is lak a rowboat, out on de stormy sea,
> It's wid me right now, in de mawnin' where will it be?[44]

He also found that the blues poet used language to create a mood or convey a tone. For Brown, there was no mistaking Ma Rainey's abilities as a tone painter in "Hard Luck Blues."

> Mah friend committed suicide, whilst I'se
> away at sea.
> They wanted to lock me up fo' murder
> in first degree.[45]

Brown saw the blues poet intimately connecting his subject matter with folk life, conveying his people's spontaneity, their love for fabling, their superstitions, and their reliance on the wisdom of shrewd proverbs.[46]

> My mamma tole me, my daddy tole me too:
> Everybody grins in yo' face, son, ain't no friend to you.[47]
> When de hog makes a bed, yuh know de storm is due,
> When a screech-owl holler, means bad luck to you.[48]

The blues poet also shared with other lyric poets a preoccupation with the lover in absentia. According to Brown, "Love is not presented, however, in a single aspect"; faithlessness, fickleness, careless love, and tormenting love are presented in tones that range "from tenderness to cynicism, from tears to laughter."[49]

Making a close study of the blues, Brown found the images, at their best, to be "highly compressed, concrete, imaginative, and original." He found—"among the cliches, the inconsecutiveness, the false rhymes"—"the startling figure."

> My gal's got teeth lak a lighthouse on de sea.
> Everytime she smiles she throws a light on me.[50]

For Brown, the blues resulted when the folk combined their two great loves: "the love of words and the love of life." And at their most genuine, they belong "to the best of folk literature."[51]

While the folk tradition offered a credible self-portrait of folk life and folk imagination, it also was a repository of social, historical, and, to some extent, psychological information about Black Americans. As an editor of Negro affairs in the Writers' Project in the 1930s, Brown approached folk material as a reliable source of social and historical information. In his work with John Lomax and B. A. Botkin collecting ex-slave narratives, Brown saw the "picture of the Old South" unfolding before his eyes. He was interested in what the narratives revealed about Black life, character and language and the social culture that shaped them.[52]

During his tenure in FWP, Brown encouraged and guided the collection of ex-slave narratives such as those gathered in Virginia under the direction of Roscoe Lewis. Brown saw this project, among others, as crucial if authentic material was to be saved that could provide answers to "questions about the slave system that can be answered only by one who has experienced slavery."

How did it "feel" to be owned? What were the pleasures and sufferings of the slave? What was the slave's attitude toward his owner, toward the white man's assumption of superiority, toward the white man's God? Did the slaves want to be free? Did they feel it was their right to be free?[53]

These were among the questions which the Virginia project workers sought to answer. Though some of the narrators perhaps "mixed fact and fancy" and tended "to exercise the best of their histrionic talents" in playing up to an appreciative audience,[54] Brown agreed with Ros-

coe Lewis when Lewis concluded that "the sum total of the ex-slave
stories recreates a picture without which posterity would have been the
poorer." [55]

Also Brown saw many of these accounts carrying the same irony,
cynicism, and clear-eyed realism that he had already found in slave
seculars.

> A little streak o' lean, an' a little
> streak o' fat,
> Ole massa grumble if you eat much o' dat. [56]

or

> Our Father, who are in heaven
> White man owe me 'leven, and pay me seven.
> Thy kingdom come, they will be done
> And if I hadn't tuck that, I wouldn't a got none. [57]

Such attitudes were as much a part of the heritage as submissiveness
and, as far as he was concerned, should not go undocumented. As Brown
suggested in *The Negro Caravan*, the seculars provided a vivid and
convincing side of folk character.

The tussles with "pattyrollers," the contempt for "po' white trash," the com-
plaints at short rations and tough masters, appear in swift biting lines. There
is very little in the seculars like Stephen Foster's gentle "Massa's in De Cold,
Cold, Ground." The spirit is closer to Louis Armstrong's "I'll be Glad When
You're Dead, You Rascal You." [58]

For Brown, this tradition provided information that from another
source would have been suspect. Drawing on ideas that Richard M.
Dorson explored in an article "Ethnohistory and Ethnic Folklore,"
Gladys Fry in *Night Riders in Black Folk History* insists on the historical value of Black folklore as a record of "the lives of illiterate or
semi-illiterate people who leave no formal record of their experience
to balance written narratives." [59] Another historian, Sterling Stuckey,
extending a line of reasoning that Brown explored in many of his writings on Black folklore, contends that "slaves were able to fashion a
life style and set of values—an ethos—which prevented them from being
imprisoned altogether by the definitions which the larger society sought

to impose."[60] Refuting the thesis formulated by Stanley Elkins that the institution of slavery so dehumanized Black people as to reduce them to the level of Sambos, Stuckey saw the majority of slaves "able to maintain their essential humanity," by drawing upon, in Brown's term, "a well spring" to which they could return in times of doubt to be refreshed.[61]

Brown also saw folk literature serving to keep alive in the group the spirit of struggle, the conviction that freedom must be every man's condition. Sharing this concern with so much Black expression, folk literature caught, especially in the spirituals, the undeniable quest for freedom in this life, not necessarily in the hereafter. The slave and the freedman drew from "the storehouse of Christian ideas and idioms" to create poetry that told convincingly of their struggle for freedom and equality.[62] The determination to be free came clearly through some spirituals, as in the incomparable "No More Auction Block For Me."

> No more auction block for me,
> No more, no more,
> No more auction block for me
> Many thousand gone.[63]

or in "Go Down Moses"

> Go down, Moses
> Way down, in Egyptland
> Tell old Pharaoh
> To let my people go.[64]

Though some spirituals speak openly of the slave's determination to be free, most of the spirituals, composed in an atmosphere charged with the slaveholders' suspicion and near hysteria, have veiled messages.[65] Brown gave credence to the reports of Douglass and other fugitive slaves that several spirituals had a double meaning, like the haunting, penetrating lyrics in "Steal Away" or the defiant and challenging lines in "Didn't my Lord deliver Daniel, and why not every man?" To the claims of Newman White that the slave "never contemplated his low estate," and that references to freedom connote only freedom from sin, Brown argued that the largest body of slave spirituals undoubtedly "reflect the slave's awareness of his bitter plight more than his consciousness of the oppression of sin."[66] Brown made his case clear.

Free individualistic whites on the make in a prospering civilization, nursing the American dream, could well have felt their own bondage to be that of sin, and freedom to be religious salvation. But with the drudgery, the hardships, the auction block, the slavemart, the shackles, and the lash so literally present in the Negro's experience, it is hard to imagine why for the Negro they would remain figurative. The scholars certainly did not make this clear, but rather take refuge in such dicta as "the slave never contemplated his low condition.[67]

Therefore, it was very easy for him to reject the notion that the spirituals were mainly other-worldly. Brown saw many lines in the spirituals telling, often poignantly and sometimes tragically, of "rollin' through an unfriendly world."[68] "Oh, bye and bye, bye and bye, I'm going to lay down this heavy load." "My way is cloudy." "Oh, stand the storm, it won't be long, we'll anchor by and by." "Lord keep me from sinking down."[69] And for Brown, the following lines spoke in the strongest terms of the slaves' yearnings for escape:

Don't know what my mother wants to stay here fuh,
Dis ole worl' ain't been no friend to huh.[70]

As the folk and cultural tradition continues to provide a window into the past, in the absence of psychoanalysis and psychological observation, folk material remains an authentic and persuasive repository of information about the Black mind. The relatively unselfconscious offerings were nurtured in a matrix where each participant felt in harmony with his community. The oral tradition with a build-in sieve, through which filtered group values, inspired confidence and group identity. The distortions, self-consciousness, and imitativeness endemic to more artificial literary modes were absent.

The social milieu in which the slave and the freedman lived, as seen in the tradition, is patently clear. The folklore leaves little room to wonder about the slave's desire to be free or his attitude concerning those who would keep him enslaved. The contented, submissive, childlike images that have been the stock-in-trade for several American writers stand in sharp contrast to those that appear in the tradition. The complexity of Black relationships, within and without racial boundaries, the community values, and the range of human responses would confound those who advocate an easy acceptance of racial characteristics and social determinism. Indeed, it was this point that took much of Brown's critical attention; the folk tradition was a key to a more credible view of Black life and character.

Besides seeing folk literature as a chronicle of the socio-historical experience of the group and as a record of its spiritual struggle, Brown also affirmed it as the surest aesthetic foundation for a Black literary tradition. As Brown saw it, folk art was characterized by vitality, spontaneity, terseness, intensity, and emotional and spiritual depth and offered not only a source but a challenging model for Black artists who would mine its vast reserves. Writers such as Paul Laurence Dunbar, Charles Chesnutt, James Weldon Johnson, Langston Hughes, Richard Wright, Margaret Walker, and Ralph Ellison have dug with varying degrees of skill and penetration into the folk tradition and, in doing so, achieved an originality and depth rare in the American literary tradition. Far from accepting the prevailing attitude of nineteenth-century critics—that Blacks did not have a culture to speak of—Brown pointed to the achievements of such early writers as Dunbar, Chesnutt, and Toomer, in large measure, as springing from and drawing upon the earliest oral expressions of illiterate slaves.

Sterling Brown considered the interpretation of folk experience and character as one of the important tasks of Black poetry and by extension, all Black writing. He pointed to Paul Laurence Dunbar, considered the first Black poet of real distinction, as a highly gifted man who "took up the Negro peasant as a clown, and made him a likeable person".[71] According to Brown, Dunbar benefited from a heritage of folk sense that poured out in "flashes of unforced gay humor," "well-turned folk phrases," and "virtuoso rhythms."[72] Brown added that "his rhythms almost never stumble" and are frequently catchy at times as in "Itching Heels."[73]

Fu' de peace O' my eachin' heels, set down;
   Don' fiddle dat chune no mo'.
Don you see how dat melody stuhs me up
   An baigs me to tek to de flo'?
You knows I's a Christian good an' strong;
   I wusship f'om June to June;
My pra'ahs des ah loud an' my hymns ah long;
   I baig you don' fiddle dat chune.[74]

According to Brown, however, Dunbar was perhaps too strongly influenced by the local color poetry of Irwin Russell and the plantation tradition formula of Thomas Nelson Page and compromised his interpretation of folk life by seriously omitting mention of the hardships that were undoubtedly a part of it. Unfortunately, Dunbar came no closer to full folk portraiture in his prose. In a 1937 critique of Dunbar's novels, Brown saw the land of "Happy Hollow," the typical setting for Dunbar's fiction, as symbolic of a never, never land that is "all too happy for words . . . or for truth."[75]

On the other hand, Brown felt that Charles Waddell Chesnutt revealed notes in folk life that Dunbar ignored. As a clue to his approach, Chesnutt creates Uncle Julius, who at a glance appears to be a tired imitation of Uncle Remus or Pages' Uncle Billy, but, upon a second and more careful look, is closer to the crafty and malevolent Brer Rabbit or the shrewd John of the John and Master tales. A pivotal character in *The Conjure Woman* (1899), Uncle Julius beguiles a naive couple with plantation tales, told not for entertainment as Harris demands of his venerable Uncle, but for a concealed, self-promoting purpose. Present in these stories are folk wit and humor with notes of irony and biting sarcasm truer to authentic Black folktales told when "old massa and missus" were not around. Chesnutt generously handled other folk motifs and forced upon them, as George Kent suggests, a "tough modernist consciousness." The slave in his tale "The Passing of Grandison" is in "the tradition of John-fooling-old massa" slave narrative, and his minor characters "are sometimes reminiscent of the bad niggers of the folk ballads."[76] In the critical survey of Chesnutt's writing in *The Negro in American Fiction*, Brown anticipated Kent's interpretation by suggesting Chesnutt's clever merger of plantation lore and folklore in *The Conjure Woman* and his modernistic handling of the problems of race and color within a framework that remained idealized and conventional.[77]

More influenced in approach by Dunbar than by Chesnutt, James Weldon Johnson relied heavily on conventional characters and attitudes in a group of poems appropriately called "Jingles and Croons," in *Fifty Years and Other Poems* (1971). Speaking of this work Brown said that "there are lullabies to pickaninnies, rivalries between rustic swains, stealing of turkeys, and warning to possums. . . . But there is little true to folk life." Later, Johnson admitted the "triteness" of these earlier pieces and attacked them, "together with all the conventionalized Negro dialect poetry, for exaggerated geniality, childish optimism, forced comicality, and mawkish sentiment."[78] In the introduction of *The Book of American Negro Poetry* (1922) Johnson claimed:

Negro dialect is at present a medium that is not capable of giving expression to the varied conditions of Negro life in America, and much less is it capable of giving the fullest interpretation of Negro character and psychology.[79]

On the contrary, Brown believed that dialect, "or the speech of the people, is capable of expressing whatever the people are."[80] Consequently, Brown was careful to separate the honest handling of dialect from the affected minstrelized treatment. Brown admitted that Johnson's "very acute" criticism of dialect was deserved. In a 1930 article, Brown observed that Negro dialect, though it has been exploited for its quaintness since Lowell's *Bigelow Papers*, in the hands of such writers as Julia Peterkin, Howard Odum, and Langston Hughes, is capable of expressing much more than pathos and humor. Brown emphasizes that the excesses of writers like Arthur Akers and Octavus Roy Cohen have nothing to do with the fitness of the medium of expression. "The fault is not in the material."[81] Though aware of the limitations of dialect as parodied on the minstrel stage and in the farces of Southern apologists, Johnson realized that to neglect the folk idiom completely would be to deny, as Alvin Aubert put it, "the essential rhythm of Afro-American life."

James Weldon Johnson seems to have recognized also, that the artistic embodiment of the essential rhythm of black life requires as a model, not the everyday speech of the black community but the speech stylistically formed to the uses of folk art. In his poems in *God's Trombones*, which grew from the poet's memories of the performances of the old time negro preacher, Johnson captures the essential rhythm of black life. He does not attempt a duplication of the folk rhythm, but plays the rhythm of the poems contrapuntally against the remembered cadences of his folk source.[82]

In the first poem in *God's Trombones: Seven Negro Sermons in Verse* (1927), "The Creation," Johnson fashioned God in human form and presented him in the rhythm of the folk sermon.

And God stepped out on space,
And he looked around and said:

I'm lonely—
I'll make me a world.[83]

Johnson rendered the powerful, evocative lines of "The Prodigal Son" in the call and response pattern of African origin, as well as the following lines from "The Judgment Day":

And the sun will go out like a candle in the wind,
The moon will turn to dripping blood
The stars will fall like cinders,
And the sea will burn like tar.[84]

Johnson matched the apocalytic imagery of the spirituals and captured their lyric beauty, "Material usually made ludicrous," Brown writes, "is here invested with dignity, power and beauty."[85]

In the handful of poems that Jean Toomer included in *Cane*, Brown also saw "a mastery of the best rhythmical devices of Negro folk music." Toomer's skillful repetition of sound, his variation of the tempo, and his juxtaposition of different metrical patterns create poetic resonance, especially in his strikingly beautiful "Song of the Son." According to Brown, the poem "expresses the return of the younger Negro to a consciousness of identity with his own," a return to folk sources, "caroling softly souls of slavery."[86] As Johnson suggested the powerful rhythms and cadences underlying the folk idiom, Jean Toomer revealed group spirit, with broad strokes of pantheism, in the pine and cane scented images in "Georgia Dusk."

Their voices rise . . . the pine trees are guitars,
    Strumming, pine-needles fall like sheets of rain..
    Their voices rise . . . the chorus of the cane
Is caroling a vesper to the stars.
O singers, resinous and soft your songs
    Above the sacred whisper of the pines,
    Give virgin lips to cornfield concubines,
Bring dreams of Christ to dusky cane-lipped throngs.[87]

While Toomer fused the landscape of the South with "soul-sounds," Langston Hughes, eminently the poet of the urban scene, celebrated a Harlem gone mad with jazz. With the accuracy of one who has listened late into the night to jazz bands belting out their sounds, Hughes, with flights of atavism, got syncopated rhythms into "To Midnight Nan at Leroy's":

Strut and wiggle,
Shameless gal
Wouldn't no good fellow
Be your pal
Hear dat music . . .
Jungle night
Hear dat music . . .
And the moon was white.[88]

In the title poem of his first volume of poetry, *The Weary Blues* (1926), Hughes weaved the blues song and sentiment around the extraordinary portrait of a blues singer.

With his ebony hands on each ivory key
He made that poor piano moan with melody,
    O Blues!
Swaying to and fro on his rickety stool
He played that sad raggy tune like a musical fool.
    Sweet Blues!
Comin from a black man's soul.
    O Blues!
In a deep song voice with a melancholy tone
I heard that Negro sing, that old piano moan—
    "Ain't got nobody in all this world,
    Ain't got nobody but ma self.
    I's gwine to quit ma frownin'
    And put ma troubles on the shelf."[89]

The "ruined gals," the elevator boys, and the jazz dancers in his second book of poetry, *Fine Clothes to the Jew* (1927), shocked the genteel, yet they were drawn with the starkness of folk portraiture.

Hughes pioneered in using blues and jazz forms as prototypes for his poetry. Brown, who was also writing and publishing his poems in the late twenties, was influenced by his work. Certainly, Hughes was one of those poets "who have taken folk types and folk-life for their province" and "no longer accept the stereotyped view of the traditional dialect writers, nor lapsing into gentility, do they flinch from an honest portrayal of folk life."[90]

Alain Locke, in the classic anthology *The New Negro* (1925), saw these writers speaking in distinctive overtones, "with a particular representativeness" about a unique racial experience.

All classes of a people under social pressure are permeated with a common experience; they are emotionally welded as others cannot be. With them, even ordinary living has epic depth and lyric intensity, and this, their material handicap, is their spiritual advantage. So, in a day when art has run to classes, cliques and coteries, and life lacks more and more a vital common background, the Negro artist, out of the depths of his group and personal experience has to his hand almost the condition of a classical art.[91]

The number of Black writers who have benefited from an acquaintance with Black folklore is legion. However, Brown belongs with a smaller group of writers and critics—including Alain Locke, Richard Wright, Ralph Ellison, Darwin Turner, George Kent, Stephen Henderson, and Houston Baker—who see Black folklore standing at the foundation of the Black American literary tradition. Despite the efforts of some literary critics to reject even the concept of a Black American literary tradition, Brown has never doubted the existence of such a tradition, has shown evidence of its continuity, and has further recognized those common characteristics that inform and enrich the larger American literary tradition. According to Brown, the record of the Black literary tradition goes back as far as America's colonial period when consciously literary artists like Phillis Wheatley, Jupiter Hammon, and George Horton "wrote down their thoughts in the forms approved by their times."[92] Though, as Brown noted, "different traditions sired different poets," their reliance on accepted models was great.[93] While these writers are "poetizing," in an effort to win respect from the American literary public by proving their skill in artistic patterns approved by the public,[94] the folk were creating poetry of depth and originality.[95] Even then, in an elaborate oral tradition that took in every aspect of their lives, they were creating artistic patterns and rhythms appropriate as a basis for a serious literature.

For Brown, the folk tradition provided the literary artist with a perspective for both examining and creating literature. He was aware that Black writers brought substantially more to their writing than the mere imitation of European and American models—as undiscerning critics too easily charged. Brown's understanding of the oral and written traditions of Blacks precluded the errors in judgment made by a critic like Robert Bone, who attempted to explain the work of Black writers wholly in terms of available white models. Darwin Turner, in a perceptive seed piece on the Black literary tradition, pointed out Robert Bone's simplistic and consequently inept view of both traditions as he fails to understand the *raison' d'être* of the oral tradition and attempts to find white sources in every Black "woodpile."[96]

In contrast to Bone, Brown did not force comparisons of Black writers with approved white models because he did not accept the assumption that a work, to be significant, must follow such a model. In his thinking, a far more accurate assessment must take into account the strong influence of a folk tradition, the existence of which did not depend upon white approval. Consequently, Brown could not dismiss the significance of the folk sermon in James Weldon Johnson's *God's Trombones*, "where he had taken up the caricatured old preacher and revealed him . . . with his own dignity and power."[97] Nor could Brown deny the importance of Black music in supplying appropriate rhythms for Langston Hughes' poetry. Further, Brown saw that Richard Wright's bold use of the "bad nigger"—a mainstay in Black folk balladry—in his characterization of Bigger Thomas was no accident. As Brown suggested in his review of *Native Son*, Wright did not need to use Camus or Dostoevsky to bring meaning to Bigger's character or experience. Similarly, in his critique of Zora Neale Hurston's work, Brown saw that she did not rely on Du Bose Heyward, Julia Peterkin, or any other regionalist in her depiction of rural Southern life and, therefore, found it quite unnecessary to explain her in terms of their work. In Brown's estimation, Hurston was "saturated" (to use Stephen Henderson's term[98]) with the folk tradition, and her novels and short stories "showed a command of folklore and idiom excelled by no earlier Negro novelist."[99]

Beyond recognizing the continuity in the Black literary tradition, Brown discovered that an essential clue to this continuity is the recurrence of common themes that are handled by one generation of Black writers and then passed on to another. Significantly, as he implies throughout his writing, the folk tradition is a repository for themes that recur in the literature. For example, in the spirituals, Brown identified liberation and freedom as unmistakable themes. Despite the "ingenious" attempts of some historians to convince their readers that reference to "freedom" in the spirituals meant "freedom from sin," Brown emphasized that the message was in most cases "freedom from oppression."[100] Extending the significance of this theme, Stephen Henderson, in *Understanding the New Black Poetry*, identifies "liberation" as the arch theme in Black poetry. Whether Black people struggled to deal with slavery, oppression, segregation, or the banalities of assimilation, the goal of freedom was always clear.[101] According to Henderson all forms of the oral tradition—"the dogged determination of the work songs, the tough minded power of the blues, the inventive energy of jazz, and the transcendent vision of God in the spirituals and the sermons," energize the idea of liberation.[102]

More than forty years before, Brown had identified other pervasive themes that range throughout both Black oral and written expressions. In the blues, Brown found a vague longing for travel and escape, humor and melancholy, endurance in the face of disaster; in the ballads, the exploits of Black heroes and heroic episodes from American history; in the work songs, resistance and protest; and in the folk tales, familiarity with nature, survival against oppression. In truth, Brown found these themes emerging in several forms, indicating their persistence. Darwin Turner, who has undoubtedly been influenced by Brown's concept of the continuity of the Black literary experience, isolates several of these same themes as ones that recur in more than one generation. Thus, "liberation, alienation, reaction against oppression, satiric portrayals of foolish Blacks, and pride in Black people generally" link the works of writers of the 1920s and the 1960s and 1970s.[103] Turner also states that these themes also serve to distinguish/differentiate the Black literary tradition from the general American tradition.

Finally, as Brown worked with the critical considerations of authenticity, vitality, originality, density, and complexity, he was convinced that the folklore provided an essential touchstone for evaluating literature. In his criticism of nineteenth-century poetry, he rubbed this touchstone against the efforts of such poets as Frances Ellen Harper and Alberry Whitman and found them wanting. In his evaluation of early twentieth-century Black playwrights, Brown saw none of them showing "the structural skill of white dramatists like Marc Connelly, or the power and scope of Paul Green." Though he attributed part of their lack of distinction to inadequate opportunities for Black playwrights to learn technique, he also suggested that they "devote themselves to the observation of the lives of their people."[104] Indeed, as evidenced in much of his criticism, Brown has a second sense, a quality of awareness that Stephen Henderson calls "saturation." This sense comes from having been immersed in the Black literary experience, the entire range of patterns that are present in both the oral and written traditions. As a result, Brown's aesthetic was shaped. Consequently, he quickly detected the lack of authenticity, the false notes, the condescension, and what passed for Black speech and psychology in American fiction.

Notably, Brown was the first critic to explore fully and consistently the inexhaustible possibilities of the folk tradition for the writer. To date, only Ralph Ellison has rivaled Brown in his conceptualization of the beauty and universality of its arts. In a 1955 Paris interview, Ellison emphasized several of the same functions of folklore which Brown had repeatedly suggested throughout his interpretations on the subject: offering the first drawings of the group's character; preserving in history those situations that help define the group's experience; describing the group's rituals and customs and the boundaries of feeling, thought, and action that particularize its human condition; and projecting the values and symbols that express its will to survive. Above all, Black folklore, in presenting the specific forms of that humanity, "announced the Negro's willingness to trust his own experience, his own sensibilities as to the definition of reality, rather than allow his masters to define these crucial matters for him." [105]

For the length of his career as a creative writer and critic, Brown has interpreted folk literature. His efforts in the extensive and excellent introduction "Folk Literature," included in *The Negro Caravan*, and in articles printed in *Phylon* and other journals, were directed at building an appreciation and understanding of folk forms, life, and character. Like leading race interpreters such as Frederick Douglass, Booker T. Washington, W.E.B. Du Bois, James Weldon Johnson, and Alain Locke, Brown celebrated Black folk songs and their power to reveal authentic strains in Black experience. Brown also honored the singers of these songs. Often invoking the names of the pioneers in the blues tradition such as W. C. Handy, Bessie Smith, Ma Rainey, Blind Lemon Jefferson, and Cottonfield Thomas, Brown transformed his articles into veritable anthologies.

However, Brown eschewed the role of race promoter. Unlike some critics who were tempted to see in Black character special racial gifts of adaptability, musical genius, or great emotional range, he did not argue any peculiar endowment. His balanced, even-handed approach to folk literature was evident when he called down enthusiasts like Roark Bradford and Zora Neale Hurston for overpraising folk speech "at the expense of the speech of white Americans." He knew that "the folk Negro's imaginativeness and pith can easily be recognized; they stand in no need of dubious comparison."[106]

Thus, Brown's belief in the intrinsic value of the folk tradition prompted him to make the study of this source a lifelong interest. Brown saw documented in folk material the tragedies, catastrophies, and triumphs of human struggle. Faithfully rendered in song and lore were the folk's deeper concerns. Their desires to express, in their own terms, their collective wisdom; to preserve the ritual community, the patterns of life, and the accounts of heroic struggle; and their desire to bequeath this, their sole possession, to those who followed—all were there for Brown's discovery.

NOTES

1. Sterling A. Brown, "Conference on Character and State of Studies in Folklore," *Journal of American Folklore*, 59 (October-December 1946): 506.

2. Alan Lomax, "Conference on Character and State of Studies in Folklore," *Journal of American Folklore* (October-December 1946): 507–10.

3. Sterling A. Brown, "Negro Folk Expressions: Spirituals, Seculars, Ballads and Work Songs," *Phylon*, 14 (1953): 60. Hereafter cited as "Spirituals, Seculars, Ballads and Work Songs."

4. Ibid., p. 61.

5. George Kent, "Self-Conscious Writers and the Black Folk and Cultural Tradition," NCTE, *The Humanity of English*, 1972., p. 73.

6. Ralph Ellison, "The Art of Fiction: an Interview," *Shadow and Act* (New York: New American Library, Inc., 1966), p. 172.

7. Ralph Ellison, "The World and the Jug," *Shadow and Act*, p. 119.

8. Ibid., p. 121.

9. Brown, "Character and State of Studies in Folklore," p. 506.

10. Sterling A. Brown, "Negro Folk Expression," *Phylon*, 11 (Autumn 1950), p. 319, hereafter cited as "Negro Folk Expression."

11. These lines from a nineteenth-century spiritual were cited in Brown, "Spirituals, Seculars, Ballads and Work Songs," p. 46.

12. Ibid., p. 46.

13. Brown, *Southern Road*, p. 50.

14. These lines from a nineteenth-century spiritual were cited in Brown, "Spirituals, Seculars, Ballads and Work Songs," p. 46.

15. Brown, *Southern Road*, p. 98.

16. Brown, Davis, and Lee, *The Negro Caravan*, p. 451.

17. Brown, *Southern Road*, p. 98.

18. Interview with Sterling A. Brown by Steven Jones and Stephen Henderson at Howard University, Washington, D.C., May 10, 1973, IAH transcript, p. 28.

19. Traditional blues as cited by Brown, *Southern Road*, p. 12.

20. Sterling A. Brown, "The Blues as Folk Poetry," *The Book of Negro Folklore*, ed. Langston Hughes and Arna Bontemps (New York: Dodd, Mead, and Company, 1958), p. 372.

21. Ibid., p. 376.

22. A traditional blues as cited by Brown in "The Blues as Folk Poetry," p. 377.

23. Ellison, *Shadow and Act*, p. 90.

24. Brown, Davis, and Lee, *The Negro Caravan*, p. 428.

25. Traditional blues lines as cited by Brown in "The Blues," *Phylon*, 13 (Autumn 1952): 287.

26. Ibid.

27. Ibid.

28. Ibid.

29. Ibid., p. 289.

30. Brown, "The Blues as Folk Poetry," p. 379.

31. Brown, *Southern Road* p. 95.

32. Frederic Ramsey, Jr., "Leadbelly's Last Session," Folkways Record Notes, reprinted from *High Fidelity Magazine* (November-December 1953).

33. Brown, "Spirituals, Seculars, Ballads and Work Songs," p. 54.

34. Brown, "The Blues as Folk Poetry," p. 372.

35. Brown, "Negro Folk Expression," p. 318.

36. Brown, Davis, and Lee, *Negro Caravan*, p. 5.

37. Sterling A. Brown, "Seventy-Five Years of the Negro in Literature: Backgrounds of Folklore in Negro Literature," *Jackson College Bulletin* 2 (September 1953): 27–29.

38. Brown, *Negro Poetry and Drama*, p. 29.

39. Ibid., p. 13.

40. Brown, Davis, and Lee, *The Negro Caravan*, p. 414.

41. Jack L. Daniel and Geneva Smitherman, "How I Got Over: Communication Dynamics in the Black Community," *Quarterly Journal of Speech* 62 (February 1976): 33–34.

42. Ibid.

43. Traditional blues lines as cited by Brown in "The Blues As Folk Poetry," p. 373.

44. Ibid., p. 372.

45. Ibid., p. 376.

114   Sterling A. Brown

46. Brown, "The Blues," p. 289.
47. Brown, "The Blues as Folk Poetry," p. 375.
48. Ibid.
49. Brown, "The Blues," pp. 382 and 383.
50. Traditional blues lines as cited by Brown, "The Blues as Folk Poetry," p. 383.
51. Ibid., p. 386.
52. Brown, "Character and State of Studies in Folklore," p. 506.
53. Brown, Davis, and Lee, The Negro Caravan, p. 848.
54. Ibid.
55. Ibid., pp. 848–49.
56. Slave secular as cited in Brown, Davis, and Lee, The Negro Caravan, p. 855.
57. Slave secular as cited by Brown in "Spirituals, Seculars, Ballads and Work Songs," p. 51.
58. Brown, Davis, and Lee, The Negro Caravan, p. 422.
59. Fry, Night Riders in Black Folk History, pp. 16–17. Also see Richard M. Dorson, "Ethnohistory and Ethnic Folklore," Ethnohistory, 8 (Winter 1961): 12–30.
60. Sterling Stuckey, "Through the Prism of Folklore: The Black Ethos in Slavery," in New Black Voices, ed. Abraham Chapman (New York: New American Library, 1972), p. 440.
61. Ibid., p. 441.
62. Brown, Davis, and Lee, The Negro Caravan, p. 6.
63. Nineteenth-century spiritual as cited by Sterling A. Brown in "The Spirituals," The Book of Negro Folklore, p. 291.
64. Ibid., p. 292.
65. Ibid., p. 286.
66. Brown, "The Spirituals," p. 287. Newman White in American Negro Folk-Songs (1928; Folklore Associates, Inc., Hatboro, Pa., 1965) was, according to Brown, ingenious but not convincing when he argued against the "abolitionist use of the spirituals as an instrument of propaganda." (p. 286).
67. Brown, "Spirituals, Seculars, Ballads and Work Songs," p. 48.
68. Ibid., p. 47.
69. These lines from traditional nineteenth-century spirituals were cited in Brown, "Spirituals, Seculars, Ballads and Work Songs," p. 47.
70. Ibid.
71. Brown, Negro Poetry and Drama, p. 35.
72. Ibid.
73. Ibid.
74. Paul Laurence Dunbar, The Complete Poems of Paul Laurence Dunbar (New York: Dodd, Mead, and Company, Inc., 1930), p. 222.

75. Brown, *Negro Poetry and Drama*, p. 77.

76. Kent, "Self-Conscious Writers and the Black Folk and Cultural Tradition," p. 83.

77. Sterling A. Brown, *The Negro in American Fiction* (Washington, D.C.: Associates in Negro Folk Education, 1937), pp. 78–82.

78. Brown, *Negro Poetry and Drama*, p. 41.

79. James Weldon Johnson, ed., *The Book of American Negro Poetry* (New York: Harcourt, Brace and World, Inc., 1922; reprint ed., 1959), p. 42.

80. Brown, *Negro Poetry and Drama*, p. 43.

81. Brown, "Our Literary Audience," pp. 44–45.

82. Alvin Aubert, "Black American Poetry, Its Language, and the Folk Tradition," *Modern Black Literature*, ed. by S. Okechukwa Mezu (Buffalo: Black Academy Press, Inc., 1971), p. 76.

83. James Weldon Johnson, *God's Trombones: Seven Negro Sermons in Verse* (New York: Viking Press, 1969 (1927)), p. 17.

84. Ibid., p. 56.

85. Brown, *Negro Poetry and Drama*, p. 68.

86. Ibid., p. 67.

87. Jean Toomer, *Cane* (New York: Liveright, 1923), p. 23.

88. Langston Hughes, *The Weary Blues* (New York: Alfred A. Knopf, Inc., 1926), p. 30.

89. Ibid., p. 23.

90. Brown, *Negro Poetry and Drama*, p. 80.

91. Locke, "Negro Youth Speaks," *The New Negro*, p. 47.

92. Brown, *Negro Poetry and Drama*, p. 12.

93. Ibid.

94. Darwin T. Turner, "Introductory Remarks About the Black Literary Tradition in the United States of America." *Proceedings: Comparative Literature Symposium, Ethnic Literature Since 1776: The Many Voices of America*, eds. Wolodymyr T. Zyla and Wendell M. Aycock (Lubbock, Texas: Texas Tech University Press, 1978), p. 75.

95. Brown, *Negro Poetry and Drama*, p. 12.

96. Turner, "Introductory Remarks About the Black Literary Tradition," p. 77.

97. Sterling A. Brown, "The Negro in American Literature," *A Biographical Sketch, James Weldon Johnson* (Nashville: Fisk University, 1938).

98. Henderson, *Understanding the New Black Poetry*, p. 62. By "saturation" in Black poetry Henderson means (a) the communication of Blackness in a given situation, and (b) a sense of fidelity to the observed and intuited truth of the Black experience.

99. Brown, *The Negro in American Fiction*, p. 159.

100. Brown, "The Spirituals," p. 286.

101. Henderson, *Understanding the New Black Poetry*, p. 18.
102. Ibid., p. 21.
103. Turner, "Introductory Remarks About the Black Literary Tradition," p. 82.
104. Brown, *Negro Poetry and Drama*, p. 123.
105. Ellison, *Shadow and Act*, p. 173.
106. Brown, "Negro Folk Expression," pp. 319–20.

6

THE POETRY OF STERLING A. BROWN: A STUDY IN FORM AND MEANING

One of the New Negro writers to emerge during the early 1930s, Sterling A. Brown attempted to represent Black life against the aesthetic background of the Black folk and cultural tradition. He, along with such writers as Jean Toomer, James Weldon Johnson, and Langston Hughes, explored folk art as a way of understanding and interpreting the truth concerning the life and character of Black Americans. Brown, using the folk tradition as a prism through which to see the Black experience, also infused his own poetry with folk themes, symbols, forms, and narrative techniques in an effort to express more fully the ethos of Black life. A survey of his poetry will reveal an extensive absorption of the folk tradition, as well as the complex sensibility of a self-conscious artist who has a firm grounding in the American critical realism and other literary traditions.

In fact, Brown's skill as a poet is clearly demonstrated in his ability to synthesize the diverse traditions at hand. This process of synthesis Brown prefers to call ''cross-pollination'' and credits it with the creation of some of his best poetry. For example, in the comic ballad ''Slim in Hell,'' Brown crosses the ancient legend of Orpheus and Eurydice with the elaborate lore of the folk trickster and presents them in the socio-historical context of twentieth-century Dixie. The result is a vigorous product that maintains the strength of both traditions, while simultaneously exhibiting vital new combinations and varieties.

As Brown explores the fertile field of oral and literary traditions, the folk tradition shows the greatest vitality and, consequently, has a strong influence on his poetry. However, the impress of the American tradition of critical realism in shaping, sharpening, and deepening his treatment of folk material is also significant. Brown joins the democratic voices of Robinson, Frost, and Sandburg as they say "yes" to their people. Often in a voice that melds the American vernacular with folk speech, Brown says a resounding "yes" as he has his compelling portraits and narratives reveal the reality and vision of America.

PART ONE

With the publication of his first volume of poetry in 1932, Sterling A. Brown introduced what was to be his most pervasive metaphor, the Southern road. As one scholar of Brown's poetry writes, Brown "adopted one of the most persistent symbols and thematic motifs in folklore to unify *Southern Road*."

The road has been a central metaphor in the black experience, and it has been essential that the traveler keep "movering," "keep inchin' along." As a symbol, the road takes various forms: the river, the railroad, the Underground Railroad, the road to Glory, the road to Freedom, the way of survival, the path winding through the lonesome valley, the hard road of Life. It could not have been by accident that Brown selected the road as his central symbol, entitled his book *Southern Road*, and derived his themes from the implications of that symbol.[1]

In the initial quotation on the frontispiece of the book, the road is transformed into a path of knowledge and experience.

O de ole sheep dey knows de road,
Young lambs gotta find de way. (Spiritual)[2]

By extension, the road becomes the road of life itself, the path from childhood to old age, from naiveté to wisdom. Appropriately, these lines suggest Brown's purpose in *Southern Road* and in several poems that followed its publication. Once taught by wise "ole sheep" the ways of the folk, he intends to construct a road that will link the cultural past with New Negro awareness, establishing, as Alain Locke claimed, "a sort of common denominator between the old and the new Negro" and giving credence to the idea that the Black literary tradition is one continuous line of development issuing from the earliest folk thought and utterance.[3]

Prefacing Part One of *Southern Road* with lines from the spiritual, "Road may be rocky, won't be rocky long," Brown suggests the struggles of its travelers.[4] The road has the power to tempt a man away from home or take a son or daughter to sin. The traveler in "Long Gone," who has "a itch fo' travelin'/He cain't understan," must leave his sweet woman "though it's homelike and happy" at her side.[5] In the tragic ballad of "Maumee Ruth," a woman's children are lured to the city. The physical distance, as well as the spiritual distance, is so great, "they cannot come again" to mourn their mother, now dead. The road has been rocky for Maumee Ruth, and the final reward for her wayfaring is the open grave.

> Might as well drop her
> Deep in the ground,
> Might as well pray for her,
> That she sleep sound. . . . [6]

The road also has a way of reducing dreams to hard reality. In "Bessie," a young girl "with her bird voice and laughter like the sun" leaves "behind the stupid, stifling shanties" for the promise of city fun. However, the youthful Bessie finds the cost of her adventures far more than she bargained for; the hardness of the city takes its toll. Those who knew her once would not recognize her now, "gaunt of flesh and painted,/Despair deep bitten in her soft brown eyes."[7] Underlying the story of Bessie's pathetic downfall is the poet's clear perception of the disparity between expectation and reality, the dangers of inexperience, and the ever-present risk involved in living.

In Part Two, the road is transformed into a river, "O, de Mississippi River, so deep an' wide. . . . " Brown imbues the landscape with a blues sentiment. Rivers are restless, like bluesmen who rove the countryside. Unpredictable, they may bring death and destruction almost as often as not. In "Children of the Mississippi," Brown captures the fear and despair of those who are at the mercy of the river.

> These folk know grief.
> They have seen

Black water gurgling, lapping, roaring,
Take their lives' earnings, roll off their paltry
Fixtures of home, things as dear as old hearthgods.
These have known death
Surprising, rapacious of cattle, of children,
Creeping with the black water
Secretly, unceasingly.[8]

In "Foreclosure," Father Missouri is as merciless as the Mississippi. The "whimsical and drunkenly turbulent" forecloser, "cuts away the banks, steals away the loam. . . . " Heedless of the curses of Uncle Dan who "sees years of laboring turned into nothing . . . the old river rolls on, sleepily to the gulf."[9] Arthur P. Davis, author of *From a Dark Tower*, writes that in "these bitter verses on the tragic experience of Negro life, Sterling Brown uses the river as a symbol of God's or nature's total indifference to the lot of the poor."[10]

Blues lines also introduce Part Three:

I'm got de tin roof blues
Got dese sidewalks on my mind.[11]

When road and river converge on city streets, the life becomes treacherous like a hot, slippery tin roof. In several poems, Brown exposes the harshness and artificiality of city life. Streetwalkers, rowdy cabaret goers, satin clad youth mindless of traditional values, all populate this perverted promised land. Brown closes this section of the book with a poem entitled "Cabaret." With the setting in "Black and Tan Chicago" of 1927, the poem is undoubtedly a satire of that place and time. The rich "grandees" who frequent the cabarets attempt to experience vicariously Black "Life upon the river." What they see is sheer fantasy acted out by a jazz band and chorus girls who know there is little romance in "Muddy Water."

Muddy Water round my feet
Muddy Water
Muddy Water, river sweet
I've been away a year today
To wander and roam
I don't care if it's muddy there
Still it's my home sweet home.[12]

As Brown intersperses the raw blues lines in the poem, he sets up a powerful antithesis. The destructive floods, the stench, and the death at no time intrude upon the papier-mâché artificiality of the scene, and the fantasy is played out for the coins of "rich, flashy, puffy-faced" overlords who demand its reality.

In the final section of *Southern Road*, called "Vestiges," the road is Brown's path of remembrance. His subjective offerings in this section link him to such New Negro poets as Jean Toomer and Arna Bontemps. As Toomer, seeking his own cultural heritage in Georgia, had saved for himself vestiges of the slave past, so Brown gathers his thoughts on love and life as vestiges of his identity. Several of these poems also echo the quiet questioning of Bontemps in "Noctune at Bethesda," or his steely hope in "A Black Man Talks of Reaping."

Opening this section with lines from the A. E. Housman poem, "When I Was One and Twenty," [13] Brown has the road realize its final metaphor—the way from naiveté to wisdom, from innocence to experience. These lines hark back to the initial folk quotation of knowledge, thus unifying the book thematically. Remembering the wisdom of old folk who know the way, Brown culls vestiges from a folk past to enrich his perceptions of Black life and character.

In the 1920s, Brown embarked on a road that led him into the world of the rural Black laborer: the tobacco fields of Virginia, the corn fields of Maryland, the coal mines of West Virginia, the turpentine camps of Mississippi, the rice fields of Georgia. All were endemic to his world. The road led to Jim Crow South where caste and class manipulated the lives of both Blacks and whites enmeshed in the system. Back doors behind porticoes, Jim Crow cars, shanty towns, crooked commissaries, roads built by convict labor, and lynching trees provided part of the spectrum of the reality of Black life in the South. As highway narrowed to village road and country footpath, Brown's road led into a world that Brown has made into his own Spoon River, Tilbury Town, or Yoknapatawpha County. [14]

Above all, Brown's road is a corridor to the personal histories of Black folk. It is no wonder that in Brown's title poem the road is transformed into human drama. In "Southern Road," Brown dramatizes the poignant story of a "po' los' boy," who faces the rest of his life on a chain gang, and Brown renders the details of the man's life in the form of the folk work song. Using this form—traditionally intended to convey the commonality of hard work—Brown, the self-conscious artist, gives, as George Kent suggests, "a particularization to the experience that the folk poet avoids."[15] As his hammer strikes in time with those of others "doubleshackled," the man grunts out his personal tragedy:

> Burner tore his—hunh—
> Black heart away;
> Burner tore his—hunh—
> Black heart away;
> Got me life, bebby,
> An' a day.
>
> Gal's on Fifth Street—hunh—
> Son done gone;
> Gal's on Fifth Street—hunh—
> Son done gone;
> Wife's in de ward, bebby,
> Babe's not bo'n,
>
> My ole man died—hunh—
> Cussin' me;
> My ole man died—hunh—
> Cussin' me;
> Ole lady rocks, bebby,
> Huh misery.[16]

The convict's grunts serve to punctuate the heaviness of his lot: a life sentence on the chain gang, a streetwalker daughter, a wayward son, a pregnant wife, a father who died "cussin' " him, and a mother grown old with misery. Nevertheless, his response to existence is charged with a realistic acceptance of his circumstances and a fortitude and tough-ness of spirit that crowd out any hints of creeping self-pity.

To express the resignation and toughness of his convict-speaker, Brown fuses the form and tone of the blues with the work song, creat-ing an innovative hybrid—the blues work song. Using the basic stan-zaic pattern of the blues, Brown slightly reorders it into shorter lines to accommodate the caesura and the "grunt" that mark the work song. With the first four lines presenting the situation or the problem, and the last two lines resolving the problem or reacting to the situation, Brown emphasizes simultaneously the speaker's blues-ridden sense of hopelessness and despair, and a stoic brand of resilience that will keep him going.

> Chain gang nevah—hunh—
> Let me go;
> Chain gang nevah—hunh—
> Let me go;
> Po' los' boy, bebby,
> Evahmo'. . . . [17]

Like this tragic character, the ordinary people who live alongside the roads and byways live again in Brown's poetry. Some are real personalities, like Ma Rainey, Revelations, Big Boy Davis, and Mrs. Bibby—the magnificent old woman portrayed in "Virginia Portrait." Others—like Maumee Ruth, Sporting Beasley, Deacon Zachary, Elder Peter Johnson, the tragic Johnny Thomas, Sam Smiley and Old Lem, Georgie Grimes, Scotty, Lula and Jim, Fred, and Sallie—the names are legion—become real as Brown attributes to them the mind, the vernacular, and the concerns of real folk.

These people stirred Brown's creative imagination and provided the stimulus for his writing. They had not lost the ability to communicate. In declaring their sense of themselves, they expressed their stoicism, humor, fatalism, toughness, profaneness, reverence, and blues spirit. Through them, Brown discovered the Black folk tradition and found a way to translate the gestures of this tradition in terms that spoke intimately to the concerns of the New Negro. The folk's preoccupation with elegant Black heroes, their drive for survival and resistance, their reach to the universal in human experience through deep revelation of the particular were among the major concerns in his poetry as well as in the poetry of other New Negro Renaissance writers. Brown also desired to communicate to a broad audience in a language that combined folk authenticity and creativity with the craftsmanship of the self-conscious writer. And like Alain Locke, the interpreter of the New Negro movement, Brown was aware of the resources in the collective wisdom of the folk and explored what Locke called "the real treasure-trove of the Negro poet." [18]

Shortly after the publication of *Southern Road*, Locke hailed Sterling Brown as "the New Negro folk poet," claiming that the book ushered in "a new era in Negro folk-expression" and brought "a new dimension in Negro folk portraiture.''[19] If Brown is a ''folk poet,'' it is because he registered the people's sentiment in their terms. Brown dared ''to give quiet but bold expression'' to their private thoughts and speech. Applauding such a poem as ''Ruminations of Luke Johnson,'' Locke said that Brown ''recaptured the shrewd Aesopian quality of the Negro folk-thought. . . . ''[20] Locke saw Brown revealing with certain insight the very small triumphs allowed Black folk. In ''Ruminations of Luke Johnson,'' Luke reflects on Mandy Jane, who tramps home each evening carrying her basket loaded with the ''greasy'' spoils of kitchen pilfering. Possessing a wit grown cynical with the knowledge of ''how things be,'' Luke justifies Mandy Jane's stealing in the full context of reparations, a predominant undercurrent in Black radical thought. And as Robert G. O'Meally suggests, ''Her theft is not mere revenge; it is masking, suggestive of a rich, dancing, *well-fed* life behind the face shown to the white employers.''[21] For what the lady's ''grandfather'' took from Mandy Jane's ''grandpappy,'' Luke rationalizes, ''Ain' no basket in de worl'/what kin tote all dat away.''[22]

In another poem, Sporting Beasley is allowed to forget the insults and drabness of his inconsequential life as he, resplendent with Prince Albert coat, white spats, and cane, struts it ''till the sun goes down.'' In a tone that is decidedly mock epical, the speaker describes the bon vivant at a concert as he strides down the aisle to his seat in row A and majestically pulls out his opera glasses amid the laughter of the crowd.[23] One of Brown's folk transplanted in the city, Sporting Beasley is a character based on a hero from Brown's youth called Sporting Daniels, ''who used to walk up and down in front of the Howard Theater in all his sartorial excellence.'' In actuality, Sporting Daniels did come into a huge auditorium about twenty minutes late, walked slowly down the aisle to give those seated ample time to admire his clothes and cane, and, once at his seat in the very front of the auditorium, pulled out opera glasses in order to see the gigantic Paul Robeson in concert.

While Brown captures in the poem much of the fun remembered from boyhood days, his portrait of Beasley achieves intensity because he brings together a complex of attitudes. Beasley is at once the object of praise, ridicule, and sympathy. Forgetting the indignities of ''snippy clerks'' he must wait on and capturing the attention of ''pointing children,''[24] whose admiration will turn into scoffing as they grow up, Beasley is ''Mr. Peacock, before the drab barnfowl of the world.''[25] Brown also achieves an ironic dimension by making his canvas massive. His portrait of Beasley must encompass the world. He is "Mr. Missionary" bringing light to the heathen world. Celestial, Sporting Beasley also makes a grand entrance through the "jasper gates of heaven . . . ." "cane and knees working like well-oiled slow-timed pistons."

On the surface the poet's attitude appears to be mocking and playful, as the tags that introduce each section bear out: "Step it, Mr. Beasley, oh step it till the sun goes down" and "Great glory, give a look" are examples. However, subsumed in the tone is an element of pathos, Brown's humor notwithstanding. In the last section the speaker petitions the Lord:

> Don't make him dress up in no night gown, Lord,
> Don't put no fuss and feathers on his shoulders, Lord.
> Let him know it's heaven.
> Let him keep his hat, his vest, his elkstooth, and everything.
> Let him have his spats and cane
> Let him have his spats and cane.[26]

The effective repetition of the last line emphasizes the smallness of his possessions and, on another level, the inconsequence of his life. Beasley is only one in a gallery of characters whose lifestyles reflect an attempt to deal with the chaos about them by carving out of it some meaning.

Brown's second volume of poetry, *No Hiding Place*, is included in *The Collected Poems of Sterling A. Brown* published in 1980. Brown again focuses upon his interpretation of character the subtle and complex currents of Black thought. In the poignant statements of "Old Lem," he captures the bitter resentment of a man grown weary of mob violence.

> Their fists stay closed
> Their eyes look straight
>   Our hands stay open
>   Our eyes must fall
>   *They don't come by ones*
> They got the manhood
> They got the courage
>   *They don't come by twos*
> We got to slink around
> Hangtailed hounds.

They burn us when we dogs
They burn us when we men
   They come by tens. . . . [27]

With stark simplicity devoid of false sentimentality, Lem tells the story of his buddy, "Six foot of man/Muscled up perfect/Game to the heart," who defied the traditions of caste and "spoke out of turn at the commissary. . . . " For his "insolence" he is murdered.

Much of the power of the poem emanates from the complex and fully realized sensibility of Old Lem. His cogent wisdom and clarity of vision allow him to articulate simply and directly the consequences of racial injustice. In one part of the poem Brown has Old Lem recycle the wisdom of the folktale, "Old Sis Goose," in which a common goose seeks justice in a courthouse of foxes and ends up having her bones "picked." Brown has Lem say:

They got the judges
They got the lawyers
They got the jury-rolls
They got the law
   They don't come by ones
They got the sheriffs
They got the deputies
   They don't come by twos
They got the shotguns
They got the rope
   We git the justice
   In the end
   And they come by tens.[28]

Lem's voice is charged with the vibrancy of the folk secular. Within this large body of non-religious music which includes the blues, songs of ridicule and recrimination, game songs, and numerous varieties of work songs, Brown recognized not only innovative musical elements but also attitudes, language, and circumstances—often cynical, ironic, signifying, and scatological—that are not the metier of the collectors of spirituals. It is the irony, the pithiness, and the elemental force of this material that informs Old Lem's speech. A comparison of a slave secular recorded by Frederick Douglass in *My Bondage and My Free-*

dom with a passage from "Old Lem" reveals Brown's skillful assimilation of the form.

> We raise de wheat,
> Dey gib us de corn;
> We bake de bread,
> Dey gib us de crust;
> We sif de meal,
> Dey gib us de huss;
> We peel de meat,
> Dey gib us de skin;
> And dat's de way
> Dey take us in;
> We skim de pot,
> Dey gib us de liquor
> And say dat's good enough for nigger.[29]

In Old Lem's speech Brown achieves a similar syntactical pattern and cadence.

> They weigh the cotton
> They store the corn
>   We only good enough
>   To work the rows;
> They run the commissary
> They keep the books
>   We gotta be grateful
>   For being cheated;
> Whippersnapper clerks
> Call us out of our name
>   We got to say mister
>   To spindling boys
> They make our figgers
> Turn somersets
>   We buck in the middle
>   Say, "Thankyuh, sah."[30]

Patterned on a rhythm prevalent in Black folk speech, the passage contains lines with two stresses each, often irregularly arranged. Several of the lines have verbs used near the beginning of the line that must be strongly stressed. Also, with a tightly controlled satiric tone, Brown contrasts what "they" do to what "we" are forced to accept, thereby having his structure effectively convey the great disparity that exists between the position of whites and that of Blacks in a caste-ridden society.

In another poem, published first in *Nation* in 1939, called "Bitter Fruit of the Tree," Brown has the speaker reveal bitterness caused by a history of oppression. Coming through the speaker's tale of three generations of abuses suffered by his family is a bitterness that is controlled, poised, and intense. This is achieved with a carefully worked out reportage that serves to present the racism, exploitation, and hypocrisy of the oppressor group and simultaneously to highlight the silence of the embittered group. Appropriately, the diction reflects the standard speech patterns of the more privileged group.

> They said to my grandmother: "Please do not be bitter,"
> When they sold her first-born and let the second die,
> When they drove her husband till he took to the swamplands,
> And brought him home bloody and beaten at last.
> They told her, "It is better you should not be bitter,
> Some must work and suffer so that we, who must, can live,
> Forgiving is noble, you must not be heathen bitter;
> Those are your orders: you *are* not to be bitter."
> And they left her shack for their porticoed house.[31]

Brown ingeniously suggests a folk bitterness fraught with Christian guilt and demands for forgiveness as well as an acute knowledge of the menacing code of White control. Those who argue, "What is past is over, and you should not be bitter," are met with a resolute silence, as suggested by the poet's superb understatement, "But my brother is bitter, and he does not hear."[32]

Brown offers, it seems, another alternative in "An Old Woman Remembers." The speaker in this poem sees her people's distress changed into militant defiance as a result of the atrocities inflicted on them during the Atlanta riot. Having absorbed the rage and horror she felt because of the killing and maiming of large numbers of her people, the woman, years later, recounts what happened when they "got sick and tired of being chased and beaten and shot down."

All of a sudden, one day, they all got sick and tired
The servants they put down their mops and pans
And brooms and hoes and rakes and coachman whips,
Bid niggers stopped their drinking Dago red,
Good Negroes figured they had prayed enough,
All came back home—they had been too long away—
A lot of visitors had been looking for them.
They sat on their front stoops and in their yards,
Not talking much, but ready; their welcome ready:
Their shotguns oiled and loaded on their knees.
"An then
There wasn't any riot any more."[33]

With this quietly ironic denouement, Brown ends a poem which appears prosy upon first encountering it, yet his simple narrative provides the frame for what Stephen Henderson calls the "Soul-Field," "the complex galaxy of personal, social, institutional, historical, religious, and mythical meanings that affect everything we say or do as Black people sharing a common heritage."[34] This "Soul-Field" gives the poem its power. The narrative is studded with "personally and communally recognized meanings which are more felt than named," meaning that reflects a quality Henderson calls "saturation."[35] For example, "sick and tired," "beaten," "bad niggers," "good Negroes," "home," and "too long," are "mascon" words and phrases that are saturated with Black experiential energy, making the reader feel more than is written.

As Brown exposes the notes of bitterness and cynicism often kept from the ear of an outsider, the circumstances of life, what George Kent calls the radical contingencies of existence, "that openness to the free and unconstrained flow of an unstructured, unfenced in reality" become apparent.[36] Kent cites in Faulkner's *Absalom, Absalom* one instance of the root uncertainty in existence in the impuissance of a slave girl and her family to prevent her sexual exploitation by her white master. Like the slave girl, the old woman (and the poem is at its root a portrait of her) had to stare at this specter and make definitions that would allow her to "escape the *boiling heat* of chaos."[37]

Other of Brown's characters, also, appear destined to confront chaos and to negotiate the radical contingencies that issue from it. In "Georgie Grimes," Brown presents one such victim of life's accidents.

Georgie, in a fit of passion, kills his woman and "with a fear behind him" runs away from his crime. Muttering over and over, "No livin' woman got de right to do no man dat way," Grimes must accept his living hell.[38] Georgie Grimes is only one character in what French critic Jean Wagner calls "The Tragic Universe of Sterling Brown." Wagner writes that before Brown, no one had brought to his poetry a keener understanding of the tragic universe of Black Americans, and no one had more convincingly showed the wall of the prison-house crowding in.[39]

In Part One of *Southern Road*, Brown introduces the tragic characters Johnny Thomas, Sam Smiley, and Frankie's lover (also named Johnny) who rush headlong towards predictably violent deaths. Johnny's fast life of gambling and entanglements with a fancy woman lead to stealing and a hard-labor gang. When Johnny splits open a guard's head in retaliation for "an awful lick" the guard had dealt him, his end comes swiftly.

> Dey haltered Johnny Thomas
> Like a cussed mule,
> Dey hung Johnny Thomas
> For a consarned fool.
>
> Dropped him in de hole
> Threw de slack lime on,
> Oughta had mo' sense
> Dan to evah git born.[40]

The disturbing suggestions that Johnny, like poor Oedipus, was doomed before he was born and that nonexistence is preferable to Black life drive home the cynicism of the last two lines.

Another Johnny becomes a victim when he forgets his mother's warnings and consorts with a half-witted white girl named Frankie. "Frankie and Johnny were lovers/Oh Lordy how they did love!"[41] Reshaping the subject of the traditional folk ballad "Frankie and Johnny," Brown changes the story to comment on the specter of sexual racism and fear in the rural South. In the traditional ballad that deals with the revenge of a scorned woman, Black Frankie shoots Johnny dead when she finds him with another woman. The ballad refrain tells the story. In Brown's ballad, however, Frankie is a "cracker hussy" who seduces the "nigger" Johnny to make love to her. Driven by "a crazy love of torment" she tells her "pappy" about the relationship and sadistically derives pleasure when her lover is lynched.

> Frankie, she was spindly limbed with corn silk on her crazy head,
> Johnny was a nigger, who never had much fun—
> They swung up Johnny on a tree, and filled his swinging hide with lead,
> And Frankie yowled hilariously when the thing was done.[42]

Brown transforms the urge for revenge into the psychotic whims of a deranged girl and his Johnny, traditionally a careless, sporting man, becomes the hapless victim of racial violence. Brown makes a switch inventing a poem of protest.

However, as Brown suggests in another poem called "Sam Smiley," the punishment for sexual mixing is not evenly meted out. Sam, a Black soldier, returning from the war in France, finds his girl in jail. He soon learns the full circumstances of her fall; however, he learns about them too late to save her from her shame and from the "narrow gaping hole" that eases it. Sam—whom "the whites had taught . . . to rip a Nordic belly with a thrust of bayonet" and who had realized "that shrapnel bursts and poison gas were inexplicably color blind"— "sent a rich white man his woman's company to keep," and the mob completes the scenario. With the same penchant for irony that prompts the poet to call this pathetic soldier "Sam Smiley," Brown has the man who had danced to cheer the steerage on his return home buck dance "on the midnight air."[43]

Like Edward Arlington Robinson, Brown takes the lives of ordinary people for his province. Much of the effect of the poem can be attributed to Brown's use of the traditional ballad form which sustains the narrative. As E. A. Robinson used this form in several of his poems in *The Children of the Night* to enhance their dramatic effects, Brown finds this framework suitable to support the conflicts and reversals that add the dramatic dimension to the portrait of Sam Smiley. The speaker in the poem is an omniscient and somewhat ironic observer who reports the action in clipped, cool Anglo-American speech. Here again a parallel may be drawn between Brown and Robinson, for it is the diction of E. A. Robinson's "Richard Cory" and "Bewick Finger" that appears to be Brown's model in this poem. Also, much of Brown's effectiveness lies in his ability to make sense out of the chaos that surrounds his folk. Understanding the taboos, the written and unwritten codes, the "contingencies of existence," he portrays Black people without pity or melodrama. When Brown's folk suffer, the reader's response is more likely to be one of empathy that comes from identification in lieu of a response predicated on empty pathos.

Brown knows, however, that Black folk cannot be wholly explained in terms of their desperation and powerlessness; he knows that he must also account for their indomitable spirit, their insistence on survival, and their willingness, if necessary, "to tear the building down." With this range of possibilities open to him, his men often attain heroic status. In "He Was a Man," a poem published in 1932, Brown portrays the quiet heroism of a Black man named Will.

> He wasn't no quarrelsome feller,
>   And he let other folks alone,
> But he took a life, as a man will do,
>   In a fight for to save his own,
>   He was a man, and they laid him down.
> He worked on his little homeplace
>   Down on the Eastern Shore;
> He had his family, and he had his friends,
>   And he didn't expect much more,
>   He was a man, and they laid him down.
> He wasn't nobody's great man,
>   He wasn't nobody's good,
> Was a po' boy tried to get from life
>   What happiness he could,
>   He was a man, and they laid him down.[44]

In a confrontation with a white man, Will is forced to pull his gun to defend himself. The white man is killed, and Will is wounded. The ubiquitous mob finds Will in the hospital, drags him from his bed, and lynches him in broad daylight, "another uppity nigger gone." The crime and the criminals are winked at by the maintainers of the justice system.

Part of the poignancy of this ballad is the knowledge that Will's only tragic flaw was his awareness of his manhood. With this thematic idea at hand, Brown conveys the somber details of the man's outcome in the framework of the folk ballad, which has a built-in effect of elevating the deeds of this ordinary man to legendary status. Also the refrain, serving as more than an incremental function, subtly emphasizes the essential conflict and dilemma: "He was a man, and they laid him down."[45]

In another poem, "Break of Day," the hero, like Will, is "nobody's great man." Big Jess "fired on the Alabama Central," had a pleasing woman—name of Mame, and "had a boy growing up for to be a fireman, just like his pa." Yet Big Jess is denied his full man's right to life and happiness, for he is ambushed and killed by "crackers" who "craved his job."[46] In presenting Big Jess' tragic story, Brown avoids a sentimental and melodramatic treatment by effectively conveying it in an adapted form of folk work song. Written in an idiom that is direct, terse, and brimming with the vernacular of the railroad work song, the poem has a series of four-line stanzas. The first and third lines advance the story, and the second and fourth lines add emphasis as well as a distinctive musical quality. In the lines two and four, Brown uses internal rhyme by repeating a phrase in the line, sometimes repeated exactly, as in, "Man in full, babe, man in full," or with slight variation as in, "Sweet-hipted Mama, sweet-hipted Mame."[47] Each line is marked by a ceasura, and the "babe" punctuates the line, as Brown incorporates the work song rhythm into the poem. Thus, through repetition and well-placed emphasis, Brown intensifies the tragic circumstance of Big Jess' bid for a decent life. His refusal to quit his job and his laugh in the face of retaliation were, for Brown, marks of courage.

And, significantly, Brown incorporates this master theme into several poems in which courage is manifest in terms of survival and resistance. In "Strange Legacies," he celebrates those people, the famous and the nameless, who have bequeathed legacies of defiance and strength. The great Black hope, Jack Johnson, "taking punishment with a golden, spacious grin" and John Henry, sticking to his hammer until he died, taught lessons of manliness, pride, and courage that were sorely needed.[48] Their magnificent feats are celebrated along with the quieter courage of anonymous folk like the "old nameless couple in Red River Bottom."[49] They have looked upon destruction, and they have not killed off their hope; they have faced the irrational forces of nature and man— the hermeneutical puzzles of the universe—and they have remained poised in the midst of chaos; they have absorbed their group's collective fear, and, with their antidote of stoicism, they have routed their "own deep misery and dread."[50]

As Brown dots this poem with the voices of these folk, his poem takes on immediacy, and his heroes become familiar and accessible. Also, in a ryhthmical verse, free of rhyme except for the occasional repetition of a line for emphasis, Brown uses a variety of tones. Jack Johnson confidently challenges: "Heah ah is, big boy, yuh see whah Ise at. Come on in. . . . "[51] Yet the poem resolutely ends, "Guess, we'll give it one mo' try." According to one critic, Brown's voice in "Strange Legacies" reflects his "fidelity to a vernacular shared by all Americans . . . to utter their will to continue in the teeth of their lives' devastation . . . they use a vernacular similar to that spoken by Frost's and Robinson's people."[52] Each line carries the dominant message of the poem: courage and strength to resist, to survive, to endure in the face of great odds.

So if we go down
Have to go down
We go like you, brother
Nachal men. . . . [53]

Perhaps no poem of Brown's expresses more powerfully this theme than "Strong Men," the poem that best lays claim to being his signature poem. Taking the leitmotif from Carl Sandburg's line, "The strong men keep coming on," Brown celebrates the indomitable spirit of Black people in the face of racism and economic and political exploitation.[54] As Brown recounts the horrors of the Middle Passage, the scourges of slavery, and the humiliation of economic peonage and social segregation, his message is not one of unrelieved suffering and victimization but one of stoicism. In a perceptive article entitled "Sterling A. Brown and the Afro-American Folk Tradition," Charles A. Rowell sees the development of the "idea of black stoicism" as Brown's central purpose in the poem. According to Rowell, Brown, in developing this idea, "juxtaposes his catalogue of inhumanities against black people to passages from the spirituals and secular songs" which bespeak their hope, strength, endurance, and dogged will to survive.[55] Following is the first section of "Strong Men":

They dragged you from homeland,
They chained you in coffles,
They huddled you spoon-fashion in filthy hatches,
They sold you to give a few gentlemen ease.

They broke you in like oxen,
They scourged you,
They branded you,
They made your women breeders,
They swelled your numbers with bastards. . . .
They taught you the religion they disgraced.

You sang:
  Keep a-inchin' along
  Lak a po' inch worm. . . .
You sang:
  Bye and bye
  I'm gonna lay down dis heaby load. . . .
You sang:
  Walk togedder, chillen
  Dontcha git weary. . . .
      The strong men keep a-comin' on
      The strong men git stronger.[56]

Through the use of these songs, which have given comfort and encouragement to Black people from their earliest experiences in this country, Brown comments on their strength and endurance. The songs further symbolize the continuity of Black people as well as their contributions of toil, art, and spirit.

"Strong Men" is also technically effective, for its structure functions to convey this dominant theme. Much of the force of the poem may be attributed to syntax. Brown launches most of his lines with heavily stressed verbs that are preceded by contrasting pronouns "they" or "you," which must also be strongly stressed. The cadence of the poem suggests the rhythm of a martial approach which quickens and becomes more pronounced as the poem reaches its conclusion.

What, from the slums
Where they have hemmed you,
What, from the tiny huts
They could not keep from you—

One thing they cannot prohibit—
  The strong men . . . coming on
  The strong men gittin' stronger.
  Strong men. . . .
  Stronger. . . . [57]

In the assertive tone of the poem lies an awareness that the race has been able to resist hostile forces and endure despite adversity. This is also in the rhythm of Brown's line: the "irresistible advance not even all the humiliations and cruelties would bring to a halt."[58]

Though courage, strength, stoicism, resistance, and survival remain among Brown's thematic concerns, sometimes he chooses to convey them in tones that are not serious but humorous and ironic. In "Bad Bad Man," Brown creates John Bias.

> . . . a squinchy runt
> Four foot two,
> Married to a strapping broad,
> Big-legged Sue.[59]

With comic hyperbole, Brown tells how little Johnnie interrupts a lynching and saves a man's life. When told what he has done, he scratched his head, "Well, I be dam!" Johnnie had merely been looking for his wife.

With humor as an instrument, Brown often goes beyond simply stating the nature of human experience; he makes his readers laugh satirically. Perhaps nowhere else does Brown take humor more as his metier than in the Slim Greer tales. Brown bases his character on a virtuoso tall tale-teller who waited tables in the Hotel Jefferson in Jefferson City, Missouri, in the late twenties. Brown quips, "He says I owe him some money because I shouldn't have taken his name." In the poem "Slim Greer," Brown first uses the name and embroiders upon one of the waiter's favorite tales.

> Listen to the tale
> Of Ole Slim Greer,
> Waitines' devil
> Waitin' here;
>   Talkinges' guy
>   An' biggest liar,
>   With always a new lie
>   On the fire.[60]

Ole Slim Greer tells of skirmishes in Arkansas "where he passed for white" ("An' he was no lighter/Than dark midnight!") Slim, palming himself off as a dark foreigner, takes up residence with a "nice white woman," who suspects nothing until she hears Slim "agitatin' those ivories."

> Heard Slim's music—
> An' then, hot damn!
> Shouted sharp—"Nigger!"
> An' Slim said, "Ma'am?"[61]

Slim is the familiar trickster in the folktale who by strength of his wit and his agility deceives, eludes, and outsmarts his opponents. The outcome of Slim's adventure could have been the same as that delivered in the tragic tale "Frankie and Johnny." Yet here Brown, turning the events around for his hilariously funny purpose, has Slim make tracks "with lightnin' speed." He skillfully takes the timeworn material of racial jokes, exploited and repeated on the minstrel stage, and reshapes it in such a way that the humor is intraracial. The butt of the joke is no longer the ludicrously dressed "coon" who wears "no. fourteen shoes" but the hypocrisy of sexual racism.

In "Slim Lands a Job?" Brown tells how Slim remains on the rolls of the employed. The ballad pokes fun at the ludicrous demands often made by Southern white employers on their Black employees. With considerable effect, Brown builds up the humor of the poem by overstatement. "Poppa Greer" is seen in striking contrast with "the slow nigger" who is going to be fired.

> "Nigger, kin you wait?"
>   Is what Pete ast;
> Slim says, "Cap'n
>   I'm jes' too fast."
>
>   Pete says, "Dat's what
>   I wants to hire;
>   I got a slow nigger
>   I'm gonna fire—
>
> Don't 'low no slow nigger
>   Stay roun' hyeah,
> I plugs 'em wid my dungeon!"
>   An' Slim says "Yeah?"

A noise rung out
  In rush a man
Wid a tray on his head
  An' one on each han'

Wid de silver in his mouf
  An' de soup plates in his vest
Pullin' a red wagon
  Wid all de rest . . .

De man's said, "Dere's
  Dat slow coon now
Dat wuthless lazy waiter!"
  An' Slim says, "How?"
    An' Slim threw his gears in
      Put it in high,
  An' kissed his hand to Arkansaw,
    Sweetheart . . . good-bye!⁶²

Also part of the effect can be attributed to Brown's use of the rhythmic
effects in the quatrains that carry the narrative. Each line contains two
stresses, the short line contributing to the lightness of the tone and the
musical sound of the verse. Also implicit in the language is what Stephen Henderson calls "hyperbolic wisecracks, rooted in the tradition
of masculine boasting."⁶³ In strokes of virtuosity and intellectual agility that would delight even Slim Greer himself, Brown serves up his
wit with appropriate proportions of wisecracking, punning, signifying,
and hyperbolic imagery. (Slim says he is "So ragged, I make a jay-
bird/About to moult/Look like he got on gloves/An' a overcoat."⁶⁴)
Edward A. Jones, one of Brown's colleagues at Atlanta University,
describes Slim as a "master raconteur often with a risqué flavor."
(Brown, too, admits that some of the tales are of the rare scatological
vintage uncorked only on the right occasions.) Jones also perceptively
adds that Slim Greer is Brown's *poetic alter ego*.⁶⁵

"Slim in Atlanta," "Slim in Hell," and "Slim Hears the Call"
complete the series. In each, the reader finds the hero in humorous
situations that obliquely comment on the absurdity of Southern life. In
the first two tales, Brown exposes forms of Southern racism and
oppression with a kind of laughter out of hell. Turning the inanity of

racial codes into an ingenious joke, he has Slim encounter Atlanta and
its laws "for to keep all niggers from laughin' outdoors."

> Hope to Gawd I may die
>   If I ain't speakin' truth
> Make de niggers do deir laughin'
>   In a telefoam booth.[66]

In "Slim in Hell," the joke is extended to all Southern fixtures when
Brown's unsuspecting hero makes a discovery on his visit to hell. "De
place was Dixie/Dat I took for Hell."[67] In Brown's blast at corrupt
money-grabbing "colored" preachers, "Slim Hears 'The Call,' " Slim,
capitalizing on his "good looks," his ability to "rap," and his winning ways with women, decides, after the example of an old "coon-
can playing" buddy, to become a bishop.

> "Gonna be me a bishop
>   That ain't no lie,
> Get my cake down here,
>   An' my pie in the sky.[68]

Exposing the con games of designing clergy, the poet shows his candor at revealing exploitation emanating from within the race as well as
from without. Though the Slim Greer tales are successful examples of
American balladry, they also join the ranks of the finest American tall
tales. "In addition to the ballad tradition," as Charles H. Rowell writes,
"it is the black tradition of storytelling and folk humor that inform
these ballads. Implied in them is the black man's ability to see not
only the tragic aspects of his life, but those comic elements also—even
in the absurdity of white racism."[69]

Herein lies one of Brown's distinctive contributions. As he explores
the themes often handled by folk artists, he brings to his exploration
the broader perspective of the literary artist. For example, informing
the "Slim in Hell" poem is not only the Black folk tradition from which
the familiar images found in sermons and spirituals are drawn, but also
allusions to the Orpheus and Eurydice story in classical mythology.
Slim, like the favored Orpheus, is allowed to go to the underworld and
is allowed to leave it. Here also is Cerberus, the terrible dog which

guards the entrance to the infernal regions, now transformed to a "big bloodhound . . . bayin' some po' devil's track."[70] By a synthesis of two viable traditions, Brown creates this ballad through a process mentioned earlier called "cross-pollination." Brown accomplishes the fusion of the folk ballad using, as well, other resources of the literary artist: allusion as a means of reinforcing the idea of the descent into hell; language and imagery that have fidelity to the folk sermon; the right combination of irony, overstatement, and humor for an effective tone; and the use of the ballad form which accommodates the narrative.

PART TWO

With the same literary perspective used in recreating folk subjects and themes, Brown adopted the language and form of Black folklore. In his poetry the language of Black folk—the dialect, the idioms, the imagery, the style—retains its richness and verve. Likewise, the spirituals, blues, ballads, work songs, tall tales, and aphorisms achieve another level of expressiveness as they are absorbed and integrated. Not once doubting the efficacy of folk speech to express all that the people were, Brown brought the use of dialect in poetry to new respectable heights, despite a debate over its value as a literary medium.

In 1922 James Weldon Johnson, writing in the preface of *The Book of American Negro Poetry*, recognized that Black writers were breaking away from the use of conventionalized Negro dialect. The long association of this kind of dialect with the conventionalized treatment of Black character had convinced Johnson and other writers like Countee Cullen that the poet could not "adequately or artistically" treat a broad spectrum of Black life using this medium.[71] Though Johnson generally applauded the tendency to discard dialect, he feared that Black poets, in an attempt to disassociate themselves from the spurious, often demeaning, traditions of dialect poetry, would lose the "quaint and musical folk speech as a medium of expression."[72] Johnson's indictment, then, was not against dialect, as such, "but against the mold of convention in which Negro dialect in the United States had been set."[73] In his now classic call for originality and authenticity in racial poetry, he anticipated a form of expression that would not limit the poet's emotional and intellectual response to Black American life.

What the colored poet in the United States needs to do is something like what Synge did for the Irish; he needs to find a form that will express the racial spirit by symbols from within rather than by symbols from without, such as the mere mutilation of English spelling and pronunciation. He needs a form that is freer and larger than dialect, but which will still hold the racial flavor; a form expressing the imagery, the idioms, the peculiar turns of thought, and the distinctive humor and pathos, too, of the Negro, but which will also be capable of voicing the deepest and highest emotions and aspirations, and allow the widest range of subjects and the widest scope of treatment.[74]

Ten years later Brown, with the publication of *Southern Road*, comes as close to achieving Johnson's ideal of original racial poetry as any Black American poet had before. Appropriately, Johnson had the distinction of introducing Brown's poems to the American reading public.

Mr. Brown's work is not only fine, it is also unique. He began writing just after the Negro poets had generally discarded conventionalized dialect with its minstrel traditions of Negro life (traditions that had but slight relation, often no relation at all, to actual Negro life) with its artificial and false sentiment, its exaggerated geniality and optimism. He infused his poetry with genuine characteristic flavor by adopting as his medium the common, racy, living speech of the Negro in certain phases of real life.[75]

In Brown, Johnson recognized a poet who mined the "unfailing sources" of Black poetry to enrich his own poems. He saw Brown exploring with uncompromising honesty the range of characteristically folk responses—the stoicism in "Memphis Blues," the tragic despair in "Southern Road," the ironical humor of the Slim Greer series, the alienation of "Revelations," and the impulse to keep moving in such poems as "Odyssey of Big Boy" and "Long Gone"—which rang true to Johnson as they would have to the folk themselves.

Brown's exploration of the range of their responses led him to the sacred songs, the spirituals. "As the best expression of the slaves' deepest thoughts and yearnings," the spirituals are emotional, imaginative, and visionary.[76] They reflect, often in rhythms as striking as the melodies are beautiful, the religious nature of Black folk. Their expression of emotions that move to tears and joy, their imaginative interpretation of life and scripture, their fascination with Biblical characters, their preoccupation with sin, evil, and the devil, their personal relationship with "King Jesus" and God, and their visionary treatment of heaven, hell and judgment day are all revealed in these songs.[77]

Many of the essential qualities, themes, and idioms of the spirituals, Brown succeeds in transferring to his own poetry. In "New Steps," an infrequently quoted poem in *Southern Road*, Brown imaginatively handles the themes of saints and sinners competing for the soul of a young man. Here the battle of good and evil is worked out in a rather homely fashion. Sister Annie, overjoyed with the fine "new steps a-climbing to de little Church do'," remains strong in the faith that the church will save her son from ruin. Encouraged that the church is now fine enough to attract her wayward son, she "struts herself down to the sinful Foot." To her disappointment, she sees that the sinners are busy sprucing up the dens of iniquity, "puttin' green paint" on "poolroom den" and "sportin' new lace next the dirty panes." Brown uses a language whose cadence and tone are reminiscent of the spiritual "By an' By," in which the unknown bard sings, "O, by an' by/I'm gwinter lay down my heavy load." He shows Sister Annie continuing the battle against sin in a gesture of one-upmanship though the weight of her armor seems onerous.

> Up de new steps that meetin' night
> Sister Annie drug a heavy an' a weary load.
> New steps a-climbin'—
> O my Lawd
> Lace curtains snow white
> Snow white curtains
> O my Lawd
> Upstairs, downstairs,
> New steps
> O my Lawd. . . . [78]

Though the poet does not reveal who finally wins out, his message is clear and parallels thematically that of the traditional religious song, "Workin' on the Building."

> If I wus a sinner man, I tell you what
>   I'd do,
> I'd lay down all my sinful ways an' work
>   on the building too.

I'm workin' on the building
  fer my Lord,
  Fer my Lord, fer my Lord,
I'm workin' on the building fer my Lord
I'm working on the building, too.[79]

Continuing to work on the building, Sister Annie is a symbol of religious faith and spiritual fortitude.

"New Steps" mirrors the form of spiritual songs and projects the Christian concepts of faith, love, humility, and salvation. Many of the songs retell in capsulized, often dramatic, form significant events and stories recorded in the Old and New Testaments. Some, however, make no direct allusion to Biblical scenes but are inspired by local events, sermons, or the desire for religious social comment.[80] In "New Steps," Brown adopts the dramatic form of many spirituals to spotlight Sister Annie's attempt to bring her boy to salvation. The characters in the story are allegorized (Brother Luck, Miss Joy, Victory). They add to the symbolic richness of the poem in which every element of the setting—"new steps," "the dingy house," "the big white letters," "snow white curtains"—is charged with a metaphorical meaning like that evoked by the chariot, the wheel, and gospel shoes, standard images in the spirituals.

The language in the poem is characterized by economy of statement, and vivid, fresh images: "An the dingy house . . . /Runnin' over wid jazz an' scarlet noise." Brown also punctuates the poem with interjections—"Oh my Lawd"—a typical feature of Black music, and he occasionally "worries the line" as he has his narrator interject bits of wisdom.

Good times, seems like, ain't fuh las'—
Nebber de real good times, dey ain't—

Finally Brown uses an effective incremental style in the chorus to evoke the most powerful image of the poem.

O my Lawd
Upstairs, downstairs
New steps
O my Lawd. . . . [81]

The themes, the qualities, and the idiom characteristic of the spiritual receive their fullest exploration in another poem appearing in *Southern Road*, "When De Saints Go Ma'ching Home." Using two carefully selected similes and incorporating into his poem a line from this spiritual, he suggests the quiet dignity and solemnity of Big Boy Davis as he tunes up his guitar to play his "mother's favorite."

> Carefully as an old maid over needlework,
> Oh, as some black deacon, over his Bible, lovingly,
> He'd tune up specially for this. There'd be
> No chatter now, no patting of the feet.
> After a few slow chords, knelling and sweet—
> *Oh when de saints go ma'chin' home,*
> *Oh when de sayaints goa ma'chin' home . . .*
> He would forget
> The quieted bunch, his dimming cigarette
> Stuck into a splintered edge of the guitar;
> Sorrow deep hidden in his voice, a far
> And soft light in his strange brown eyes;
> Alone with his masterchords, his memories. . . . [82]

As Big Boy sang the saints' triumph song, he would see "a gorgeous procession" of the faithful, those who had held out to the end, marching to the "Beulah Land." [83] There would be Ole Deacon Zachary and Sis Joe. Elder Peter Johnson, "steamin' up de grade/Lak Wes' bound No. 9," and "little brown skinned chillen/Wid deir skinny legs a-dancin' would join the heavenly band." [84] However, white folk, as goes his dream, would "have to stay outside." In keeping with God's promise to take care of his own, those who had shunted him would not be kept behind. Heaven is a place reserved for the righteous, and his folk shall occupy the best place. There would be "another mansion fo' white saints." [85] Ironically, his vision of heaven takes on the pattern of earthly existence; segregation will be preserved.

According to Big Boy's dream, God's judgment was not color blind; it would fall as evenly on the Black folk as the white. Big Boy's buddies—Sportin' Legs and Lucky Sam, Smitty, Hambone, and Hardrock George—would go the way of "guzzlin', cuttin' shines" and bootleggers. [86] Even Sophie, his strappin' brown, could not fit in with the saints of God. One, though, was assured a place. He sees his mother's "wrinkled face,/Her brown eyes, quick to tears—to joy."

Mammy
With deep religion defeating the grief
Life piled so closely about her,
Ise so glad trouble doan last alway,
And her dogged belief
That some fine day
She'd go a-ma'chin'
When de saints go ma'chin' home.[87]

Part of the effectiveness of the poem lies in Brown's skillful mixture of idiom and his evocation of religious imagery and lyrics in the spiritual. In profiling the saints in the heavenly band, Brown uses folk dialect to clothe the humble and simple faith they brought to their religion. Interspersed with the more formal language, these passages stand in bold relief.

"When de Saints Go Ma'ching Home" is one of the best examples of Brown's effective use of structure. Using the music of the spiritual as his dominant poetic referent, Brown has Big Boy's rendition of this favorite spiritual come alive with the fervor, ecstacy, and drama of Black religious music. Brown uses several of the techniques identified by Stephen Henderson in his important book *Understanding the New Black Poetry*. Brown makes a clear allusion to the song title and adopts it as the title of his poem. The title has the power to evoke the image of a bodacious New Orleans band parading from the cemetery amid the rejoicing of those who are very much alive, or Louis "Satchmo" Armstrong irreligiously belting out the "chant of saints," in one hand his handkerchief which has become a cliché and in the other hand his trumpet which will never be one. Brown forces the reader to incorporate into the structure of the poem his memory of specific passages from the spiritual. Here Big Boy sings the song with solemn, slow chords from his guitar. Brown takes care to write in the inflection and the syncopation.

Oh when de saints go ma'chin' home
Oh when de sayaints goa ma'chin' home. . . . [88]

Above all, "When De Saints Go Ma'ching Home" is performance. Brown presents in six dramatic scenes the singer's remarkable vision. Attributing to his singer the skill of the visionary minister who, touched by the Holy Fire, recreates heaven's alabaster gates, the streets of gold, and the manna on celestial tables to coax his reluctant sheep to the fold, the poet imaginatively reenacts the singer's performance. Each section relates a different aspect of the singer's vision, as though the vision were a series of stills that could be viewed separately or run together to produce the moving picture. Kimberly W. Benston, in a brilliant exegesis of the poem, writes that it is "the mode of seeing the hero's songs, the perspectivizing of performance, which constitutes the inner concern" of the poem.[89] In each section the "envisaged saints exist as possibilities not memories, which none is actually present but everyone, under the hero's watchful 'gaze' is immanently represented."[90]

As performance, the poem speaks to the separation between singer and audience, between the self and the community. Bentson sees the disjunction between the singer and the audience producing the "deep tension" in the poem and representing its "true subject." This "disjunction" is readily apparent in the structures of the poem. Bentson writes, "The poem is framed by acute recognition of this discontinuity: 'He'd play after the bawdy songs and blues . . . he'd go where we/Never could flow'—divorce figured in the distinctions between 'he' and 'we' (self and community) and between the hero and poet (voice/dialect and text/formal diction)."[91] Ultimately, by separating himself from his audience, the singer is capable of a higher vision that has the power to convince his hearers of their own possibility of revision, renewal and re-creation.

In Brown's "Sister Lou," one of the most remarkable monologues in American literature, the speaker—much like the Indian-looking woman Brown met in Coolwell, Virginia—compresses her higher vision of heaven in images as familiar as hearthside implements. Sister Lou at the bedside of an ailing friend bolsters her courage with the familiar images of old dear friends that she will meet "When de man/Calls out de las' train."[92]

Sister Lou has the train, the dominant symbol of escape and separation in folk parlance, serve as the heavenly chariot to take her friend "home." As with the folk, in the imagination of Sister Lou "the scenes of everyday life form continuous allegories" with the material found in the Bible.[93] The woman, when she gets home, would show "Marfa" how to make "greengrape jellies" and bake "a passel of Golden Biscuits" for poor Lazarus, "scald some meal for li'l box plunkin' David and tell the Hebrew children her stories."

> Give a good talkin' to
> To yo' favorite 'postle Peter,
> An' rub the po' head
> Of mixed-up Judas,
> An' joke awhile wid Jonah.[94]

Matching the pantheon of Biblical heroes given in the spirituals, Brown establishes what he believes to be the intimate relationship that exists betweeen Black folk and the heavenly host. Among them, they would be accepted.[95] In heaven, there would be no back doors. "No mo' dataway/Not evah no mo!" There would be pearly gates and their own room, "Openin' on cherry trees an' plum trees/Bloomin' everlastin'."[96] The saints would be compensated for enduring hardship and suffering pain. The folk had faith that their "belief in God enabled them to cling on to life, though poor, miserable, and dying, looking to God and expecting Him, through miraculous and spectacular means, to deliver them from their plight."[97]

Sometimes, however, their faith is shaken. In the poem, "Children of the Mississippi," the victims of the Mississippi flood recall the story of Noah but wonder why they did not receive the sign.

> De Lord tole Norah
> Dat de flood was due,
> Norah listened to de Lord
> An' got his stock on board,
> Wish dat de Lord
> Had tole us too.[98]

In another poem, "Crossing," Brown fuses the doubting of escaping slaves with the spiritual doubting of Christians. As in the spirituals, the freedom from sin gets all mixed up with physical freedom from oppression.

> We do not know
> If any have reached that Canaan
> We have received no word.
>
> Behind us the belling pack
> Beyond them the hunters
> Before us the dismal swamp.
>
> We do not know. . . . [99]

It is appropriate that Brown couches their doubts in the poignant language of the sacred songs, for each journey involves uncertainty. Incorporating lines from several traditional songs, Brown effects, as Stephen Henderson suggested in *Understanding the New Black Poetry*, "a particularized response" resulting from the subjective feeling stirred by the reference. Henderson calls this technique the use of "subjective correlative," in contrast to the objective correlative that gained currency in the New Criticism.[100] The following lines illustrate the technique:

> We know only
> That there lies not Canaan
> That this is no River Jordan.
>
> Still are we motherless children
> Still are we dragging travelers
> Alone, and a long ways from home.
>
> Still with the hard earth for our folding bed
> Still with our head pillowed upon a rock
>
> And still
> With one more river,
> Oh, one wide river to cross.[101]

These lines evoke several spirituals. Dominating the poem is an allusion to the spiritual, "Wasn't Dat a Wide River."

> Oh, Jordan's River is deep and wide
> One mo' river to cross
> I don't know how to get on de other side
> One mo' river to cross.[102]

The "ancient dusky rivers," that Hughes made symbols of the continuity of his people's racial spirit, for Brown become symbols of obstacles that must be bridged. Those who "leapt/From swamp land/Into marshes," those who "grow footsore/and muscle weary" inherit the hardships of their ancestors and stand in need of the encouragement and solace provided by the spirituals.[103] Intrinsic to Brown's language are references to the spiritual lyrics: "Sometimes I feel like a motherless child . . . A long ways from home"[104] and "Let us cheer the weary traveler, along the heavenly way."[105] However, his language is formal; departing from the dialect of the sacred song, it reflects a new period of struggle. The "crossing" is not to be considered entirely otherwordly—"This is not Jordan River/There lies not Canaan"—but the crossing represents also the immediate and real crossing over to freedom.

The folk, according to Brown, "had many other moods and concerns than the religious; indeed, some of these ran counter to the spirituals. Irreverent parodies of religious songs, whether coming from the black-face minstrelsy or from tough-minded cynical slaves, passed current in the quarters."[106] These secular folk rhymes, sometimes called "jig-tunes" and "devil-tunes," were also regarded as "upstart crows" because of their sacrilegious use of "biblical phrases in a satirical, free-thinking way."[107] This mood transformed the "Lord's Prayer."

> Our Fader, who art in heaven
> White man owe me 'leven, pay me seven,
> Thy kingdom come, they will be done
> And if I hadn't tuck that, I wouldn't git none.[108]

The mood is present in Brown's poem "Chillen Get Shoes." In a cynical inversion of the spiritual "All God's Chillen Got Shoes," the hoped-for heavenly shoes become silver slippers worn by Moll, the neighborhood prostitute.

> Hush little Lily
>   Don't you cry;
> You'll get your silver slippers
>   Bye and bye.
>
> Moll wears silver slippers
>   With red heels,
> And men come to see her
>   In automobiles.
>
> Lily walks wretched,
>   Dragging her doll,
> Worshipping stealthily
>   Good-time Moll;

> Envying bitterly
>   Moll's fine clothes,
> And her plump legs clad
>   In openwork hose.
>
> Don't worry Lily,
>   Don't you cry;
> You'll be like Moll, too
>   Bye and bye.[109]

Certainly, the odds are stacked in Lily's favor that she will someday be like Moll, and Brown's message of cynicism is complete. By borrowing from religious imagery the silver slippers associated with the saints' paraphernalia, Brown brings the other-worldly idealism of the spirituals in conflict with the immediacy of life.

In "Memphis Blues," Brown uses folk rhymes, working in concert with "the rhythm and imagery of the black folk sermon," to convey "the black folk preacher's vision of the threat of destruction" and a deeper, more pervasive "comment on the transitory nature of all things man-made." [110] Charles H. Rowell recognizes Brown's "excellent employment of the rhythm of black folk rhymes" to emphasize the speakers' indifference to the inevitable destruction of Memphis.

> Memphis go
> By Flood or Flame;
> Nigger won't worry
> All de same—
> Memphis go
> Memphis come back,
> Ain' no skin
> Off de nigger's back.
> All dese cities
> Ashes, rust. . . .
> De win' sing sperrichals
> Through deir dus'.[111]

Rowell recognizes in the lilting rhythms of these lines something of the folk rhyme "Aunt Kate."

> Ole Aunt Kate, she died so late
> She couldn't get in at the Heaven Gate.[112]

As Rowell suggests, Brown, projecting on the speaker a child's indifference to death, uses playful, teasing, lines to heighten the poem's message. The Black man is indifferent to the destruction of Memphis, for he has never seen it as his own.[113]

In part two of "Memphis Blues," Brown employs the call and response patterns of certain spirituals to create voices similar to the folk preacher's exhorting his congregation to salvation and those of the members responding to his call.

> Watcha gonna do when de tall flames roar,
>   Tall flames roar, Mistah Lovin' Man?
> Gonna love my brownskin better'n before—
>   Gonna love my baby lak a do right man,
>   Gonna love by brown baby, oh, my Lawd!
>
> Watcha gonna do when Memphis falls down,
>   Memphis falls down, Mistah Music Man?
> Gonna plunk dat box as long as it soun',
>   Gonna plunk dat box fo' to beat de ban'
>   Gonna tickle dem ivories, oh, my Lawd![114]

Here, however, is a difference. "Ironically, the response of each speaker in the poem has nothing to do with the impending destruction; while Memphis is being destroyed, each speaker plans to do what he thinks is best for him." Implicit in their responses is "the sensibility of the blues singer—his stoic ability to transcend his deprived condition."[115] Also present is the blues song's emphasis "on the immediacy of life, the nature of man, and human survival in all of its physical and psychological manifestations."[116] The preacher man, the drinking man, the gambling man, and so on, see themselves as outsiders. As they have been excluded from the society by proscription and prejudice, they define their survival in their own terms; they take their pleasure and their meaning from within the boundaries set for them. However, moving at a deeper level is Brown's paradox. Being outside will not keep them from destruction. Even those distinctions made and boundaries set among men will have no meaning then.

As Brown brings into play a combination of folk forms—the secular rhyme, the sermon, the blues, and the scattered notes of the gospel shout—in "Memphis Blues," they function not only to further the meaning of the poem but also to suggest the essential interrelatedness of the forms. In the poems, the rituals associated with the blues come together. The tendency in the folk community was to keep the so-called "devil-tunes" from the religious songs. The religious community objected to the raw overt lines of the blues songs that scandalized the moral attitudes and accepted modes of conduct required by its ministers. Though the blues resulted from the same feeling that informs the spirituals and gospel songs, these songs reflected radically different world views.[117] Mahalia Jackson had such a strong perception of the distinction between sacred and secular music that she never sang blues songs and refused to cast herself in the role of an entertainer. However, as Larry Neal observes, "Although the blues are an extension of the emotional and tonal qualities inherent in the spirituals, their chief emphasis is on the material world—the world as flesh, money, survival, freedom, lost love, unrequited love, and instable love."[118]

In a striking vignette of Buddy Bolden, Neal captures the essence and feeling of the Blues/God syntheses. He hears Bolden playing something on his coronet that "for a while sounds like the blues, then like a hymn." Though at first he cannot make out the tune, after a while he realizes that Bolden "is mixing up the blues with hymns."[119] As Neal listens to the melancholy sounds of his horn, he imagines a pitch battle between the Lord and the Devil, and only heaven knows who will win. For Brown, also, the faint line that separates the two forms was not as important as "the Afro-American ethos" that they share.

Sterling Brown and his contemporary, Langston Hughes, more than any other New Negro writers, explored the oral tradition and experimented with its forms in the belief that Black folk were creating valuable, original art. They put great stock in the virtuosity of folk expression; they prized its innovation, its freshness of style, and its inclusive quality as artistic exemplars. Of all the forms, the blues received the greatest exploration in their poetry. According to Stephen Henderson, Hughes and Brown "expand and amplify the form without losing its distinctive blues flavor. Poems like Hughes' 'The Weary Blues' and 'Montage of a Dream Deferred' and Brown's 'Memphis Blues' suggest something of their range, even in their respective first volumes of poetry."[120]

Brown's absorption and intensification of the blues form and feeling vary from poem to poem. In "Long Track Blues," Brown, handling the twin blues themes of loving and leaving, departs from the three-line stanza typical of the classic blues but uses the two-line form, the sentiments, the language, and verbal conventions of the standard blues. As folk artists had done before, he makes the railroad ''the favored symbol of escape.'' He renders with fidelity the melancholy of a man who has lost his ''lovin' babe.''

> Heard a train callin'
> Blowin' long ways down the track;
> Ain't no train due here,
> Baby, what can bring you back?[121]

The familiar ingredients are all here: the distant whistle of the train, the howling dog, the beckoning signal lights, the brakeman's lantern, all of which combine to express the man's lament. A comparison of the stanza from a folk blues and one from Brown's poem shows his close study of the form.

> I went down to do depot, I looked
>   upon de board,
> Couldn't see no train, couldn't hear no
>   whistle blow.[122]

> Went down to the yards
> To see the signal lights come on;
> Looked down the track
> Where my lovin' babe done gone.[123]

An analysis of these two stanzas shows that Brown approximates the cadence of the blues line with four stresses. He also uses an idiom that captures the sound and sense of railroad lore. However, in this poem the poet runs the risk of being, as George Kent suggests, ''too reliant upon a folk form that has, itself, the alliance of the singing voice, instrumental music, facial expression and jester, to drive itself into our spirit.'' Yet, to articulate the deeply personal feeling of departure and loss, Brown utilizes symbolism, among other literary conventions, to increase the power of the blues poem, stripped of the oral resources of the blues song. An example is the following stanza:

> Red light in my block,
> Green light down the line;
> Lawdy, let yo' green light
> Shine down on that babe o' mine.[124]

The red light and green light that usually function to keep the rail traffic unsnarled, here have symbolic significance. The red light is a symbol for hard times, bad luck and danger; the green light is a symbol of good times, success, and safety. And on another level the green light represents the presence of spiritual grace and protection. Out there, somewhere down the line is grief, ugly grief—not to be denied. Hauntingly, the poem suggests the poignancy that comes with preparing to face grief and loss and death.

In another poem, "Rent Day Blues," Brown, using extended dialogue, tells the story of a couple facing rent day without any money. As the man wonders where they will get the rent, his woman turns up with the money from a mysterious source. Though the man is briefly troubled, he finally resolves to let their good fortune stand. In "Rent Day Blues," Brown clearly presents one of the major themes of the blues—poverty and economic uncertainty—within the context of the blues' preoccupation with the love relationship. Here, Brown breaks with the blues tradition by having his blues poem "proceed in a narrative fashion." According to blues critic Charles Keil, the blues lyric rarely proceeds in this fashion but "is designed primarily to illustrate a particular theme or create a general mood." [125] Using dialogue as a narrative technique, Brown is able to add a dramatic dimension and bits of characterization not typical of the blues lyric. For example, in the following stanzas the willingness of the woman to get the rent money any way she can and the man's suspicions and cynicism come through clearly.

My baby says, "Honey,
Dontcha worry 'bout the rent.
Looky here, daddy,
At de money what de good Lord sent."

Says to my baby,
"Baby, I been all aroun';
Never knowed de good Lord
To send no greenbacks down." [126]

Brown is also experimenting with the rhythm of the blues poem. For example, he infuses a jazz-style offbeat rhythm in the poem. The established pattern appears to be iambic trimeter. However, in the first stanza cited above, the last line breaks from this basic pattern with a syncopated pentameter line. In a solidly aesthetic gesture, Brown is taking on the risk and challenge of the literary rather than the oral poet. Brown is, however, not as experimental in his blues trilogy entitled "New St. Louis Blues." Undoubtedly, Brown had in mind the man reputed to be the Father of the Blues when he wrote these three poems. Twenty years before, in 1912, W. C. Hardy wrote "the most widely known blues of all," the "St. Louis Blues." The plaints of a lonely, love-sick woman filter through its lines.

In "Market Street Woman," Brown retains the cadence of the popular Handy song with its quickened pace in the first half of the line, while he transforms the St. Louis temptress into an aging streetwalker whom the men now ignore.

> Put paint on her lips, purple powder on her choklit face,
> Paint on her lips, purple powder on her choklit face,
> Take mo' dan paint to change de luck of dis dam place.

> Gettin' old and ugly, an' de sparks done lef' her eye,
> Old an' ugly an' de fire's out in her eye,
> De men may see her, but de men keeps passin' by—[127]

Brown, in portraying this hard luck woman to whom life is "dirty in a hundred ornery ways," uses the softened, elided sounds of folk speech and song.[128] However, the strong racial flavor is not dependent upon dialect. As Alain Locke had predicted several years before—that someone would reveal the soul of the Black man "in a characteristic way of thinking and in a homely philosophy rather than in jingling and juggling of broken English"—Brown achieves the "deeper idiom of feeling" in the "New St. Louis Blues" trilogy.[129] The "deeper idiom" that Locke speaks of is conveyed in Brown's sensitive treatment of the ironies, paradoxes, and near tragic situations of Black life.

In the first poem of the trilogy, "Market Street Woman," the old prostitute is a symbol of a demoralized Black community in which only the slimmest prospect of "luck" can change an agonizingly desperate situation. And ironically, unlike her diamond-studded prototype, she has no power to entice. The dispossessed man in "Low Down," bumming tobacco from passers-by, views himself as worthless and views life as a gamble in which the dice are loaded and the cards are "all marked to hell." He is heard saying:

Bone's gittin' brittle, an' my brain won't low no rest,
Bone's gittin' brittle, an' my brain won't let me rest,
Death drivin' rivets overtime in my scooped out chest.[130]

Diseased, lonely, and spiritually lost, the man sees his personal worth reduced to "bummin' cut plug from de passers by." Significantly, in these poems, Brown is consistent with the blues mode and presents more than "a woman's plaint for her departed or departing lover"; he handles the human concerns over aging, fear of death, and the confrontation with natural disasters.[131]

Recognizing in the best folk blues "their elemental honesty, depth of insight and strong original phrasing," Brown fuses these qualities with the resources of the literary artist to give genuine expression to "the soul of the Negro."[132] For example, in "Tornado Blues," he personifies the death and destruction wrought by the St. Louis Cyclone.

Destruction was a-drivin' it and close behind was Fear,
Destruction was a-drivin' it and hand in hand with Fear,
Grinnin' Death and skinny Sorrow was a-bringin' up de rear.[133]

Death, Destruction, Fear, and Sorrow are allegorical figures taunting the victims of this deadly tornado. The following lines, created by nameless blues singers, commemorate its victims.

The wind was howling, buildings began to fall
I seen dat mean ol' twister comin' jes lak a cannon ball.

De world was as black as midnight, I never heard such
   a noise before.
Like a million lions, when turned loose, dey all roar

De people was screamin', runnin' ev'y which-a-way,
   (Lord, help us, help us)
I fell down on my knees an' began to pray.

De shack where we were livin' reeled an' rocked but
   never fell.
How de cyclone started, nobody but de Lawd can tell.[134]

In this poem, "Tornado Blues," Brown heightens the treatment of this theme. His poem begins with these remarkable lines:

> Black wind come a-speedin' down de river from de Kansas plains,
> Black wind come a-speedin' down de river from de Kansas plains,
> Black wind come a-roarin' like a flock of giant aeroplanes—[135]

Couched in a convincing folk idiom, Brown's "aeroplanes" simile is strikingly original; it parallels the folk figure "lak a cannon ball." In the next line, Death, Destruction, Fear, and Sorrow take on flesh as they allegorically express the truth of the dirty work wrought by merciless tornado winds. Also implicit in the poem is a subtle irony that demands that the tornado visit the poor Black people and Jews, rather than the wealthier whites, especially since "they had little to offer their cruel guests."[136]

In "Ma Rainey," one of the finest poems in *Southern Road*, Brown skillfully brings together the ballad and blues forms and, demonstrating his inventive genius, creates the blues-ballad. On one level, the poem gives a glimpse of the folk heroine, Ma Rainey. Gertrude "Ma" Rainey, on the vaudeville circuit at the age of fourteen, "heard the blues while trouping up and down her native south land, and started singing them herself to audiences that were spellbound as her deep, husky voice gave them back their songs."[137] In many ways the mother of the blues, she took a youngster named Bessie Smith in her care and lovingly taught her the blues, and the child grew strong in timbre, cadence, and resonance, like her "Ma." Befitting the title Madam "Ma" Rainey, she made her entrance on innumerable stages with a sequined gown hugging her short, stocky frame, an elaborate gold necklace, tasseled earrings, and a brilliant gold-tooth grin crowning it all. Her professionalism was hard won in the Black minstrel shows, medicine shows, traveling road shows, and vaudeville shows where she trained her raspy voice to complement the new instrumental blues stylings.

But even more than being a portrait of the venerated blues singer, the poem serves as an emotional portrait of the people who flocked to hear "Ma do hear stuff."

> An' some jokers keeps deir laughs a-goin' in de crowded aisles,
> An' some folks sits dere waitin' wid deir aches an' miseries,[138]

These are the same folk the reader meets in "Foreclosure," "Children of the Mississippi," "Old King Cotton," and "Strange Legacies," the nameless folk who know endless toil and live with misery and dread. For them Ma Rainey sings, "Backwater Blues."

> 'It rained fo' days an' de skies was dark as night,
> Trouble taken place in de lowlands at night.

> 'Thundered an' lightened an' the storm begin to roll
> Thousan's of people ain't got no place to go.

> 'Den I went an' stood upon some high ol' lonesome hill,
> An' looked down on the place where I used to live.[139]

Ma Rainey is the high priestess who has the power to articulate the pain and suffering of her people. She sings "about de hard luck/Round," their "do' " and "de lonesome road" they "mus' go. . . . " Her power over her audience emanates from her ability to translate the chaos and uncertainty of their lives into terms that can be understood and confronted. When she sings "Backwater Blues," she catches hold of the folks "somekindaway."

> An' den de folks, dey natchally bowed dey heads an' cried,
> Bowed dey heavy heads, shet dey moufs up tight an' cried,
> An' Ma lef' de stage, an' followed some de folks outside."
> Dere wasn't much more de fellow say:
> She jes' gits hold of us dataway.[140]

Brown celebrates Ma Rainey's charisma that is more than flashy jewelry and sequined gown. He celebrates her skill in the art of improvisation, which Albert Murray says "will enable contemporary man to be at home with his sometimes tolerable but never quite certain condition of *not* being at home in the world and will also dispose him to regard his obstacles and frustrations as well as his achievements in terms of adventures and romance."[141] Like Larry Neal and Ralph Ellison, Brown also celebrates the power of the blues singer "to reflect the horrible and beautiful realities of life"[142] and to affirm "the value of the group and man's ability to deal with chaos."[143]

In "Ma Rainey," Brown has the blues mode function thematically and structurally to heighten the effect of the poem. In the poem he also uses a technique that is a common practice among several poets. Henderson describes the practice as "forcing the reader to incorporate into the structure of the poem his memory of a specific song or passage of a song, or even of a specific delivery technique." Throughout Brown's poetry there are several examples of this technique. "When the Saints to Ma'ching In," "Strong Men," and "Revelations" are among the most notable examples. In the final section of the poem, Brown incorporates Bessie Smith's popular "Backwater Blues." The song, by suggesting the hardships and suffering of the victims of the Mississippi Valley floods, illustrates the dire problems faced by these people and gives, as Charles H. Rowell suggests, an "air of immediacy to the poem." [144]

Brown has also fused the blues form with the ballad to invent the "blues-ballad," which Henderson hails as "a literary phenomenon . . . as distinctive as Wordsworth's lyrical ballad." [145] As structurally effective as it is innovative, the blues-ballad combines the narrative framework of the ballad and the ethos of the blues. The ingenuity of his invention can be best appreciated when one sees how the two traditions come together in a blues-ballad like "Ma Rainey."

Ballads telling of the exploits of Black folk heroes, similar to sixteen-bar or eight-bar ballads of Anglo-Saxon origin, began to appear in America during the second half of the nineteenth century. With the abolition of slavery, Black folk, facing the prospect of freedom, were inspired to compose songs dedicated to the virtues and deeds of their heroes. These ballads bear their names: "John Hardy," "John Henry," "Casey Jones," "Railroad Bill," "Stagolee," and "Frankie and Johnny," among others. Aware of English, Irish, Scottish, and French ballad styles, Black balladeers adopted the classic ballad form which tells a story in a series of stanzas, usually in a progressive, chronologically developed narrative with or without a refrain. [146]

At the close of the century, blues developed as a form out of the hollers of the solitary farmers who worked the rows of Southern fields. Often they sang their hollers, repeating the lines until new lines came to mind that completed the thought and expressed the emotion.

With the introduction of the guitar, capable of producing the moaning, whining, flattened sounds of the human voice, blues took shape. Though the early blues had the eight-bar or sixteen-bar stanzaic structure like the ballads, with the experimentation with the "blues notes" and the African pentatonic scale, the "twelve-bar blues" evolved. The most common but by no means the only structure consisted of three lines of four bars each.[147]

Within this structure, the blues singer improvises his music, and in the act of creation he draws from a stock of favorite verses and familiar rhythmic patterns, and combines them with new lines extemporized out of his melancholy experience. He sings of love and infidelity, poverty and economic uncertainty, lonely travel and dislocation, drinking and drugs, and disasters and death. Unlike the balladeer who extolls the virtues of a distant hero, the blues singer is the central character in this song. Therefore, the blues singers themselves become heroes to their hearers. Brownie McGhee, Blind Willie McTell, Haddie "Leadbelly" Ledbetter, Blind Lemon Jefferson, Gertrude "Ma" Rainey, Bessie Smith, Clara Smith, Mamie Smith, Ida Cox—the names are legion—look on their personal calamities and are not destroyed.[148]

Clearly in this cultural tradition, Brown, with a conscious artistry, combines the intensely personal music of the blues singer with the heroic tales and epic scope of the balladeer. The genius of his invention is apparent in "Ma Rainey." Brown takes the explicit, chronological, and narrative elements of the ballad to tell how the people flock in to hear "Ma Rainey do her stuff." And though the ballad form functions well to spotlight this magnificent woman with the "gold-toofed smiles," it cannot accommodate the intimacy, the immediacy, and the emotional intensity that Brown intends for the poem. He needs the blues ethos to suggest the massive concentration of emotion present among the folk in Ma's audience—the work-weary soul, the laughing to keep from crying, the unspeakable sorrow, the needful catharsis.

In a superb creation of his own blues, Brown employs the standard twelve-bar, three-line structure in a moving blues phrase that captures the "botheration" experienced by the folk who heard her.[149] He sets up the pattern in the first line: "An' den de folks, dey natchally bowed dey heads an' cried." He improvises around the theme in the second line: "Bowed dey heavy heads, shet de moufs up tight an' cried."[150] "Worrying the line," he alters the phrasing to amplify the poignance of their response.[151] In the closing line, Ma Rainey, the priestess-exorcist-medicine woman—her work done—has, in Albert Murray's terms, dislodged their blues "before the botheration degenerates into utter hopelessness."[152] Part of the strength of this poem lies in its blues language. Brown, in every part of the poem, has reproduced the people's speech. "I talked to a fellow, an' say, 'She jes, catch hold of us, somekindaway.' '' The compressed phrasing, the elimination of un-necessary tense and adverb construction, the speech is what people say to each other—''it's the language they use when they stand on a street corner talking, when a mother talks to a child, when a man and woman make love.''[153]

Like the blues singer, the poet punctuates his phrases with glottal stops and vocal snaps, and he elides words and syllables.[154] And with great dexterity, he effects a bluesy sense of time (we are not sure how long the audience waits for Ma Rainey to appear or how long she stays out there, and slides in and out of tempo, varying the tempo in each section).

As with Brown's masterful recreation of the guitar player's perfor-mance in ''When de Saints go Ma'ching Home,'' here too is perfor-mance. However, there is a difference. Here the separation between the audience and the singer is bridged by the transforming power of the blues. Though her purpose may be self-centered, even selfish, as she raises the awful specter of her own melancholy, she ''fingers the jagged edges'' of their collective hurt; and, by doing this, she helps them to confront and, perhaps, transcend those problems that weigh heavily on their minds. Brown has each section contribute to this act of catharsis which is ultimately the goal of the performance. Part one is the gathering; part two deals with anticipation emanating from deep within souls that laugh and cry in unison; part three is appearance; and part four is the actual performance and response. Thus the poem's structure accents the essential roles the performer and audience play. And magically, at the end of the poem, performer and audience be-come one. ''An Ma lef' de stage, an' followed some de folks out-side.''

Of the folk forms that Brown adopted for his poetry, the ballad is his most versatile and most frequently used. Brown is drawn to the ballad form for a number of reasons. Certainly, one is the ballad's tra-dition of presenting a story in a moving and dramatic manner. Em-ploying the form used by the folk for centuries to commemorate events of catastrophe, tragedy, and good fortune as well as the people that shaped them, Brown creates his own memorable tales. They tell the tragic story of convicts on chain gangs as in ''Convict'' and ''Johnny Thomas,'' and they follow the comic exploits of the trickster-con man Slim Greer or the supra-sensitive race patriot ''Crispus Attucks McKoy.'' They record the odysseys of traveling men like Big Boy or Long Gone and expose the heroic figures of bad men and men of defiance, inspired by the Black folk's own heroes—Railroad Bill, Po Lazarus, Stackolee, and Roscoe Bill.

Second, the topical nature of ballads, especially American balladry, coincided with Brown's own interest in treating a variety of subjects in a narrative medium. Charles Rowell notes Brown's extensive use of themes, some of which were not previously handled by Black folk ballad makers.

His poems in the ballad tradition are not confined to the subjects iterated in Gordon Hall Gerould's *The Ballad of Tradition* or those G. Malcolm Laws sees as the prevailing themes of the black folk ballad. Brown's literary ballads, while sometimes adhering closely to the folk ballad form, cover numerous subjects from black folk life. Racial injustice, exploits of folk heroes, tragic love affairs, religion, suffering in poverty, freedom, the need for travel—all of these and many others constitute the subjects of Brown's ballads. His poems in the ballad form alone, more than his poems employing other forms of Afro-American music, give us a broad slice of black life in America.[155]

The theme of immortality even finds its way into Brown's ballad "Odyssey of Big Boy." Big Boy, a guitar playing roustabout, here confronts thoughts of death and craves immortality with his heroes.

> Lemme be wid Casey Jones
>   Lemme be wid Stagolee,
> Lemme be wid such like men
>   When Death takes hol' on me,
>   When Death takes hol' on me. . . . [156]

Big Boy represents the strong, resourceful Black worker who, denied the adventure of vertical movement in American businesses and industry, has wandered from job to job, from state to state, earning his wages with sweat and grit. He has "skinned" mules and "druv steel" in Kentucky, "stripped tobacco" in Virginia, "shocked de corn" in Maryland, "cut cane" in Georgia, and "planted rice" in South Carolina. He has "slung hash" and "busted suds," and "seen what dey is to see." He has had his share of women, too, from the "stovepipe blond in Macon" to the Creole gal in New Orleans." But the one that "put it over dem" was "a gal in Southwest Washington/At Four'n half and M."[157] As Big Boy tells of his exploits in love and life, he assures his place in legend. Here, Brown is myth-maker. As the title helps to suggest a relationship between Big Boy and other heroes who had made their odysseys (Homer's Odysseus, Virgil's Aeneas, Dante's Pilgrim), Big Boy is raised to the level of mythic hero who embodies the value, attitude, *Weltanschauung* of his people.

> An' all dat Big Boy axes
>   When time comes fo' to go,
> Lemme be wid John Henry, steel drivin' man,
>   Lemme be wid old Jazzbo,
>   Lemme be wid ole Jazzbo. . . . [158]

While Brown shows Big Boy laying claim to an immortality open to this common man, he sketches broadly and vividly aspects of Black life in America.

Perhaps a third reason for Brown's extensive use of the ballad form is its characteristic stanzaic pattern. It satisfied Brown's appreciation for "rattling good verses." [159] Starting with the standard quatrain with a typical rhyme scheme of a b c b, Brown sometimes added a fifth line of refrain as in the "Odyssey of Big Boy" and "He Was A Man." Echoing the refrain from the popular ballad, "Frankie and Johnny," the line, "He was a man, and they laid him down," not only serves to advance the theme of the story but also significantly sustains the tragic tone of the poem. Sometimes Brown alternates the four-line stanzas with couplets as in the poem "Scotty Has His Say." Recasting lines from the "Original Talking Blues," Brown punctuates Scotty's flippant challenge with:

> Whuh folks, whuh folks; don' wuk muh brown too hahd!
> Muh brown what's tendin' chillen in yo' big backyahd. [160]

Though his lines occasionally fit the conventional meter of four stressed syllables per line, they often have irregular stress, giving an angular effect to his rhythm, as in the long ballad poem "The Last Ride of Wild Bill."

Finally, the ballad-maker's penchant for improvisation especially appealed to Brown's own high sense of creativeness. Noting the habit of folk singers to borrow stanzas from one song to incorporate in another, Newman I. White calls the Black folk's tendency toward improvisation "highly characteristic, a racial trait."[161] (Perhaps this tendency is better termed a cultural trait instead of a "racial" one.) G. Malcolm Laws, in a comparison of white ballad singers and Black singers, also notes "the Negro's unusual power of improvisation." Law writes:

> As in all balladry, there is a central event to be recounted. But the Negro is not usually content merely to pass along the ballad as he heard it. In a sense he performs the ballad, sometimes adding comments between stanzas as well as incorporating in it details of interest. . . . [162]

Consistent with "the folk habit of lifting what they want and using it how they will,"[163] Brown experimented by combining "narrative techniques of the ballad with artistic techniques of the other forms."[164] Earlier, it was shown how Brown, in a poem like "Ma Rainey," combines the blues form and feeling with the ballad and, in effect, invents the blues-ballad.[165] Also, within the ballad framework of "Memphis Blues," Brown captures rhythms borrowed from folk sermons and children's rhymes. In fact, Brown's skill at inventing or improvising is extensive. For instance, in a poem called "Puttin' on Dog," Brown cleverly alternates stanzas that echo the rhythms and rhyme of a folk children's gamesong with ballad stanzas. Also apparent is Brown's handling of the snappy dance rhythms of the day. The story tells of old Scrappy, a flamboyant showoff, who runs up against bad man Buck.

> Look at old Scrappy puttin' on dog,
> Puttin' on dog, puttin' on dog,
> Look at old Scrappy puttin' on dog,
> Callin' for the bad man Buck.
>> Buck saw him comin', pulled his thirty-two forty,
>> Got him once in the arm, and twice in the side;
>> Scrappy switched his gat, like they do it in the Western,
>> And let the daylight into Buck's black hide.
> Look at old Scrappy puttin' on dog,
> Puttin' on dog, puttin' on dog,
> Look at old Scrappy puttin' on dog,
> Waitin' for the undertaker's wagon.[166]

Brown achieves effect through a subtle employment of understatement. For Brown, then the ballad form affords a versatile, dramatic, and distinctively musical medium for his numerous themes.

Influencing nearly half of all of Sterling Brown's poems, the ballad form is frequently used to relate the heroic exploits of Black men. In his second published book of poems, *The Last Ride of Wild Bill* (1975), Brown skillfully tells stories of men who, each in his own way, confront injustice, brutality, and adversity. Though the tone of his ballads changes from the serious-tragic attitude of "Sam Smiley," to the bravado of "The Ballad of Joe Meek" and the flippant cynicism of "Crispus Attucks McKoy," his forte is his ability to explore the characters and situations that reflect a segment of Black life.

Sharing with the Black ballad singers an interest in violence and murder, Brown has six of the twelve ballads in *The Last Ride* end in murder. G. Malcolm Laws, who recognizes the folk's preoccupation with murder and crime, offers several explanations.

More than half the Negro ballads are based on murder, a percentage far higher than that of the white ballads. Several possible explanations of this phenomenon spring to mind. For one thing, much native balladry has originated among cowboys, lumbermen, sailors, soldiers and others whose lives were sufficiently dramatic and hazardous to lend themselves to ballad treatment. The Southern Negro's circumscribed life has offered little of comparable excitement to sing about except crime. Then, too, Negro balladry, as the Lomaxes have shown, flourishes in prisons, where songs about crime are presumably of general interest. It may also be suggested that the social distinctions drawn among white men between criminal and non-criminal have not been equally emphasized among Negroes, who so often have been victims of the white man's laws.[167]

As victims of the white man's laws or his lawlessness, the characters gain the sympathy, if not the admiration, of the audience. Similarly, Brown's heroes are drawn in such a way as to prompt a response that parallels that of the folk audience to heroes who "outtrick and outspeed the law."[168] For instance, in Black folk balladry, Long Gone, Lost John—a hero noted for his speed and skill at evading the sheriff, the police, and the bloodhounds—is heard saying, "The hounds ain't caught me and they never will." When "Lost John 'doubled up his fist and knocked the police down' " his deed wins approval from the audience as much as his winged heels do. The audience's approval, Brown suggests, is rooted in the folk's "bitter memories and suspicion of the law."[169]

In Brown's ambitious ballad, "The Last Ride of Wild Bill," he presents the exploits of a fully developed contest hero who, reminiscent

of Long Gone, Lost John, is all but unbeatable in eluding the authorities. In part one of the poem, entitled "The Challenge," the conflict
between Wild Bill, numbers-runner par excellence, and the new Chief
of Police is revealed. Brown gives his hero, who flaunts his numbers-
running activities in the face of authorities, the necessary "cool" of
an urban folk hero. Wild Bill is lawless, even down to depositing a
slug in the telephone to call the Chief of Police. Wild Bill, who has
heard that the new Chief intends to put an end to his activities, says:

> "I just heard the news
> You spread over town.
> I raise you one,
> I call your bluff.
> Your cops
> Are not quite tough
> Enough.
> And you ain't so smart,
> I will be bound,
> To run the
> Great Wild Bill
> To ground.
> I'd like you to know,
> What I thought you knew,
> You have bit off more
> Than you'll ever chew.
> As long as loose change
> Is in this town
> Wild Bill
> Will still
> Run the numbers down." [170]

In part two, the news of the challenge creates the predicted flurry of
activity. And with a touch of irony, the poet has all humanity side with
Wild Bill against the impudent police chief. In the next section, "Civic
Response," Brown shows the betting heavy and the money mounting
as all manner of folk bet on their boy. Here, too, the poet does not
deny himself the small ironies of the situation.

> On Druid Hill
> An old-stock cavalier tried to bet
> His yard-boy part of his back-pay due
> But Mose he believed in Wild Bill too.

The next two sections handle, in some detail, the character development of the two opponents, whom Brown is careful to make worthy
of each other. What Wild Bill has in cockiness and cool, the Chief
matches in game and determination. In establishing Wild Bill's character, Brown must draw in the essential quality of "badness." Badness, as Laws defines it, is "an extreme form of meanness or bravado" exhibited "by a bully to whom crime gives a sense of power." [171]
It is also the orneriness of Stackolee who shoots down Billy Lyons or
the meanness of Railroad Bill as he gathers a string of crimes to his
credit. Bad men are the notorious characters in folk balladry who are
noted for their recklessness and swagger and build reputations as gam-
blers, robbers, and killers. Thomas W. Talley, in his pioneer work,
Negro Folk Rhymes, offers several folk descriptions of badmen, and
one, in particular, Wild Nigger Bill, appears to have been the prototype for Brown's hero. [172] Inheriting Nigger Bill's bravado, Brown's
hero is seen preparing for his "last ride."

At eleven-thirty
Wild Bill was ready,
His voice was steady
But his temper dirty.
He got up from his business lunch
They fixed him up
A Planter's Punch.

He looked at the cherry and the lime with scorn,
Threw the fruit mixture in the sink
"No salad for me,
When I drink I drink."
Got a two-by-four scantling for a bracer,
Drank a tumbler of corn
With rye for a chaser. [173]

The following sections of the poem focus on "the chase." Wild Bill,
allegorically seen as the fox, is able to elude the hunter (the Chief) and
the hounds (the police). Here, Brown shows a good knowledge of the
ballad conventions used by Sir Walter Scott. In the divisions of *The
Last Ride*, the titles which are similar to those used in Scott's long
poem, *The Lady of the Lake*, Brown heightens the excitement by detailing the places, people, and events that go into the drama. Using a

technique of Black speech that Stephen Henderson calls "virtuoso naming and enumerating," the poet confounds his readers with a long list of names and details that have a specificity that convinces them that he "really must know what he is talking about."[174] Brown's use of this technique is evident in the following passage:

> He turned to his jumper
> By his side.
> The jumper was beaming
> And his grin was wide.
> They checked
> The collect
> And were satisfied.
> They had picked up the bags
> As per schedule:
> Third Baptist Church,
> The Vocational School,
> The Registrar's office
> At the City Jail,
> Braxton Bragg's statue
> On the horse's tail,
> Behind a hedge on the Courthouse lawn,
> The Parish-House of the Cathedral
> Of Saint John
> Who saw the holy number
> And so on.[175]

The detailing also helps make the point that the number's business has widespread popularity.

As the tale goes, Wild Bill's luck is incredible. On three occasions he is aided by fellow citizens who stall the police. His success is almost assured until he meets with the Chief's final trick.

> Then Bill saw a bag
> In a new place.
> He looked at his jumper
> With doubt in his face.
> "Must be a new agent
> We ain't checked.
> But the bag is fat
> And it looks correct,

It's a territory
We don't know,
But we better make a clean sweep
As we go.''
The jumper brought it to him
Laid it on his knee
It was heavier than a bag
Had right to be.
Bill held it to his ear,
Heard something tick,
Then he understood
The Chief's last trick.
As he threw it from him,
He heard the roar,
And then the great Bill
Knew no more.[176]

In the final section, "The Last Collect," Wild Bill finds himself "Hell bent on wheels" bound for Hell. However, even there Wild Bill retains his "cool" and his clientele.

They climbed all over
His running board,
"Wild Bill, Wild Bill!"
'Their shouting roared
And rang through all the streets of Hell:
   "Give us the number,
   Wild Bill,
   Tell us
   What fell."[177]

In this poem, Brown, with a folk spirit of improvisation, lifts some standard fixtures from the traditional English ballads, combines them with the rhythms, the imagery, and the idiom of the Black folk ballad to create a memorable poem.

In conclusion, what Black folk expressed in story, proverb, and song, Brown thoughtfully considered and absorbed in poetic imagination, and infused in his own creative writing. He adopted themes and symbols from the folk storehouse; catastrophe, hardship, superstition, religion, poverty, murder, death, loneliness, travel, and courage were among the themes that Brown handled with telling originality. In his work folk themes and symbols are amplified and intensified by the application of his own poetic vision and made to perform a distinct literary function. Besides adopting themes and symbols from folk life, Brown made the folk his subjects. From his poems emerge personalities whose words are often bitter, humorous, cynical, tragic, gay, but never sentimental. Brown succeeded in capturing the frankness and honesty of people talking among themselves. They are Black folk whose labors, loves, and hardships reflect in very real terms the texture of Black character.

Also present in Brown's poetry is a pervasive racial consciousness, an awareness of the historical and social circumstances that have kept Black people in America sensitive to oppression. His race consciousness, far from being "isolating and limiting" as one reviewer of *Southern Road* feared,[178] has the effect of revealing in realistic terms the thoughts, feelings, and perspectives of people whose image and voice have been corrupted again and again on the mistrel stage, in Southern "plantation" literature, and in the mindless imitations of Black writers seeking a receptive market.

In Brown's hands, dialect sheds its conventional artificiality and resembles natural speech with strong rhythms and striking "imagery, idioms, peculiar turns of thought, distinctive humor and pathos . . . the deepest and highest emotions and aspiration."[179] In line with James Weldon Johnson's high criteria, Sterling Brown reaffirms its suitability as an appropriate literary medium.

Brown embraces forms from oral folk art and succeeds in going beyond mere transcriptions in rendering them in literature. His poems recreate the blues ethos and the dignity and solemnity of the spiritual. Also, with varying notes of tragedy, humor, and bravado, his narratives achieve more than the virtuosity of anonymous folk tales and ballads.

PART THREE

As Brown has taken the forms of Black folklore and has given them broader and deeper application, he has brought to his poetry written in traditionally "literary" forms a practiced craft and a cultural and aesthetic perspective enriched by the folk tradition. Less dramatic and less innovative in style than his folk-inspired poetry, his formal poems are personal, lyrical, and, to some extent, pastoral. The poems appearing in the last section of *Southern Road* provide a good sample for analysis. These poems generally revolve around thematic and philosophical axles, which also serve to promote the movement of the entire book. Though set apart by Brown's exclusive use of Euro-American literary forms—including the sonnet, the quatrain stanzaic form, and free verse—the poems are linked to the rest of the book, and Brown's other poems, by the repetition of dominant themes and the reintroduction of attitudes and philosophical perspective explored in former sections of the book. Prominent among these poems are two of Brown's favorite themes: enduring strength and wisdom. These master themes have the power to carry along with them other themes including youth and old age, the dichotomy of town and country, and the triumvirate—life, love, and death.

In "Salutamus," the only poem in the section that is recognizably racial in tone, Brown returns to the theme of enduring strength. At crucial points in the book—including "Strong Men" in Part One, "Strange Legacies" in Part Two, and "Salutamus," in Part Four—Brown reveals unmistakably his "belief in the potentialities of a handicapped minority." [180] "Salutamus," taking its epigraph from Shakespeare's *Henry IV*—"O Gentlemen the time of Life is short"—carries the message of change. Those hampered by bitterness, despair, disappointments, and the "searing brand" of racial hatred know that their race's strength lies in their ability to endure.

> What though some roads wind through a gladsome land?
> It is a gloomy path that we must go.[181]

The lines resemble the lyrics of James Weldon Johnson's "Lift Every Voice" as well as "echo the spiritual lyrics." For example, Part One of *Southern Road* is introduced by the following epigraph: "Road may be rocky/Won't be rocky long." [182] As these various voices act to amplify the message, the reader understands that change will come; it is inevitable but must be paid for with long suffering.

> And yet we know relief will come one day
> For these seared breasts; and lads as brave again
> Will plant and find a fairer crop than ours.
> It must be due our hearts, our minds, our powers;
> These are the beacons to blaze out the way.
> *We must plunge onward; onward, gentlemen. . . .* [183]

Subsumed in these lines is a tradition of protest which includes Dunbar's "We Wear the Mask," Du Bois' "A Litany at Atlanta," and Johnson's "Fifty Years." With its conventional imagery of the sowing and reaping, the poem bears a close resemblance to Cullen's sonnet, "From the Dark Tower," which appeared in *Copper Sun* (1927). Also using the form of the sonnet, Brown achieves a lyrical intensity which results from the compression of the emotions of hate, hope, love, and despair. Thus, Brown has the very structure of the poem become a metaphor of a constrained, oppressed race.

Six of the ten poems that make up the final section of *Southern Road* are in sonnet form. They signal a shift from the dramatic to the lyrical. Brown's focus is now personal and his poetry subjective. With these poems Brown again demonstrates the great value he places in technical skill. His extensive use of the sonnet, what D. G. Rossetti calls "a moment's monument," makes the best case for Brown's continued interest in exploiting form and technique. The opportunity to create musical effects is just as accessible here as in the blues poems and the ballad. The compressed, concentrated thought, the economy of language, and the exactness of expression that he prizes in the folk literature are required in the sonnet.

In the companion poems "Challenge" and "Telling Fortunes," the theme is wisdom. The message in both these poems seems to be that wisdom is often the gift of mature age and youth is sometimes foolish and predictably vulnerable. The speaker in "Challenge" says:

> I said, in drunken pride of youth and you,
> That mischief-making Time would never dare
> Play his ill-humoured tricks upon us two,
> Strange and defiant lovers that we were.[184]

He is confident and undaunted even in the face of Time and Death. Yet the reader knows that his stance is foolish even though his personal tragedy remains understated.

> And thus, with you believing me, I made
> My prophecies, rebellious, unafraid . . .
> And that was foolish, wasn't it, my dear?[185]

The young speaker in "Telling Fortunes" echoes the message in Housman's poem "When I Was One and Twenty," two lines from which supply the epigraph for the entire section. As in the Housman poem, the young man becomes easy prey for "women with dark eyes." A mature woman, gypsy-like, with a red cloth tied on her hair and her face tinted "with dark rose mysteries," dispenses wisdom the young man cannot comprehend.

> "This card a trip," you said. "You go your way,
> Another foolish way, boy, joked by men,
> Whether alone or not it does not say."
> And this, "Beware of women with dark eyes,"
> You teased; I laughed. . . . Oh you were very wise
> Who could have understood such wisdom then?[186]

Both sonnets end with a question. Structurally correct, the questions function to convey the confusion of the young lovers and to leave suspended the specific consequences of their lack of wisdom.

In another sonnet titled "Rain," the speaker is no longer a young, brash lad who laughs at fortune; he is a melancholy, solitary singer whose experience "with the old hag, Sorrow" has made him resilient and accepting of the harsh realities of his life. The tone of the poem is melancholic, like in the blues, and two of the themes popular with the blues singer—unrequited love and separation—are here refined. Primarily the painter of people and not of landscape or scene, the poet achieves in this poem clear, crisp images in a description of a gloom-ridden room that are among the best he has ever drawn.

> Outside the cold, cold night; the dripping rain. . . .
> The water gurgles loosely in the eaves,
> The savage lashes stripe the rattling pane
> And beat a tattoo on November leaves.
> The lamp wick gutters, and the last log steams
> Upon the ash-filled hearth. Chill grows the room.
> The ancient clock ticks creakily and seems
> A fitting portent of the gathering gloom.[187]

The poet directly communicates the feelings of sorrow and loneliness through aural imagery. He also skillfully uses the first five lines in the sestet to comment on the happy future that the speaker and his love had planned but, because of some unknown circumstance, will not realize. These lines serve to intensify the speaker's sorrow as they evoke the vision of what could have been. And in the final line, which is marked off by a space, the speaker has come full circle in the course of his introspection. "Outside the dripping rain; the cold, cold night." Nothing has changed except, as with the blues singer, there has been self-confrontation that may lead to transcendence.

In "Return," Brown again is drawn to the landscape and limns it vividly with "bits of cloud-filled sky . . . framed in bracken pools" and "vagrant flowers that fleck unkempt meadows." Wordsworthian in theme and emphasis, the poem described the quietude and peacefulness that come over the speaker who returns "in boyish wonderment" to a familiar rustic spot.

> There I have lain while hours sauntered past—
> I have found peacefulness somewhere at last,
> Have found a quiet needed for so long.[188]

The reader's sense of the beauty and calm of the place is heightened by the knowledge that the speaker's experience always has not been so idyllic.

The theme of the dichotomy of town and country, only hinted at in "Return," is fully realized in "To a Certain Lady, In Her Garden" and "Mill Mountain." In the first poem, Brown, as Stephen Henderson suggests, "contrasts Mrs. Spencer's idyllic garden to the rough mankilling streets beyond" in a treatment of the *hortus conclusus* theme.[189]

> A step beyond, the dingy streets begin
> With all their farce, and silly tragedy—
> But here, unmindful of the futile din
> You grow your flowers, far wiser certainly.[190]

Here in this garden the poet expects to find relief from the "belittered, grimy ways" of crowded streets, escape from the "farce" and futility of the city. Here, too, he expects to find quiet wisdom.

> Lady, my lady, come out the garden,
> Clay-fingered, dirty-smocked, and in my time
> I too shall learn the quietness of Arden,
> Knowledge so long a stranger to my rhyme.[191]

He seeks to know how she, the "profiteer," has snatched "a sense of strange and momentary pleasure/and beauty . . . "[192] and has "gained so easily the dear/Capricious largesse of the miser soil?" For the poet, the lady has "life's puzzle solved."

"To a Certain Lady, In Her Garden" is dedicated to New Negro poet Anne Spencer whom Brown describes as "a wise, ironic but gentle woman." Stephen Henderson sees in the portrait of Spencer a connection between her and the wise old lady in "Virginia Portrait," in Part One of *Southern Road*. Despite differences in class and lifestyles, the two women share an inner strength of purpose that allows them to rise above "the futile din."[193]

Significantly, Brown uses other means to establish the connection between this poem and the rest of the book. With two dedications to Anne Spencer, Brown links Part One, which is dedicated to the poet, to the final section. Brown also accomplishes an effective repetition of the theme of strength in quiet wisdom and reintroduces a philosophical perspective that essentially states that wisdom and dignity are often found where they are unexpected. Also, subtly embroidered throughout this poem is the leifmotif of the book.

O de ole sheep dey knows de road,
Young lambs gotta find de way.

As one who knows the way, who has life's puzzle solved, Anne Spencer imparts meaning and direction to the younger poet on the road from innocence to experience.

The poems in "Vestiges" are dedicated to another lady, the poet's wife Rose Anne, also known as Daisy. Though remembrances of their courtship and their love provide the aura for most of these poems, Daisy's presence is most deeply felt in "Thoughts of Death" and "Against That Day." Even at the writing of these poems almost fifty years before her death in 1979, the thoughts of her loss urges forth Brown's most personal reflections.

Thoughts of death
Crowd over my happiness
Like dark clouds
Over the silver sickle of the moon.

He sees death coming to some like "a grizzled gangster/Clubbing in the night," or "like a gentle nurse/Taking their toys and stroking their hot brows." However, he imagines that death will come to her "Like an old shrewd gardener/Culling his rarest blossom. . . . "[194] In "Against That Day," the image of her "mirth," "nimble grace," and "the sweet flesh of (her) lovely face" vanquished by the destroyer death, leads the poet to ponder the eternal questions of immortality and the despotism of time.

> What will there be then to rebel
> Against Time's crazy tyranny,
> What wretched substitute to tell
> Your loveliness and bravery?[195]

In "Mill Mountain," the last poem in the section, Brown returns to the theme of the dichotomy between town and country. Personal in tone and strongly characterized by the pastoral mode, the poem contrasts the turbulence and squalor of an unnamed city with the tranquility and beauty of Mill Mountain. Under the glow of moonlight, the speaker sees the dirty city transformed into a "distant fairyland" and seeks to share this revelation with a dozing child who has accompanied him.

> What has become at last, my frightened child,
> Of that brown city that we knew by day?
> What of its squalor, of its pettiness—
> What of its blatant noises and its dirt—
> Its crying children and its fretting grind—
> And hectic love close pent in sultry rooms?[196]

However, the full meaning of the poem cannot be approached through this theme alone. In a crucial passage in the poem, the speaker with the mood of "Dover Beach" addresses the large issues of life. However, his musings do not reach the sleeping child.

> . . . We have learned tonight
> That there are havens from all desperate seas,
> And every ruthless war rounds into peace.
> It seems to me that Love can be that peace
> However stormy or warlike Life has seemed.

> What do you think? Why do you never answer?
> Asleep so soon . . . And what a quiet breathing.[197]

As the speaker supplies a formulaic answer, the reader is immediately aware that it cannot be taken as absolute. The questions, syntactical metaphors for the speaker's confusions, serve to undermine his conclusion and lead invariably to the reversal in the final lines:

> Sleep, child. . . . It's better than these words of mine.
> Words that I meant sincerely to be rich
> Of healing for your fever—that have turned
> To empty words, apparently so poor.
> Sleep on. What else is there for you,—but sleep?[198]

The speaker moves back from idealism and the half-real world, cloaked by the softness of the moonlight. The "slowly creeping lights" that are in reality the headlights of cars, the railroad searchlights that "too officiously grope in the dark," and his nearly forgotten thoughts of tomorrow inveigh against his fantasies.

The subtle message of the poem is that attempts to evade or escape the unpleasant reality of life are doomed to failure. Brown's message is also Housman's message in the concluding poem of *A Shropshire Lad*, "Terence, This is Stupid Stuff." According to Terence, Housman's persona, refusing to see the world as it is, at best leads to illusion.[199] At worst, it leads to futility, for one can only return to the old world, to "begin the game anew," until life is ended with an eternal sleep.

On another more personal level, "Mill Mountain" is a tribute to the transforming power of love, and Rose Anne, the unifying figure in this section, remains the poet's haven "from all desperate seas."

Having considered at length the nature and purpose of his poetry, Brown presents interesting clues concerning these matters in the poem that concludes *Southern Road*. Poetry, to be of value, must deal with reality and not fantasy. Though it may sound notes of pessimism, it just as often conveys the notes of acceptance, encouragement, and hope. For ultimately, peace and beauty come from an acceptance of truth, however frank and harsh. With a philosophical approach to the function of poetry similar to A. E. Housman's, Brown sees his poetry providing a defense, through the acceptance of pain, against the much harsher pain of life itself.

178   Sterling A. Brown

Essentially then, Brown, the poet, becomes the blues singer, fingering the jagged grain "to keep the painful details and episodes of a brutal experience alive in one's aching consciousness."[200] The point of Brown's poetry is to give "the child"—those in search of wisdom—words that are "meant sincerely to be rich of healing" for a fretting and troubled world.

NOTES

1. Betty S. Barber, "Influence of Afro-American Folklore on the Poetry of Sterling Brown" (an unpublished paper written for Dr. Samuel Allen, English Department), Howard University, March 27, 1972, p. 7.

2. Lines from a nineteenth-century spiritual, quoted in Brown, *Southern Road*, frontispiece.

3. Alain Locke, "Sterling Brown: The New Negro Folk-Poet," in *Negro: An Anthology*, ed. Nancy Cunard (New York: Frederick Ungar Publishing Company, 1970), p. 92.

4. Lines from a nineteenth-century spiritual, quoted in Brown, *Southern Road*, p. 1.

5. Brown, *Southern Road*, pp. 8 and 9.

6. Brown, *Southern Road*, p. 11.

7. Ibid., p. 41.

8. Ibid., p. 68.

9. Ibid., p. 74.

10. Arthur P. Davis, *From a Dark Tower: Afro-American Writers* (Washington, D.C.: Howard University Press, 1974), p. 129.

11. Lines from a twentieth-century blues song quoted in Sterling A. Brown, *Southern Road*, p. 101. It is one of many blues composed and sung by those Blacks who migrated to the cities of this country during the 1910s and 1920s.

12. Brown, *Southern Road*, pp. 115–17.

13. A. E. Housman, *A Shropshire Lad* (New York: Henry Holt and Company, 1922), p. 20.

14. Blyden Jackson and Louis D. Rubin, Jr., *Black Poetry in America: Two Essays in Historical Interpretation* (Baton Rouge: Louisiana State University Press, 1974), p. 60.

15. Interview with George E. Kent at the University of Chicago, May 10, 1978.

16. Brown, *Southern Road*, p. 46.

17. Ibid., p. 47.

18. Locke, "Sterling Brown: The New Negro Folk-Poet," p. 92.

19. Ibid.

A Study of His Poetry 179

20. Ibid., p. 90.
21. Robert O'Meally, "Reconsideration," *The New Republic*, (February 11, 1978): 35.
22. Brown, *Southern Road*, p. 26.
23. Ibid., p. 113.
24. Ibid.
25. Ibid.
26. Ibid., p. 114.
27. Sterling A. Brown, "Old Lem," in *The Collected Poems of Sterling A. Brown*, selected by Michael S. Harper (New York: Harper & Row, 1980), pp. 170–71.
28. Ibid., p. 170.
29. Frederick Douglass, *My Bondage and My Freedom* (New York: Miller, Orton & Mulligan, 1855), pp. 252–53.
30. Brown, *The Collected Poems of Sterling A. Brown*, p. 170.
31. Sterling A. Brown, "Bitter Fruit of the Tree," in *The Collected Poems of Sterling A. Brown*, p. 190.
32. Ibid.
33. Sterling A. Brown, "An Old Woman Remembers," in *The Collected Poems of Sterling A. Brown*, pp. 178–79.
34. Stephen Henderson, *Understanding the New Black Poetry*, p. 41.
35. Ibid., p. 43.
36. Kent, "Self-Conscious Writers and the Black Folk and Cultural Tradition", p. 78.
37. Ibid.
38. Brown, *Southern Road*, p. 22.
39. Wagner, *Black Poets in the United States*, pp. 481–82.
40. Brown, *Southern Road*, p. 33.
41. Lines from this traditional American ballad were cited in Brown, *Southern Road*, p. 35. The song, sometimes titled "Frankie and Albert," has more than three hundred variants according to John Lomax and Alan Lomax in *American Ballads and Folk Songs* (New York: Macmillan Co., 1935), p. 103.
42. Brown, *Southern Road*, p. 35.
43. Ibid., p. 38.
44. Sterling A. Brown, "He Was a Man," in *The Collected Poems of Sterling A. Brown*, p. 136.
45. Ibid.
46. Sterling A. Brown, "Break of Day," in *The Collected Poems of Sterling A. Brown*, p. 146.
47. Ibid.
48. Brown, *Southern Road*, p. 95.
49. Ibid., p. 96.

50. Ibid.

51. Ibid., p. 95.

52. John F. Callahan, "In the Afro-American Grain," *The New Republic* (December 20, 1982): 28.

53. Brown, *Southern Road*, p. 96.

54. Line from Carl Sandburg's poem "Upstream" used by Brown as an epigraph to the poem "Strong Man" in *Southern Road*, p. 51.

55. Rowell, "Sterling A. Brown and the Afro-American Folk Tradition," p. 142.

56. Brown, *Southern Road*, p. 51.

57. Ibid., p. 53.

58. Wagner, *Black Poets of the United States*, p. 503.

59. Sterling A. Brown, *The Last Ride of Wild Bill and Eleven Narrative Poems* (Detroit: Broadside Press, 1975), p. 45.

60. Brown, *Southern Road*, p. 83.

61. Ibid., p. 85.

62. Ibid., pp. 86–87.

63. Henderson, *Understanding the New Black Poetry*, p. 38.

64. Sterling A. Brown, "Slim Hears the Call," *The Last Ride of Wild Bill*, p. 30.

65. Edward A. Jones, "On Sterling Brown: Poet and Man," *Sterling A. Brown: A UMUM Tribute*, p. 11.

66. Brown, *Southern Road*, p. 88.

67. Brown, *The Last Ride of Wild Bill*, p. 40.

68. Ibid., p. 31.

69. Rowell, "Sterling A. Brown and the Afro-American Folk Tradition," p. 152.

70. Brown, *The Last Ride of Wild Bill*, p. 38.

71. Johnson, ed., "Preface to the First Edition," *The Book of American Negro Poetry*, p. 40.

72. Ibid., p. 41.

73. Ibid., p. 42.

74. Ibid., pp. 41–42.

75. Johnson, "Introduction," *Southern Road*, p. xiv.

76. Brown, "Spirituals, Seculars, Ballads and Work Songs," p. 47.

77. Howard W. Odum and Guy B. Johnson, *The Negro and His Songs: A Study of Typical Negro Songs in the South* (New York: The New American Library, Inc., 1969), Chapel Hill, 1925, Chapter II.

78. Brown, *Southern Road*, p. 92.

79. Nineteenth-century spiritual quoted in Odum and Johnson, *The Negro and His Songs*, p. 72.

80. Harold Courlander, *Negro Folk Music USA*. (New York: Columbia University Press, 1963), pp. 35–79.

81. Brown, *Southern Road*, p. 92.
82. Ibid., p. 12.
83. Ibid., p. 13.
84. Ibid., p. 14.
85. Ibid., p. 16.
86. Ibid.
87. Ibid., p. 17.
88. Ibid., p. 12.
89. Kimberly W. Benston, "Sterling Brown's After Song: 'When De Saints Go Ma'ching Home' and the Performance of Afro-American Voice," *Callaloo* Nos. 14 & 15, 5 (February-May 1982): 37.
90. Ibid., pp. 38–39.
91. Ibid., pp. 39–40.
92. Brown, *Southern Road*, p. 48.
93. Odum and Johnson, *The Negro and His Songs*, p. 29.
94. Brown, *Southern Road*, p. 49.
95. Brown, "Spirituals, Seculars, Ballads, and Work Songs," p. 47.
96. Brown, *Southern Road*, p. 49.
97. Benjamin A. Mays, *The Negro's God as Reflected in His Literature* (New York: Atheneum, 1968), p. 25.
98. Brown, *Southern Road*, pp. 67–68.
99. Sterling A. Brown, "Crossing" in *The Collected Poems of Sterling A. Brown*, p. 194.
100. Henderson, *Understanding the New Black Poetry*, pp. 48, 59. As Henderson uses the term, the "subjective correlative" is a technique used by the writer by which he incorporates into his poem a reference to a well-known song to evoke an emotional response from the reader. Reference is made to a state of mind or feeling instead of to an object or structure, thus the term "subjective correlative."
101. Brown, "Crossing," p. 195.
102. Nineteenth-century spiritual as cited in James Weldon Johnson and J. Rosamond Johnson, eds., *The Book of American Negro Spirituals* (New York: Viking Press, 1925), p. 153.
103. Brown, "Crossing," pp. 194, 195.
104. Lines from a traditional nineteenth-century spiritual quoted in James Weldon Johnson and J. Rosamond Johnson, eds. *The Second Book of American Negro Spirituals*, (New York: Viking Press, 1926), p. 30.
105. Lines from a traditional spiritual quoted in Johnson and Johnson, eds., *The Book of American Negro Spirituals*, p. 184.
106. Brown, "Spirituals, Seculars, Ballads and Work Songs," p. 50.
107. Brown, *Negro Poetry and Drama*, p. 21.
108. Ibid.
109. Brown, *Southern Road*, p. 110.

110. Rowell, "Sterling A. Brown and the Afro-American Folk Tradition," p. 145.

111. Brown, *Southern Road*, p. 61.

112. Traditional folk lines as cited in Hughes and Bontemps, eds., *The Book of Negro Folklore*, p. 342.

113. Rowell, "Sterling A. Brown and the Afro-American Folk Tradition," p. 145.

114. Brown, *Southern Road*, p. 60.

115. Rowell, "Sterling A. Brown and the Afro-American Folk Tradition," p. 147.

116. Larry Neal, "The Ethos of the Blues," *The Black Scholar*, 3 (Summer 1972): 44.

117. Ibid., p. 45.

118. Ibid., p. 44.

119. Larry Neal, "Some Reflections on the Black Aesthetic," *The Black Aesthetic*, ed. by Addison Gayle, Jr. (New York: Doubleday, 1971), pp. 14–15.

120. Henderson, *Understanding the New Black Poetry*, p. 50.

121. Sterling A. Brown, "Long Track Blues," in *The Collected Poems of Sterling A. Brown*, p. 241.

122. Traditional folk blues as cited in Brown, Davis, and Lee, *The Negro Caravan*, p. 430.

123. Brown, "Long Tracks Blues," p. 241.

124. Ibid.

125. Charles Keil, *Urban Blues* (Chicago: University of Chicago Press, 1966), p. 52.

126. Sterling A. Brown, "Rent Day Blues," in *The Collected Poems of Sterling A. Brown*, p. 147.

127. Brown, *Southern Road*, p. 70.

128. According to Odum and Johnson in *The Negro and His Songs*, the rhyme used in folk songs by Blacks "has mainly to do with vowels rather than entire words. The Negro tends to pronounce many words with final consonants silent. The final letter of a word need not affect his rhyme if the vowels be similar." (p. 293)

129. Locke, "Sterling Brown: The New Negro Folk-Poet," p. 89.

130. Brown, *Southern Road*, p. 72.

131. Brown, Davis, and Lee, *The Negro Caravan*, p. 428.

132. Brown, "The Blues," p. 292.

133. Brown, *Southern Road*, p. 71.

134. Classic blues quoted in Brown, Davis, and Lee, *The Negro Caravan*, p. 480. This song was sung by Elzadie Robinson on Paramount Records (12573).

135. Brown, *Southern Road*, pp. 70–71.

136. Rowell, "Sterling A. Brown and the Afro-American Folk Tradition," p. 140.

137. Brown, Davis, and Lee, *The Negro Caravan*, p. 427.

138. Brown, *Southern Road*, p. 63.

139. Ibid., p. 64.

140. Ibid.

141. Albert Murray, *The Negro and the Blues* (Columbia: University of Missouri Press, 1973), p. 107.

142. Neal, "The Ethos of the Blues," p. 44.

143. Ellison, *Shadow and Act*, p. 250.

144. Rowell, "Sterling A. Brown and the Afro-American Folk Tradition," p. 142.

145. Henderson, *Understanding the New Black Poetry*, p. 51.

146. Courlander, *Negro Folk Music, USA*, pp. 176–77.

147. Paul Oliver, "Blues to Drive the Blues Away" in *Jazz*, ed. by Nat Hentoff and Albert J. McCarthy (New York: Rinehart and Company, 1959), p. 88.

148. Ibid.

149. Albert Murray, *Stomping the Blues* (New York: McGraw Hill, 1976), p. 5.

150. Brown, *Southern Road*, p. 64.

151. Stephen Henderson defines worrying the line in *Understanding the New Black Poetry*, p. 41. "This is the folk expression for the device of altering the pitch of a note in a given passage or for other kinds of ornamentation often associated with melismatic singing in the Black tradition. A verbal parallel exists in which a word or phrase is broken up to allow for affective or didactic comment."

152. Murray, *Stomping the Blues*, p. 5.

153. Samuel Charters, *The Legacy of the Blues* (New York: Da Capo Press, 1977), pp. 84, 88.

154. Hentoff and McCarthy, *Jazz*, p. 89.

155. Rowell, "Sterling A. Brown and the Afro-American Folk Tradition," p. 148.

156. Brown, *Southern Road*, p. 5.

157. Ibid., pp. 5–7.

158. Ibid., p. 7.

159. Brown, "Spirituals, Seculars, Ballads and Work Songs," p. 52.

160. Brown, *Southern Road*, p. 23.

161. White, *American Negro Folk Songs*, p. 26.

162. G. Malcolm Laws, *Native American Balladry* (Philadelphia: American Folklore Society, 1964), p. 85.

163. Brown, "Spirituals, Seculars, Ballads and Work Songs," p. 52.

164. Rowell, "Sterling Brown and the Afro-American Folk Tradition," p. 148.

165. Henderson, *Understanding the New Black Poetry*, p. 51.

166. Sterling A. Brown, "Puttin' on Dog," in *The Collected Poems of Sterling A. Brown*, p. 228.

167. Laws, *Native American Balladry*, pp. 86–87.

168. Brown, "Spirituals, Seculars, Ballads and Work Songs," p. 53.

169. Ibid.

170. Brown, *The Last Ride of Wild Bill*, p. 11.

171. Laws, *Native American Balladry*, p. 88.

172. Thomas W. Talley, ed. *Negro Folk Rhymes* (New York: Macmillan Co., 1922), p. 94.

173. Brown, *The Last Ride of Wild Bill*, pp. 15–16.

174. Henderson, *Understanding the New Black Poetry*, pp. 33–34.

175. Brown, *The Last Ride of Wild Bill*, p. 23.

176. Ibid., p. 24.

177. Ibid., pp. 26–27.

178. Review of *Southern Road*, *The Commonweal* (June 1, 1932): 110.

179. Johnson, ed., *The Book of American Negro Poetry*, pp. 41–42.

180. E. [ugene] Clay [Holmes], "Sterling Brown: American Peoples' Poet," *International Literature*, 2 (June 1934): 121.

181. Brown, *Southern Road*, p. 123.

182. These lines from a traditional nineteenth-century spiritual are quoted in Brown, *Southern Road*, p. 1.

183. Brown, *Southern Road*, p. 123.

184. Ibid., p. 126.

185. Ibid.

186. Ibid., p. 127.

187. Ibid., p. 128.

188. Ibid., p. 129.

189. Stephen E. Henderson, "*Southern Road*: A Blues Perspective," *New Directions*, 2 (October 1975): 32.

190. Brown, *Southern Road*, p. 124.

191. Ibid.

192. Brown, *Negro Poetry and Drama*, p. 66.

193. Henderson, "*Southern Road*: A Blues Perspective," p. 32.

194. Brown, *Southern Road*, p. 131.

195. Ibid., p. 132.

196. Ibid., p. 134.

197. Ibid., p. 135.

198. Ibid.

199. Housman, *A Shropshire Lad*, p. 92.

200. Ellison, *Shadow and Act*, p. 90.

7

THE CRITICAL MIND OF STERLING A. BROWN

Nowhere is Sterling Brown's legacy as builder of the Black aesthetic tradition more evident than in his career as a critic. As interpreter, reviewer, and editor, Brown has consistently raised the standards of criticism and encouraged writers to extend the possibilities of their art. In pioneer critical surveys which began the necessary work of tearing down the icons of misconception, stereotypes, and ignorance that stood fast in American society, he laid the foundations for the study of Black images in American fiction, poetry, and drama. Brown's essays on folklore, music, and history identified the cultural values that pervade the society and that shape and distinguish Black experience. But most important Brown put into place an aesthetic philosophy which has the folk tradition as the basis of art. In so doing, Brown "provided the core of identity for imaginative Afro-American writing."[1] A valuable consequence of this approach is a model for the realistic depiction of life, one that does not encourage what Brown calls "artistic aridity." A second consequence of this approach is the rescue of dialect and the lowly as subject matter from complete and shamefaced disavowal. Also this aesthetic eschews assimilation which Brown sees as a negative goal of Black writing. Brown's position is clearly that assimilation requires that Blacks approach American society as cultural beggars. The folk culture enables Blacks to approach American society as creators and innovators, thus providing the conditions for their successful integration of American culture.

Brown's criticism demonstrates a dual aesthetic approach that requires a solid grounding in several literatures as well as a broad knowledge of the folk sources. It is an aesthetic that provides the basis for judgments concerning matters of structure, language, and meaning and can be used to assess the depth and originality of the literary work when placed beside the folk model. Brown's commitment to explore the folk sources of literature appears stronger in light of the attitude of some of his contemporaries like H. L. Mencken, who called the notion that any respectable work of art could have a communal origin "wholly nonsensical."[2] For Brown, folk expression constitutes a very adept self-portraiture of a people and serves as an important source, model, and measure for literary interpretation.

Sterling Brown began his career as a critic in the late twenties. By that time he had already absorbed the cultures of rural communities in Virginia, Tennessee, and Missouri, and he had gleaned from the people living in these communities an enviable knowledge of folk character and expression. It is not surprising, therefore, that Brown's earliest critical reviews show him bringing to the task not only a thorough knowledge of literary traditions but also a profound understanding of Black folk culture, a combination few of Brown's contemporaries could boast.[3]

In Brown's first published article, "Roland Hayes," which won an *Opportunity* prize in 1925, the impact of his knowledge of the folk sources is already discernible in his criticism.[4] Conversant with the canons of the Western aesthetic, Brown describes Hayes' interpretation of Handel and the singer's superb craftsmanship in the arrangement of his repertoire. As Brown suggests to his readers the aesthetic beauty of Hayes' renditions of Dvorak's melodies, he also describes the dynamic syncopation of "Everytime I Feel de Spirit" and the weird, brooding beauty of "You hear de Lamb a-cryin'." In fact, the entire review is saturated with the music of the spirituals and the dramatic language of the Bible. It serves to illustrate Brown's skill at bringing together several traditions, with a special emphasis on the folk. As he applies his knowledge of the folk sources of literary expression to critical matters, he strengthens and clarifies his criticism by making literary judgments based upon a dual aesthetic. With this duality of approach, he can sufficiently manage the canons and techniques of Western art and the referents in Black folk expression to render the beauty of complexity of an experience like the Roland Hayes concert, even as a young critic in the mid 1920s.

Emerging as a mature critic in the 1930s, Brown introduced many concerns that later dominated his critical thought. Beginning in 1931, Brown wrote a monthly series of critical reviews in *Opportunity* called "The Literary Scene: Chronicle and Comment." For almost ten years this series provided Brown a forum for his ideas. In it Brown commented on the modern developments in American literature: the trend toward regionalism, the newer traditions of realism and naturalism, the dominance of the lowly as subject matter, the use of dialect to achieve local color, and the rising tide of social protest in literature. Beyond these topics, Brown repeatedly stressed concerns that came to comprise his critical platform. The need for a literary audience interested in the genuine development of the Black writers, the validity of portrayals of Black life and character regardless of their authorship, the distortion of historical fiction, and, generally, the achievement of a high level of craftsmanship were all problems that occupied his attention.[5]

Addressing these concerns, Brown wrote during this decade several important, pioneering studies which broke new ground in the criticism of Black literature and culture. In "The Blues as Folk Poetry" published in *Folk Say, A Regional Miscellany* (1930), Brown gave the earliest serious treatment to the structure, imagery, sound, and meaning of the blues. Two years later, he published "Negro Character As Seen by White Authors" (1933), in which he discussed the significant influence of white writers in the portrayal of Black character. In 1937 Brown published two critical surveys, *The Negro in American Fiction* and *Negro Poetry and Drama*. Published as Bronze Booklets Number Six and Seven by the Associates in Negro Folk Education, these surveys were not intended as exhaustive studies. However, as Ulysses Lee noted, they were crammed with penetrating and incisive statements that allowed Brown "to say a great deal more about the treatment of the Negro in American literature than had been done before."[6]

Four years later, Brown, along with Arthur P. Davis and Ulysses Lee, set out to present, with the publication of *The Negro Caravan*, "a more accurate and revealing story of the Negro writer than has been told before."[7] The anthology presented a body of writing by American authors that revealed a "truthful mosaic" of Black character, thought, and experience and gave perceptive literary interpretations and critical evaluations of many phases of Black writing and culture. Even today it has no rival in comprehensiveness and critical vitality. With these books and articles, Brown helped lay the basis for modern criticism of Black literature.

Throughout Brown's career as a critic, he recognizes the significance of sound criticism as a guide and catalyst for the development
of literature. He is also aware that such a literature was not likely to
develop without the support of a healthy literary audience. Beyond the
need to enlarge the audience for the artist and heighten its appreciation
for literature, Brown knows that there is a special need to educate the
readers of literature by and about Blacks to avoid the twin pitfall of
Black idealization and white stereotyping. Consequently, Brown repeatedly attempts to educate the audience to distinguish truthful exploration of Black character and life from its crass exploitation. To do
this, he must point to the truth or untruthfulness of an author's work
without trepidation. He must also bring to this task a kind of "critical
clairvoyance" that allows him to distinguish among various literary
portraits, noting those that have successfully captured Black life and
character and those whose content has been manipulated for some extra purpose.

Turning his attention to the writings of Black authors, Brown de-
tects idealism and forced gentility in some of them. He sees racial
apologists and promoters cajoling the audience into accepting less than
a frank and truthful portrayal of the race. On the other hand, he sees
an audience making unreasonable demands upon the artist to flatter and
uplift the race.

During the late 1920s, Brown recognized the tendency among several Black critics, supersensitive about racial progress, to object to any
portrayal of Black life that did not show Blacks in the best possible
light. Insisting on "elevating" literature and art, they considered trea-
sonous any attempt to show the crime, squalor, and ugliness that are
part of Black life. A number of Black writers and, by extension, Black
critics who wished to influence their work suffered from what Brown
called "the complex of a minority within (a) colony." "Negro writers
were 'strangled by practicality.' If Americans in general were concerned with 'getting on,' Negroes even after Emancipation were concerned with getting free."[8] Extending Van Wyck Brooks' diagnosis of
critical ineffectuality among American critics, Brown saw this weakness affecting the writing of Blacks. Ever conscious of the push toward freedom and respectability, some writers were "strangled by
practicality," and in many cases their work was burdened by the weight
of polemics and propaganda. Black critics were no less burdened. The
unwritten but nonetheless powerful charge to show "the best" resulted

in their disapproval of those authors who portrayed the lowly folk, used dialect, and ignored the strivings of the Black middle class.

In a 1929 review of DuBose Heyward's *Mamba's Daughters*, Brown expresses disappointment that far too many critics would fail to see the "warm humanity" of a character like Hagar because they would too easily and too uncritically dismiss the book with the statement, "But why will he select such scenes and such folk." [9] A year later, in an important article entitled "Our Literary Audience," Brown writes that the Black writer "is faced with a limited audience," especially within his own group. He emphasizes that it is limited not only in the number of readers but also in its fundamental outlook. He writes, "I submit for consideration this statement, probably no startling discovery: that those who might be, who should be a fit audience for the Negro artist are, taken by and large, fundamentally out of sympathy with his aims and his genuine development." [10] Brown charges that those "who do condescend to read books about Negroes, allow their criticism of these books to belie anything but honest evaluation." He goes on to identify four fallacies committed by the audience that invariably limit the quality of its criticism.

We look upon Negro books regardless of the author's intention, as representative of all Negroes, i.e. as sociological documents. We insist that Negro books must be idealistic, optimistic tracts for race advertisement. We are afraid of truth telling, or satire. We criticize from the point of view of bourgeois America, or racial apologists. [11]

For the audience that holds this limited point of view, O'Neill's play *Emperor Jones* is seen "as a study of the superstition, and bestiality, and charlataning of the group rather than a brilliant study of a hard-boiled pragmatist, far more American and African and a better man in courage and resourcefulness than those ranged in opposition to him." [12] Suffering a similar assessment, DuBose Heyward's *Porgy* or *Mamba's Daughters* are judged as poor and "unsatisfying" simply because they take the lowly as subject matter. Dialect, no matter how skillfully recorded, according to Brown, is eschewed as an affront to middle class respectability. Tragedy, too, should not be the metier of the Black artist; it ill suits an audience bent on elevating itself á la Hollywood. Brown is also dismayed that even Langston Hughes and Jean Toomer, "humane, fine-grained artists" are not cherished because they apparently shock the sensibilities of those Blacks who would be Victorian and Pollyanna.

Offering an alternative to this limited critical perspective, Brown argues against attitudes that condemn the treatment of the lowly as a "concerted attack" on the race and that shamefacedly scorn dialect as less than respectable. To suggest the dominance of the lowly as subject matter, he mentions more than ten writers, including Hardy, Synge, Joyce, O'Neill, Willa Cather, Sherwood Anderson, and Ernest Hemingway, who have portrayed this group. However, he makes it clear that each artist must be able to decide to which subject matter "he can best give convincing embodiment and significant interpretation." Insisting upon the portrayal of one subject matter over another, he argues, will result in stereotyping, undue hampering of the artist, and the signing of the "death warrant to the literature." [13]

Well aware of the natural inclination of Black people to want the ruthless libels against them answered by faultless pictures of exceptional Black men, he challenges them to acquire "the mental bravery" to deal with adverse criticism and to insist on standards of criticism that are based on "fidelity to the truth." [14] Otherwise, if the Black artist is hemmed into creating a view of life and character that coincides with the conceptions and requirements of a small Black audience—which insists his work be representative of the "best" of Black character, respectable, idealistic, propagandist tracts for racial uplift—his efforts and stature are necessarily dwarfed.

During the late twenties Brown recognized that the problem was not a new one. Through the pages of *The Crisis*, he was acquainted with the debate over what themes, content, and form would be considered appropriate for literature by and about Blacks. In 1926, *The Crisis* staff, under the editorship of W.E.B. Du Bois, conducted a year-long symposium in which authors were asked to respond to questions concerning how the Black man should be portrayed in art. [15] Among those responding were Carl Van Vechten, H. L. Mencken, Langston Hughes, Benjamin Brawley, and Countee Cullen. Brown read Carl Van Vechten's [16] and H. L. Mencken's [17] responses chastising Blacks for their hypersensitivity concerning their portrayal. He read Hughes' tersely worded statement that said in essence that "the true literary artist is going to write about what he chooses anyway regardless of outside opinions." [18] Brown also recognized the subtle but recognizable dif-

ferences held by Benjamin Brawley[19] and Countee Cullen[20] on the ac-
ceptable subject matter for the Black artist.

And the controversy had not abated when Brown wrote "The Negro
Writer and His Publisher" in 1941. In this article he was explicit in
his detailing of the role of the critic in influencing the theme, content,
and form of Black writing.

Charges are levelled against many of our authors of "selling the race down
the river." This is an easy charge, generally raised when our authors write
something we may not happen to like. The use of dialect and of characters
from the lower economic levels, for instance, causes some critics to cry trea-
son. The sounder way of criticism, it seems to me, would be to approach the
product and evaluate it, not to attribute motives too easily. If the author has
"sold out," the untruthfulness of the work will be obvious; and it is the critic's job to point out that untruthfulness. Many of our critics, however, still
condemn without reading, because they do not approve the way of life portrayed.[21]

The tasks then for the critic are to maintain the independence and
integrity of the critical attitude and to insist that whatever the writer's
style, form, or life and character presented, the writer's first require-
ment is fidelity to the truth of his subject matter. Brown "would have
the writer discover his characters to the reader: how they live, how
they act, and what they think; but Brown would not have the writer
exploit his character for the purpose of crusading."[22] The writer must
also have the courage to choose his subject matter, style, and form
regardless of external pressures. For instance, if the writer is cowed
into avoiding a portrayal of lowly folk or folk dialect, considered a
mark of oppression or of ignorance, he may wish to avoid any reference to Black life all together. As Brown sees it, this writer runs the
risk of artistic aridity.[23] In *Negro Poetry and Drama*, Brown sees the
tendency in the Black poet-critic William Stanley Braithwaite who "is
concerned nowhere in his poems with race but wishes them to be 'art
for art's sake.' "[24] Brown considers Braithwaite a lyricist who writes
poetry of romantic escape. A regionalist and a realist according to his
own poetic preference, Brown has little sympathy with escapism and
"would return the poet from his flight of escape to the romantic world
of love and the stars to the earth and people of here and now."[25] About
Braithwaite and other Black writers in the romantic tradition like Les-

lie Pinckney Hill, Benjamin Brawley, and George Marion McClellan, Brown writes:

The conscious reacting of these poets against dialect was good in so far as it meant a refusal to perpetuate stereotypes of Negro life. Too often, however, this reaction, in order to prove "cultural unity," seemed to mean something else. References to race were avoided or else couched in abstract, idealistic diction. Valuably insisting that Negro poets should not be confined to problems of race or pictures of Negro life, these poets too often committed a costlier error out of timidity at being Negroes: they refused to look into their own hearts and write. . . . The resulting verse . . . was escapist and derivative, and although accomplished at time, was too often without vitality.[26]

The error of "timidity" appears even more costly when Brown considers that a self-imposed alienation from Black life stalls indefinitely the writer's accepting the responsibility of being the ultimate interpreter of his own group. This self-imposed alienation has been encouraged by pressures "to be considered a poet and not a Negro poet," by unreasonable demands from his audience, and by miseducation that has taught contempt for anything "peculiarly Negro."[27] However, Brown is convinced that, in spite of these odds and despite a number of "excellent books" done by white writers, "the final interpretation of Negro life must come from within." In *Negro Poetry and Drama*, he challenges the young poet "to express his own view of life in his own way."

The reading world seems to be ready for a true interpretation of Negro life within, and poets with a dramatic ability have before them an important task. And the world has always been ready for the poet who in his own manner reveals his deepest thoughts and feelings. What it means to be a Negro in the modern world is a revelation much needed in poetry. But the Negro poet must write so that whosoever touches his book touches a man.[28]

Principally a critic of literature by and about Black Americans, Brown is especially aware of the tendency on the part of some critics to apply a double-standard of criticism to the writing of Black authors. He is also aware of the harm that such a standard could do to the development of the literature and holds unequivocally the position that the critic must insist on a single standard of criticism. In the comments introducing the cultural essays in *The Negro Caravan*, Brown, Lee, and

Davis observe that little real criticism of Black writing from the nineteenth century exists because the critics were more interested in commenting on the lives of the writers and in praising their breaking into print than in tackling solid critical issues. These critics were also limited by the pressure imposed to echo English and American "greats." [29] If indiscriminate praise and uncritical awe marred the judgments of critics in the 1800s, critical philanthropy further undermined standards of criticism when applied to Black literature in the twentieth century.

Brown says that a book is more likely to be judged by standards that are academic, moralistic, or racialistic than by its "veracity, its insight, its power." [30] Sometimes Black critics, convinced of their responsibility to inspire youth and increase respect for the creative efforts of Black artists, veered away from strict standards of judgments. Brown sees the distinguished critic and scholar Benjamin Brawley doing this. In a review of Brawley's *The Negro Genius* (1937), Brown levels a severe attack on his history of Black literary and artistic achievements. Pointing at the "inconsistencies, underemphasis, overemphasis, and errors in interpretation" in the book, Brown specifically criticized Brawley's easy attribution of "genius" to the physically blackest of the race and his vague and uncritical use of the term. Brown also points out Brawley's omission of a thorough-going study of significant literary trends. [31] In 1941, Brown again comments on what he considers to be the shortcomings of Brawley's critical approach in *The Negro Genius*. [32] He thinks Brawley's approach is biographical rather than critical; his criticism, "academic and genteel rather than realistic"; and his criteria based on considerations of racial achievements rather than considerations of craft. [33] As Brown sees it, if books by Black writers are to be judged, they must be judged "without sentimental allowances." [34]

In *The Negro in American Fiction*, Brown cites an example of what he considers overestimation in William Braithwaite's critique of the novels of Jessie Fauset. Brown is convinced that Braithwaite gives unwarranted praise to Jessie Fauset when he calls her the American woman most worthy "to wear the mantle of Jane Austen's genius." Brown argues:

This comparison is not apt: Jane Austen's satiric approach to her people and setting and neatly logical plots are not evident in Miss Fauset's four novels. Miss Fauset is sentimental, and regardless of her disclaimers, is an apologist.

She records a class in order to praise a race. Favorite characters are chauvinists, condemning "the dastardly American whites," believing that Negro blood is "the leaven that will purify this Nordic people of their cruelty and their savage lust of power." Having courageously set herself to chart the class of Negroes she knows, Jessie Fauset, at her best succeeds in a realism of the sort sponsored by William Dean Howells. Too often, however, instead of typical Negro middle class experience we get the more spectacular "passing," and exceptional Negro artists and cosmopolitans.[35]

Brown believes that proving the presence of a Black upper class or, in Braithwaite's terms, creating "an entirely new milieu in the treatment of the race in fiction" is not justification enough for lavish praise. Unlike Braithwaite, Brown is convinced that Jessie Fauset's standards are bourgeois. He believes that her characters are interpreted and represented in terms of their "color, breeding, gentility, wealth, and prestige"; her plots are seldom lifelike; and her tone generally falling short of tragic, is merely sentimental.[36] Consequently, Brown's criteria for the great fiction writer are the author's mastery of craft and his ability to interpret character and life with realism and significance. Until such standards are met, lavish praise should be withheld.

Also, as evident in much of Brown's criticism, just as detrimental to the development of creative expression is the preoccupation with counter-stereotypes. While Brown understands how Black writers and audiences have become hypersensitive as a result of the steady assaults of "psuedo-science and propaganda writers like Thomas Dixon, Roark Bradford, and Thomas Nelson Page, he cautions against their insistence on counter-stereotypes.

. . . it is natural that when pictures of us were almost entirely concerned with making us out to be either brutes or docile housedogs . . . we should have replied by making ourselves out superhumans. It is natural that we should insist that the pendulum be swung back to its other extreme. Life and letters follow the law of the pendulum. Yet, for the lover of the truth, neither extreme is desirable. And now if we are coming of age, the truth should be our major concern.

This is not a disagreement with the apologistic belief in propaganda. Propaganda must be counter checked by propaganda. But let it be found where it should be found in books explicitly propagandistic, in our newspapers, in the teaching of our youth. Even so, it must be artistic based on truth, not on exaggeration.[37]

In an article written in 1941, entitled "The Negro Writer and His Publisher," he makes it clear that he is opposed to overt propaganda.

Should the Negro author write propaganda? If by propaganda is meant the self-pity and self-justification of adolescents, the question answers itself. If by propaganda is meant the revealing of the exploitation, oppression and ignominy, the struggle and the dream, and that is what many do mean by the word, I would answer yes. But I consider the author's task to be the revelation of what he believes, after long thought, to be the truth; and the truth of Negro experience in America is strong enough propaganda for everyone. I think that the picture will not be one of unalloyed tragedy. To present counter-stereotypes of villainous whites and victimized Negroes is a temptation, but it is not worthy of our best creative and interpretative powers. . . . Truth to Negro experience must consider the Negro's ability to take it, to endure, and to wring out of life something of joy.[38]

Brown is convinced that propaganda, unwarranted praise, and critical philanthropy, no matter how well meant, are totally inimical to the development of creative expression and the development of a literary audience. In "The Negro Writer and His Publisher," Brown cites the following quotation by Langston Hughes to illustrate how publishing opportunities are limited because of a subtle yet ubiquitous double standard used in dealing with "Negro material."

Here are our problems: In the first place, Negro books are considered by editors and publishers as exotic. Negro material is placed, like Chinese material into a certain classification. Magazine editors will tell you, "We can use but so many Negro stories a year." "That 'so many' meaning very few." Publishers will say "We already have one Negro novel on our list this fall."[39]

It is the insistence on a single standard of criticism that leads Brown and other editors of *The Negro Caravan* to make an elaborate gesture in avoiding the term "Negro literature" in the anthology. Brown's main objection to the term is that its use may result in the literature's being "too easily placed by certain critics, white and Negro, in an alcove apart." He further reasons, "the next step is a double standard of judgment which is dangerous for the future of Negro writers. 'A Negro novel,' thought of as a separate form, is too often condoned as 'good enough for a Negro.' "[40] He believes that cordoning off Black literature into a special area may result in decreasing the size of the reading audience and in seriously limiting the amount of critical attention due the literature.

Brown also argues that an equally important reason for avoiding the term "Negro literature" is that Black writers are American writers and their work is an integral part of American literature. He is convinced that Black writers write in forms evolved in English and American literature and, "in spite of such unifying bonds as a common rejection of the popular stereotypes" and a common "racial cause," do not fall into "a unique cultural pattern."[41] Therefore, the terms "a Negro novel" and "a Negro play" are ambiguous, he suggests, but also misleading if used to classify works by authorship, content, or style. He argues that any classification of works by and about Negro life will include works by white authors, and rightly so, because these works have been "most influential upon the American mind."[42]

Though Brown appears to protest too much, the point he makes is that Black writers have been influenced by the same literary traditions that have influenced all American writers, and their literature is a segment of American literature. In the introduction of *The Negro Caravan*, Brown points to the intricate weave that writings by Blacks make in the warp and woof of American literature.

Negro writers have adopted the literary traditions that seemed useful for their purposes. They have therefore been influenced by Puritan didacticism, sentimental humanitarianism, local color, regionalism, realism, naturalism, and experimentalism. Phillis Wheatley wrote the same high moralizing verse in the same poetic pattern as her contemporary poets in New England. While Frederick Douglass brought more personal knowledge and bitterness into his antislavery agitation than William Lloyd Garrison and Theodore Parker, he is much closer to them in spirit and in form than to Phillis Wheatley, his predecessor, and Booker T. Washington, his successor. Frances E. W. Harper wrote antislavery poetry in the spirit and pattern of Longfellow and Felicia Hemans; her contemporary, Whitfield, wrote of freedom in the pattern of Byron. And so it goes. Without too great imitativeness, many contemporary Negro writers are closer to O. Henry, Carl Sandburg, Edgar Lee Masters, Edna St. Vincent Millay, Waldo Frank, Ernest Hemingway, and John Steinbeck than to each other. The bonds of literary tradition seem to be stronger than race.[43]

Brown applies this thesis in his appraisal of the New Negro Renaissance of the 1920s. Broadly viewing the literary stirrings of the postwar years, Brown sees the American literary renaissance and the New

Negro movement coinciding in their mutual reaction against sentimentality, didacticism, optimism, and romantic escape and in their rejection of "poetic diction" in preference for fresh, original language.[44]
The New Negro poets no longer caricatured or neglected race but attempted to express it. "At their best," Brown says, "they belonged
with the renascent American poets who 'in the tones of ordinary speech
rediscovered the strength, the dignity, the vital core of the common-
place.' "[45] The writers of both movements were drawn to realism and
naturalism, as well as to daring experiments in literary forms. They
welcomed an intense, scientific candor in the exploration of self and
society; they revolted against conventional taboos in Victorianism and
turned from Babbittry. They faced the postwar period with hope, and
they generally entrusted to youth the battle against reactionism and hypocrisy.

According to Brown, "The rise of the New Negro movement coincided with increased interest in Negro life and character in the twenties." The New Negro's discovery of Africa and his excursion into his
cultural past were matched by the predominant interest of several
American authors in exotic primitivism. Eugene O'Neill, relying on
superstition and atavism to produce power in *The Emperor Jones* (1920),
Sherwood Anderson, exploring the "Negro way of life" in *Dark
Laughter* (1925), and Carl Van Vechten, making a Harlem bohemia in
his *Nigger Heaven* (1926), share an interest in the discovery of the
exotic in Black life. These writers, Brown argues, greatly influenced
the work of Black writers, for good or for ill. Despite the brilliant experimentation and example of such writers as Jean Toomer and Eric
Walrond, several Black writers "trooped off to join Van Vechten's band
and shared in the discovery of Harlem as a New African colony."

Wa-wa trumpets, trap drums (doubling for tom-toms), and shapely dancers with
bunches of bananas girdling their middles in Bamboo Inns and Jungle Cabarets
nurtured tourists' delusions of "the Congo cutting through the black." Claude
McKay's *Home to Harlem* (1926) concentrates on the primitive, which McKay
defiantly glorifies in *Banjo* (1929), whose hero decides to "let intellect go to
hell and live instinct." *Joie de vivre* was acclimated to Harlem especially, to
Negroes generally. It was all rhythm, rhythm; jazz-bands swung out on "That's
Why Darkies Were Born"; pent-houses sprouted miraculously atop Lenox Avenue tenements; the cabin was exchanged for the cabaret but the old mirth was
still inside.[46]

Brown leaves little doubt in the reader's mind that he considers the push toward exotic primitivism prurient and perverse. It is perhaps his desire to deemphasize this side of the movement that prompts his objection to the term "Harlem Renaissance" and his hesitation to use the term "Negro Renaissance." Writing in an essay entitled "The New Negro in Literature" (1925–1955), he explains that the "five or eight years" allotted were much too brief a period for any "renaissance" and that Harlem was no more than the "show-window" and the cashier's till of the movement. According to Brown, "the New Negro had temporal roots in the past and spatial roots elsewhere in America, and the term has validity . . . only when considered to be a continuing tradition."[47]

On one level, Brown contends that the so-called "Harlem Renaissance" was a publisher's gimmick. Those who saw profit in selling the exotic promoted young Black writers and a Harlem never-never land. Songs like 'That's Why Darkies Were Born," "Harlem on My Mind," "A Train to Harlem," and "Harlem Penthouse," which lured joy seekers to Harlem nightspots, carried the tinsel-like ring of Tin Pan Alley. For Brown, the image of the "Harlem Penthouse," set against the specter of the slums and breadlines of Lenox Avenue, was "the saddest thing in the world."[48] However, for many whites caught up in the "Roaring Twenties," the image was necessary and gratifying. According to Brown, their objectives were simple and rather apolitical. "They were interested in slumming, sex, and titillation." They were content to create out of thin air the dreamy jazz-filled world ironically drawn in the poem "Cabaret."[49] Compounding the ironies, several Blacks who were flattered by the attention went along with the program and readily accepted the slogan—"White folks cornered the money but Black folks cornered the joy."[50]

This proverbial joy, however, was less familiar to the majority of people who lived in Harlem. Like Langston Hughes, Brown believes that most people in Harlem were not aware of any "renaissance" other than the Renaissance Dance Hall on Seventh Avenue, which was the predecessor of the famous Savoy. Ironically, after dark, certain spots were reserved for whites only.

In an anecdote that Brown likes to tell about the Cotton Club, he says that he, Mercer Cook, a French actress, and her brother went to the Cotton Club one night to hear Duke Ellington. When they tried to be seated, only the French actress and her brother were seated on the main floor, and he and the "tawny" Mercer Cook had to go "way up the steps." When Will Marion Cook came in with his party later that night, the waiters were obliged to seat them at ringside because he had written the songs that the Duke was performing.[51]

As Brown later came to believe, the "Harlem Renaissance" was a creation by white intellectuals with the assent of some Blacks. In "The New Negro in Literature," he points to the telltale signs of a movement that had artificial moorings. Some Blacks, "caught up along with much of America in ballyhoo," sought to make a cult of Harlem. With a youthful rebellion and hunger for attention and change, they "set up their own Bohemia" and lived out the excitement of the twenties. Very few experiments, according to Brown, escaped what was "falsely atavistic and wilfully shocking."[52] In a fascinating interview in 1974, Brown vehemently disclaims any association with the Harlem Renaissance and levels a seering attack at Carl Van Vechten, whom he charges with despoiling the first fruit of the movement. Brown says, "He corrupted the Harlem Renaissance and was a terrible influence on them [the writers whom he patronized]." Brown calls Van Vechten "a voyeur." "He was looking at these Negroes and they were acting the fools for him. And the foolisher they acted, the more he recorded them." Disassociating himself from the Harlem writers, Brown says that "when they were down there flirting with Carl Van Vechten, I was down south talking to Big Boy. One of the most conceited things that I can say is I am proud that I have never shaken that rascal's hand."[53]

On another level Brown sees the "Harlem Renaissance" mystique as detrimental to an understanding of Black literary development. First of all, he points out that the term "Harlem Renaissance," as it connotes a long-lived literary movement, is misleading. Preferring the term "New Negro Renaissance," he believes that it is more accurate in suggesting the evolution of Black writing in America. According to him, the term "New Negro" itself dates back to the Civil War and suggests the race consciousness and the political awareness of nineteenth-century Blacks. Brown recalls a magazine dedicated to Frederick Douglass in 1917 called *Champion*, in which many of the principles that New Negroes of the 1920s espoused were very much alive. "All of the race consciousness, all of the struggle for equity, all of the struggle for rights was in this magazine." But for two obvious distinctions—the rejection of poetic diction and the prevalence of the theme of Africa—the writing of the 1920s continued in the broad tradition of writing in the nineteenth century.[54] Consequently, Brown argues that the five- or eight-year period allotted to the New Negro Renaissance was only a brief line on the continuum of Black writing, and that the coming of the Depression of 1929 did not put an end to the work of the New Negro writers.

Second, Brown considered it misleading and ultimately limiting to view the writers as Harlemites. In fact, most of the writers did not grow up in New York and did not write solely about the Harlem scene. According to Brown, Countee Cullen was the only New Negro writer "born and bred in the Harlem briar patch."[55] Langston Hughes, the "best known and most versatile writer produced by the New Negro Renaissance," was born in Joplin, Missouri, in 1902. Wallace Thurman, author of *Infants of the Spring*, was born in Salt Lake City, Utah, also in 1902 and was educated in California. Zora Neale Hurston was born and reared in an all Black community called Eatonville, Florida, and never got far away from the lure of the South. Claude McKay, who wrote some of the best images of Harlem in his volume *Harlem Shadows*, was born in Jamaica, and Alain Locke, the spokesman for the New Negro and the author of the book that launched the movement, was born into a Black middle-class community in Philadelphia. Brown believes that his own contribution to the New Negro Renaissance has tended to be ignored because of the myopic way in which the renaissance has been viewed. He quips: "They say I missed the boat; I wouldn't have caught the boat if it were backed up to my yard. . . . Therefore, they leave me out; they say I'm in the thirties." Brown says not only had he started writing in the twenties, but also "When De Saints Go Ma'ching Home" and "Strong Men" won prizes in 1927 and 1929 respectively.[56]

Brown objects to restricting the locale of the renaissance and disparages the exclusion of those outside of Harlem whose efforts made the renaissance possible.[57] For Brown, any renaissance of consequence must include a consideration of the teachers and intellectuals who spark and give guidance to the movement.

According to Brown, Black writers did not deal exclusively with Harlem but looked for material anywhere they could find it. Though there were bonds that yoked the writers together—"a common rejection of popular stereotypes and a common 'racial' cause"—they were influenced by the larger literary movements and currents of thought.[58] For example, Countee Cullen was influenced significantly by Edna St. Vincent Millay and A. E. Housman. Claude McKay gained from his association with Max Eastman. The author of *Cane*, Jean Toomer, was influenced by such Greenwich Village writers as Waldo Frank, Paul Rosenfield, and Margery Latimer, who was also his first wife. Anne Spencer, "the most original of all the Negro women poets, exhibited a close affinity to Browning." Brown, too, admits that his poetry was influenced by what Sandburg, Robinson, and Frost were doing.

In the final assessment, Brown believes that part of the failure of the Harlem phase of the New Negro Movement must be attributed to the lack of a literary audience interested in the full development of its writers. It was clear to him that those who jumped on the bandwagon in praise of exoticism and those who basked in its neon glow could not sustain a serious exploration of the African past and folk culture nor appreciate the tone of impatience and self-reliance that characterized the New Negro. To build a successful movement, Brown suggests that an intelligent audience is essential to disapprove idealization of character and to move its artists to fuller, truer, less self-conscious revelation.

As Brown sees a special need to educate the literary audience to reject Black idealization and take on a critical "bravery" that will permit a frank revelation of its life, he also takes it as his task to show how attitudes to Black life, several having great influence and tenacity, have developed in American thinking and how these attitudes have circumscribed in many ways the treatment of Black life and character in literature. To do this, Brown introduces into American criticism a perspective on the treatment of Black life and character in American literature that has since dominated critical thought on the subject. Central to this perspective is his contention that "the Negro has met with as great injustice in American literature as he has in American life." [59] Brown suggests that the literature of the Black experience cannot be interpreted purely in terms of the literary movements and schools that influence American literature as a whole. If the essential truth concerning the portraiture of Black life and character is to be told, it must include an understanding of how and why social and cultural factors enter into its interpretation. In the introduction of *The Negro Caravan* (1941), Brown states what has become a fundamental assumption underlying his critical approach to the treatment of Black images in American literature.

It appears to be a truism that racial and minority groups are most often stereotyped by the majority. Today in Europe, conquered or threatened minorities receive substantially the same literary treatment that the Negro has received here for so many years. With certain honorable exceptions, more numerous in our own time, the white authors dealing with the American Negro have interpreted him in a way to justify his exploitation. Creative literature has often been a handmaiden to social polity.[60]

Black people in America, according to Brown, are faced with problems similar to those of every other minority group concerned with creating its literature and interpreting itself. Since it is the prerogative of the majority group to impose its will on the minority group at all levels of society, even in art and culture, the minority group generally finds itself submerged by the dominant group's interpretation of its life and character. Too often, the literary men of the majority group choose to limit their characterizations to hastily drawn generalizations which demonstrate their lack of understanding and sympathy. They tend to represent the dimensions of minority character in terms of stereotypes and special roles and to interpret its life in accordance with social policy. Very often, Brown suggests, justification of exploitation and persecution is the impetus for their interpretations.

For Brown, evidence of this pattern of exploitation in literature about minorities is pervasive. On several occasions he uses the following passage to illustrate its universality:

I swear their nature is beyond my comprehension. A strange people!—merry 'mid their misery—laughing through their tears, like the sun shining through the rain. Yet what simple philosophers they? They tread life's path as if 'twere strewn with roses devoid of thorns, and make the most of life with natures of sunshine and song.[61]

Though most Americans would be quick to say that the passage speaks of the American Blacks, Brown reveals that it describes the Irish in a play depicting one of the most tragic periods in Ireland's history. However, Brown points out that this statement could have been used to describe the Jew, the South African Black, or any member of a peasant or working class, for his treatment in literature fits a similar pattern. He suggests that attendant irony in this pattern when he writes, "It is a noteworthy fact that in America the three comic standbys for vaudeville jokes represent three of the people whose histories have involved so much oppression and tribulation: the Negro, the Jew and the Irish."[62]

It was, then, for Brown axiomatic that the treatment of Blacks in literature generally parallels their treatment in life. Brown would agree with Seymour L. Gross who writes that the history of the Black man in American literature "has been an unconscious, or at least half-conscious masking of issues that have been contorted by fear, guilt and rage."[63] These emotions are the by-products of the ubiquitous caste system that has developed around the conflict between Black and white. The myths of white superiority and Black inferiority, the rituals of social interaction, the postures of double consciousness among Blacks, racial self-hatred, and cultural aridity are part and parcel of a complex system of dynamics that make up the American dilemma. As the attitudes of the white majority to the Black minority result in the assignment of roles and positions in society, Brown argues that it is inevitable that these attitudes would be imposed on the literature.

Consequently, Brown's critical approach naturally proceeds from the belief that social attitudes toward Blacks in American society resulted in the grooving of Black character into a few restrictive stereotypes. Though Brown was not the first to recognize the prevalence of stereotypes in the literature, anti-stereotype criticism, according to Seymour L. Gross, culminated in his works, receiving its fullest, most thorough-going study. Before Brown began to outline his critical theories, Benjamin Brawley and Alain Locke were among those critics who first called attention to images of Blacks manipulated to conform to preconceived notions of the race. In 1916, Benjamin Brawley challenged writers "not to remain forever content to embalm old types and work over outworn ideas" and announced "the day of Uncle Remus as well as of Uncle Tom is over."[64] In 1926 Alain Locke, in his article "American Literary Tradition and the Negro," launched a critical strategy which would later reappear in the works of Sterling Brown.[65] Locke wrote:

The constant occurrence and recurrence of the Negro, even as a minor figure, throughout this wide range is in itself an indication of the importance of the Negro as a social issue in American life, and of the fact that his values are not to be read by intrinsic but by extrinsic coefficients.[66]

Seven years later, Sterling Brown would reintroduce the critical strategy suggested by Locke. In an essay titled "Negro Character as Seen by White Authors," Brown sets out to account for the prevalence of stereotypic images of Black character in American literature and to supply the historical context in which these stereotypes evolved. As he traces the development of Black character in this article and in his book-length studies, *The Negro in American Fiction* (1937) and *Negro Poetry and Drama* (1937), he argues that the majority of books about Black character merely repeat a handful of timeworn stereotypes that have come to represent it. According to Brown, several stereotypes—the Contented Slave, the Wretched Freeman, the Brute Negro, the Comic Negro, the Tragic Mulatto, and the Exotic Primitive—attached themselves so firmly to American literature that, with time, they assumed a life of their own. Despite the morphology of each of these types, Brown observes that these stereotypes, marked by "exaggeration or omissions," are often used to flatter whites by emphasizing difference between the races and to justify "social proscription." He adds that they are ubiquitous in American literature because they are "generally accepted as contributors to racial understanding."[67] Throughout his discussion, Sterling Brown makes it clear that he does not consider everything a stereotype "that shows up the weakness of Negro character." Whether the stereotyping denigrates Black character or flatters it, any stereotyping "is fatal" to the development of a great and convincing literature.

In the introduction of *The Negro in American Fiction*, Brown relates the fable of blind men who tried to describe an elephant to illustrate the distortions of truth that are the inevitable result of a myopic posture. As the fable goes, each man returned to his respective kingdom where it was advantageous to believe that the elephant was all trunk or tusk or hide.[68] The fable is suggestive of two significant ideas that underlie Brown's interpretations of the treatment of Black images in American literature. First, stereotypes are the products of a single, restricted point of view that have become fixed ideas in the mind of society. Second, stereotypes have evolved at the dictates of social policy, usually to justify the exploitation and persecution of a minority group.

Brown suggests that one way for whites to deal with the boundaries erected between the races was to exaggerate the differences to the point of ludicrousness, attributing to the subjected race more than its allotment of clowns and buffoons. From Cooper to Octavius Roy Cohen and Roark Bradford, some white writers have been delighted by their creation of the Comic Negro who "has pranced his way by means of books, vaudeville skits, shows, radio programs, advertisements, and after dinner speeches into the folklore of the nation.''[69]

Another way was to flatter themselves with a mirror image. For Brown, the prevalence and recurrence of the tragic mulatto image in American literature can be explained by a fascination, approaching hysteria, with the notion that two warring blood strains are locked in perpetual strife in an almost white body. The mulatto cannot reconcile his "divided inheritance;" his intellectual striving and his unwillingness to be a slave (his white inheritance) is forever struggling to overcome his "baser emotions, his indolence, his savagery."[70] The long line of tragic mulattoes—Longfellow's pathetic "Quadroon Girl," Cassy and Eliza in Stowe's *Uncle Tom's Cabin*, and George Washington Cable's Creoles, to name a few—show the mixed blood as the victim for whom slavery is more odious than for other Blacks.

Equally as revelatory of the majority group as the tragic mulatto is the exotic primitive. In the pages of *Opportunity*, Brown's patience with the easy conclusions drawn by writers like Carl Van Vechten, who insisted that they had discovered the essential authentic Negro, wears thin. Van Vechten's Lasca Sartoris, "exquisite, gorgeous, golden-brown messalina of Seventh Avenue,'' symbolizes the prurient abandon of Harlem nights as she vivifies the unrestrained savage emotions and spontaneity of the Harlem primitive.

As much as a restricted point of view has to do with the prevalence of stereotypes in American literature, it cannot be seen to the exclusion of the influence of social attitudes in explaining the evaluation of fixed ideas about Black character and life and their recurrence in various periods in American literary history. As Brown surveys the development of Black images, he makes use of the "swing of the pendulum'' theory to account for the action and reaction pattern.[71] For instance, in the eighteenth century, the image of the noble savage inspired romantic speculation about his ancestry and customs. While in the early nineteenth century, when slaveholders sought to secure their property and ensure the continuance of their peculiar institution, the figure of the contented slave became a necessary part of the plantation scene.[72] The Black man is naturally suited for slavery and incapable of assuming the responsibilities of freedom, so runs the logic. Brown singles out Thomas Nelson Page as "probably most persuasive in casting a golden glow over the antebellum South.'' Manipulating character and dialect, Page makes his uncles' nodding "ventriloquist's dummies agreeing upon the blessedness of slavery.''[73] Brown also suggests that this view is taken to its reactionary extreme in the image of the brute Negro, a subhuman who poses a constant threat to Southern womanhood.

Throughout his critical surveys, Brown recognized the ingenious connection between the treatment of Blacks in literature and prevailing social attitudes. During periods in American history when Blacks experienced the brunt of racial oppression and exploitation, they were portrayed as unspeakably happy in their situation. When their rapid rise in political life was the first promise of equality, they were presented as brutes and rapists incapable of and ill-deserving the responsibilities of citizenship. As the country retreated from the disillusionment of World War I and people marched to the din of machinery, Black humanity was again exploited for its disparity and became the exotic primitive incarnate. And thus Brown traces wide and sweeping arcs in the treatment of Black images in American literature. Like Locke, he sees no "more valuable record for the study of the social attitudes and their changes in literary treatment of Negro life and character."[74]

As Brown is able to show the exploitation that Black images suffered at the hands of white authors, he also shows how some writers have gone beyond the stereotype to realistic portraiture. In the pages of *Opportunity* he reviews the works of DuBose Heyward, Julia Peterkin, Howard Odum, Erskine Caldwell, William Faulkner, and others who attempted "sincere realization" of Black life and character. As candid in showing their achievement as he is in assaying their limitations, Brown suggests that their influence in fixing attitudes to Black life and in suggesting literary directions to Black writers has been great. Though constantly encouraging Black writers to discover the essential qualities of Black portraiture and to write out of their experience, Brown admits that "some of the best attacks upon stereotyping have come from white authors, and from Southerners." In an article called "The New Secession: A Review," a review of Julia Peterkin's *Black April*, Brown points to this development as one of the "paradoxes of history." Julia Peterkin, Ambrose Gonzales, and DuBose Heyward—South Carolinians—have joined North Carolinians Howard Odum, Guy Johnson, and Paul Green in "recognizing in the Negro what Synge has seen in Aran Islanders, Gorki in Russian peasants, and Masefield and Gibson in the lowly folk of England."[75]

While Brown acknowledges in some Southern writers their willingness to explore in Black character a complexity of temperament not possible within the confines of stock characterization, he also welcomes the movement among other Southern writers toward realism. In writers such as Erskine Caldwell and Roy Flannagan, Brown sees exemplified "the high qualities of accurate observation, irony, and courage."[76] For Brown, Erskine Caldwell, in his *God's Little Acre, Tobacco Road*, and *Kneel to the Rising Sun*, presents a crosscut of Southern life that reveals its brutality, its social injustice, and its exploitation of Blacks and poor whites with frank honesty. Likewise, in his review of the books *Inchin' Along, Amber Satyr, Free Born*, and *Georgia Nigger*, Brown makes note of an important tendency in the literature of the period to show frankly "the bitter irregularities" of race relations: the conditions of peonage, the convict labor system, and the practice of lynching. Though he admits that the authors are often so intent upon spotlighting the injustices of these practices that they heap on the injustices with the result of straining credence, he insists that these novels give "the broad social picture" that is not only accurate but also needed to focus attention on these conditions.[77] With the introduction of this kind of searching realism into Southern literature, it is not surprising to Brown that skillful writers have begun to tear down the flimsy props supporting the plantation tradition. He recognizes Thomas Wolfe and William Faulkner among a group of Southern writers who "convinced of the 'barren spiritual wilderness' of their section," have "stripped off cherished illusion after illusion" in repudiating the romantic legend of the plantation.[78]

Brown, though aware of the long taught patronizing, the trite generalizations, naivete, and sentimentality that creep into the best writing, applaudes the more encouraging trends in Southern fiction toward deeper and fuller characterization, an inspired use of local color to mine the folkways of a special group, a clear-eyed search for realism, and a frank and courageous exposure of social injustice. As Melville, Twain, and Albion Tourgee had attacked the plantation tradition with a growing realism in the preceding century, these Southern fiction writings advanced a portrait of the South that broke conventional molds.

While he acknowledges the significant contribution of these writers in illustrating the inadequacy of familiar stereotypes, Brown cannot accept the American conviction that the Southern white man knows the Negro best. Brown reserves the judgment that "the exploration of Negro life and character rather than its exploitation must come from

Negro authors themselves.'' However, the critic concludes with some point:

One manifest truth, however, is this: the sincere, sensitive artist, willing to go beneath the clichés of popular belief to get at an underlying reality, will be wary of confining a race's entire character to a half-dozen narrow grooves. He will hardly have the temerity to say that his necessarily limited observation of a few Negroes in a restricted environment can be taken as the last word about some mythical Negro. He will hesitate to do this, even though he had a Negro mammy, or spent a night in Harlem, or has been a Negro all his life. The writer submits that such an artist is the only one worth listening to although the rest are legion.[79]

Thus it is Sterling Brown who disturbed the waters, whose perspective of the treatment of Black image challenged the conventional categories and approved sentiments taken to explain the essence of Black life and character. Above all, he attempted to educate the audience to demand truth in the portrayal of life and character and to reject extra-literary reasons for accepting one subject matter as opposed to another. If Black writers were to be about the task of creating literature and interpreting it with understanding and sympathy, the "false images had to be discredited before a more authentic portrait could be drawn." According to Robert Bone, Sterling Brown "undertook the necessary labor of destruction."[80]

Finally, what Brown accomplishes in his criticism—through sane judgments, breadth of knowledge, and a finely controlled ironic language—is the successful interpretation of life and attitudes. Just as the power in his poetry is rooted deeply in an understanding of the folkways of his people and a mastery of the craft, his effectiveness as a critic is rooted in his awareness of the events and needs of his time. Certainly, part of Brown's contribution is his ability to discern social needs and his acute awareness of the discrepancies and distortions as well as the ironies and realities of life. In other words, Brown's criticism reflects the truth of Harry Levin's statement, "Literature is not only the effect of social causes; it is also the cause of social effects."[81] Brown's critical vision has helped those writers and critics of Black American literature who have come after him understand better the reciprocal relations between literature and society.

NOTES

1. Clyde Taylor, "The Human Image in Sterling Brown's Poetry," *Black Scholar*, 12 (March/April 1981): 13.

2. H. L. Mencken, "A Review of *Poetic Origins of the Ballad*" by Louise Pound, *Smart Set* (June 1921): 143–44.

3. Ulysses Lee, "Criticism at Mid-Century," *Phylon*, 11 (Winter 1950): 334.

4. Sterling A. Brown, "Roland Hayes," *Opportunity*, 3 (June 1925): 173–74.

5. I am indebted to Lee's article, "Criticism at Mid-Century," for some of these ideas.

6. Lee, "Criticism at Mid-Century," p. 334.

7. Brown, Davis, and Lee, *The Negro Caravan*, p. v.

8. Ibid., p. 832.

9. Sterling A. Brown, "Mamba's Daughters," *Opportunity*, 7 (May 1929): 161–62.

10. Brown, "Our Literary Audience," p. 42.

11. Ibid.

12. Ibid.

13. Ibid., p. 44.

14. Ibid., p. 46.

15. As Arthur P. Davis and Michael W. Peplou suggested in their book *The New Negro Renaissance*, included in the questionnaire were questions "which seem to have been worded in such a way as to elicit denunciations of works like Claude McKay's *Home to Harlem* and other sensationalist works in the popular *Nigger Heaven* tradition." Included were: (1) When the artist, black or white, portrays Negro characters is he under any obligation or limitation as to the sort of character he will portray? (2) Can any author be criticized for painting the worst or the best characters of a group? . . . (4) What are Negroes to do when they are continually painted at their worst and judged by the public as they are painted? . . . (6) Is not the continual portrayal of the sordid, foolish and criminal among Negroes convincing the world that this and this alone is really and essentially Negroid, and preventing white artists from knowing any other types and preventing black artists from daring to paint them? The intent and tone of the questions clearly indicate the controversial nature of the debate. See Arthur P. Davis and Michael W. Peplou, *The New Negro Renaissance: An Anthology* (New York: Holt, Rinehart and Winston, 1975), p. 464.

16. "The Negro in Art: How Shall He Be Portrayed?" *The Crisis* (February 1926): 165.

17. "The Negro in Art: How Shall He Be Portrayed?" *The Crisis* (March 1926): 219.

18. Ibid., p. 220.

19. More reserved in approach, Benjamin Brawley urged, "An artist must be free; he cannot be bound by any artificial restrictions. At the same time we heartily wish that so many artists would not prefer today to portray only what is vulgar. There is beauty in the world as well as ugliness, idealism as well as realism." "The Negro in Art," *The Crisis* (April 1926): 278.

20. Countee Cullen, however, saw the "hue and cry against misrepresentation" as futile as well as foolish. Advising the young writers with an emphasis that Brown would later use in his own criticism, he said: "Let the young Negro writer, like any artist find his treasure where his heart lies. If the unfortunate and less favored find an affinity in him, let him surrender himself, only let him not pander to the popular trend of seeing no cleanliness in their squalor, no nobleness in their meanness and no commonsense in their ignorance." This was taken from "The Negro in Art," *The Crisis* (August 1926): 193–194.

21. Sterling A. Brown, "The Negro Writer and His Publisher," *Quarterly Review of Higher Education Among Negroes*, 9 (July 1941): 145.

22. Ila Jaquith Blue, "A Study of Literary Criticism By Some Negro Writers, 1900–1955" (Ph.D. dissertation, University of Michigan, 1959), p. 24.

23. Sterling A. Brown, "More Odds," *Opportunity*, 10 (June 1932): 188.

24. Brown, *Negro Poetry and Drama*, p. 50.

25. Blue, "A Study of Literary Criticism," p. 131.

26. Brown, *Negro Poetry and Drama*, pp. 45–46.

27. Brown, "More Odds," p. 188.

28. Brown, *Negro Poetry and Drama*, pp. 80–81.

29. Brown, Davis, and Lee, *The Negro Caravan*, pp. 832–33.

30. Ibid., p. 833.

31. Brown, "Book Reviews," *Opportunity*, 15 (September 1937): 280.

32. *The Negro Genius* is a revised form of an earlier work, *The Negro in Literature and Art*, which appeared in 1910.

33. Brown, Davis, and Lee, *The Negro Caravan*, p. 833.

34. Ibid., p. 7.

35. Brown, *The Negro in American Fiction*, p. 142.

36. Ibid., pp. 139–41.

37. Brown, "Our Literary Audience," p. 43.

38. Brown, "The Negro Writer and His Publisher," p. 146.

39. Ibid., p. 143. Brown has quoted from Donald Ogden Stewart, *Fighting Words* (New York: Harcourt, Brace and Co., 1940), pp. 58ff.

40. Brown, Davis, and Lee, *The Negro Caravan*, p. 7.

41. Ibid., p. 6.

42. Ibid., p. 7.

43. Ibid., pp. 6–7.

44. Brown, *Negro Poetry and Drama*, p. 60.

45. Ibid., pp. 60–61.

46. Sterling A. Brown, "The New Negro in Literature (1925–1955)," *The New Negro Thirty Years Afterward* (Washington, D.C.: Howard University Press, 1955), p. 59.

47. Ibid., pp. 57–58.

48. Brown, interview on May 30, 1978, with James Early, Ethelbert Miller, and Stephen Henderson at Howard University (tape).

49. Brown, *Southern Road*, p. 115.

50. Brown, taped interview with Early, Miller, and Henderson, May 30, 1978.

51. Brown, taped interview with Early and Miller on May 19, 1978 at Howard University.

52. Brown, "The New Negro in Literature" p. 59.

53. Ekaete, "Sterling Brown: A Living Legend," p. 9.

54. Brown, taped interview with Early, Miller, and Henderson, on May 30, 1978 at Howard University. Also mentioned in taped interview with Miller and Early on May 19, 1978.

55. As Jean Wagner suggests, Countee Cullen's childhood has a certain degree of mystery about it. Though Cullen states that he was born in New York, there are other accounts from highly accredited sources that he may have been born in Baltimore, Maryland, or in Louisville, Kentucky.

56. Stephen Henderson agrees with Brown's criticism of the restrictiveness with which the period is viewed. He comments in the May 20, 1978 interview with Brown: "If you narrow the period to one specific locale, like Harlem, you are able to control the interpretation of the historical moment. If you say the Harlem Renaissance . . . you don't have to pay attention to what happened in Washington, Atlanta, or the rest of the country." The popular conception that makes Harlem the hub of the intellectual and creative fervor ignores the developments that were taking place outside of Harlem.

57. Davis and Peplow, editors of *The New Negro Renaissance*, confront the same problem. They write: "Without wishing to deny the importance of Harlem, we have not used the term "The Harlem Renaissance" for our title because it implies certain limitations (literature written only in or about Harlem; literature only by Harlemites). The New Negro Renaissance is a much broader term. It allows us to include representative selections from the South, for example, or from black metropolises other than Harlem." p. xx.

58. Brown, Davis, and Lee, *The Negro Caravan*, p. 6.

59. Sterling A. Brown, "The Negro Character As Seen by White Authors," *Journal of Negro Education*, 2 (April 1933): 180.

60. Brown, Davis, and Lee, *The Negro Caravan*, p. 3.

61. Brown, *The Negro in American Fiction*, p. 1.

62. Brown, "The Negro in American Literature," p. 22.

63. Seymour L. Gross, "Introduction: Stereotype to Archetype: The Negro in American Literary Criticism," *Images of the Negro in American Literature*, eds. Seymour L. Gross and John Edward Hardy (Chicago: University of Chicago Press, 1966), p. 1.

64. Benjamin Brawley, "The Negro in American Fiction," *Dial*, 60 (1910): 449.

65. Ibid., p. 10.

66. Alain Locke, "American Literary Tradition and the Negro," *Modern Quarterly*, 3 (1926): 216–17.

67. Brown, "Negro Character as Seen by White Authors," p. 180.

68. Brown, *The Negro in American Fiction*, p. 1.

69. Brown, "Negro Character as Seen by White Authors," p. 190.

70. Ibid., pp. 194–95.

71. Sterling A. Brown, "Negro Literature—Is it True? Complete?" *Durham Fact Finding Conference* (Durham, North Carolina: Fact Finding Conference, 1929), p. 26.

72. Francis Pendleton Gaines, *The Southern Plantation: A Study in the Development and Accuracy of a Tradition* (New York: Columbia University Press, 1924), p. 35.

73. Brown, *The Negro in American Fiction*, p. 51.

74. Locke, "American Literary Tradition and the Negro," p. 215.

75. Sterling A. Brown, "The New Secession—A Review," *Opportunity*, 5 (May 1927): 147.

76. Sterling A. Brown, "Amber Satyr," *Opportunity*, 10 (November 1932): 352.

77. Sterling A. Brown, "A New Trend," *Opportunity*, 11 (February 1933): 56.

78. Sterling A. Brown, "Mississippi, Alabama: New Style," *Opportunity*, 13 (February 1935): 55.

79. Brown, "Negro Character As Seen by White Authors," p. 20.

80. Robert Bone, "Preface to the Atheneum Edition," of *Negro Poetry and Drama* and *The Negro in American Fiction* by Sterling Brown.

81. Harry Levin, "Literature as an Institution," *Accent* (Spring 1946); quoted in Wilbur S. Scott, *Five Approaches of Literary Criticism* (New York: Collier Macmillan Publishers, 1962), p. 126.

SELECTED BIBLIOGRAPHY

THE WORKS OF STERLING A. BROWN

Books

The Collected Poems of Sterling A. Brown. Selected by Michael S. Harper. New York: Harper & Row, 1980.

The Last Ride of Wild Bill and Eleven Narrative Poems. Detroit: Broadside Press, 1975.

The Negro in American Fiction. Washington, D.C.: Associates in Negro Folk Education, 1937; reprint ed., New York: Atheneum, 1969.

Negro Poetry and Drama. Washington, D.C.: Associates in Negro Folk Education, 1937; reprint ed., New York: Atheneum, 1969.

Outline for the Study of the Poetry of American Negroes. New York: Harcourt, Brace, 1931. Prepared to be used with *Book of American Negro Poetry*. Edited by James Weldon Johnson. New York: Harcourt, Brace and Co., 1931.

The Reader's Companion to World Literature. Edited by Lillian H. Hornstein and G. D. Percy. New York: New American Library, 1956.

Southern Road. New York: Harcourt, Brace, 1932; reprint ed., Boston: Beacon Press, 1974.

Brown, Sterling A., Davis, Arthur P., and Lee, Ulysses, eds. *The Negro Caravan*. New York: Dryden Press, 1941; reprint ed., New York: Arno Press, 1969.

Biographical Sketches

"Arna Bontemps, Co-Worker, Comrade." *Black World* 22 (September 1973): 11+.
"In Memoriam: Charles W. Chesnutt." *Opportunity* 10 (December 1932): 387.
"James Weldon Johnson." In *Book of American Negro Poetry.* Edited by James Weldon Johnson. New York: Harcourt, Brace and Co., 1931.
"Portrait of a Jazz Giant: Jelly Roll Morton." *Black World* 18 (February 1974): 28–48.
"Ralph Bunche, Statesman." *The Reporter* 1 (December 1949): 3–6.
"Roland Hayes." *Opportunity* 3 (June 1925): 173–74. Also in *Readings from Negro Authors.* Edited by Otelia Cromwell, Eva Dykes, and Lorenzo Turner. New York: Harcourt, Brace and Co., 1931.

Selected Poems

"After Winter." In *Golden Slippers.* Edited by Arna Bontemps. New York: Harper, 1941.
"All Are Gay." In *American Stuff: An Anthology of Prose and Verse.* New York: Viking Press, 1937.
"An Old Woman Remembers." *Freedomways* 3 (Summer 1963): 409.
"A Bad, Bad Man." In *Folk Say.* Vol. 4. Edited by Benjamin A. Botkin. Norman: Oklahoma Folklore Society, 1932.
"Ballad of Joe Meek." *Freedomways.* 3 (Summer 1963): 405–11.
"Bessie." In *Southern Road.* New York: Harcourt, Brace and Co., 1932; reprint ed., Boston: Beacon, 1974.
"Bitter Fruit of the Tree." *Nation* 149 (August 1939): 223.
"Break of Day." *New Republic* 85 (11 May 1938): 10.
"Call Boy." In *Folk Say.* Vol. 4. Edited by Benjamin A. Botkin. Norman: Oklahoma Folklore Society, 1932.
"Challenge." In *Caroling Dusk.* Edited by Countee Cullen. New York: Harper, 1932.
"Children of Mississippi." *Opportunity* 9 (December 1931): 363.
"Clotile." In "Sixteen Poems by Sterling Brown." Folkways Recording, FL 9794, 1973.
"Conjured." In *This Generation.* Edited by George Anderson and Eda L. Walton. New York: Scott, Foresman, 1939.
"Crispus Attucks McKoy." *IK Ben de Nieuwe Neger.* Edited by Rosie Pool. Den Haag: B. Dakker, 1965.
"The Devil and the Black Man." In *Folk Say, the Land is Ours.* Vol. 4. Edited by Benjamin A. Botkin. Norman: Oklahoma Folklore Society, 1932.
"Effie." *Opportunity* 7 (October 1929): 304.

Selected Bibliography   215

"Foreclosure." In *Ebony and Topaz*. Edited by Charles Johnson. New York: National Urban League, 1927.

"Glory, Glory." *Esquire* 10 (August 1938): 78.

"He Was a Man." *Opportunity* 10 (June 1932): 179.

"Let Us Suppose." *Opportunity* 13 (September 1935): 281.

"Long Gone." In *Anthology of American Negro Literature*. Edited by V. F. Calverton. New York: Harcourt, Brace and Co., 1931.

"Long Track Blues." In *Folk Say, the Land is Ours*. Vol. 4. Edited by Benjamin A. Botkin. Norman: Oklahoma Folklore Society, 1932.

"Ma Rainey." In *Southern Road*. Boston: Beacon Press, 1974.

"Master and Man." *The New Republic* 89 (November 1936): 66.

"Maumee Ruth." In *Caroling Dusk*. Edited by Countee Cullen. New York: Harper and Brothers, 1927.

"Memphis Blues." In *Book of American Negro Poetry*. Edited by James Weldon Johnson. New York: Harcourt, Brace and Co., 1931.

"Mose." In *Southern Road*. Boston: Beacon Press, 1974.

"Odyssey of Big Boy." In *Caroling Dusk*. Edited by Countee Cullen. New York: Harper and Brothers, 1927.

"Old Lem." In *This Generation*. Edited by George Anderson and Eda L. Walton. New York: Scott, Foresman, 1939.

"Old Man Buzzard." *Scholastic* 32 (21 May 1938): 20.

"Parrish Doctor." In "Sixteen Poems of Sterling A. Brown". Folkways Recording, FL 9794, 1973.

"Puttin' on Dog." In *Folk Say*. Vol. 4. Edited by Benjamin A. Botkin. Norman: Oklahoma Folklore Society, 1932.

"Remembering Nat Turner." *Crisis* 45 (February 1939): 91.

"Return." In *Caroling Dusk*. Edited by Countee Cullen. New York: Harper and Brothers, 1927.

"Revelations." In *Folk Say, A Regional Miscellany*. Vol. 2. Edited by Benjamin A. Botkin. Norman, Oklahoma: Oklahoma Folklore Society, 1931.

"Riverbank Blues." *Opportunity* 7 (May 1929): 148.

"Salatamus." In *Caroling Dusk*. Edited by Countee Cullen. New York: Harper and Brothers, 1927.

"Sam Smiley." *Crisis* 39 (March 1932): 91.

"Scotty Has His Say." *Scholastic* 32 (21 May 1938): 20.

"Sharecropper." In *Get Organized*. Edited by Alan Calmer. New York: International Publishers, 1939.

"Sister Lou." *Opportunity* 10 (January 1932): 11.

"Slim Greer." In *Book of American Negro Poetry*. Edited by James Weldon Johnson. New York: Harcourt, Brace and Co., 1931.

"Slim Lands a Job." (Original title: "Slow Coon", in *Folk Say, A Regional Miscellany*. Vol. 2. Edited by Benjamin A. Botkin. Norman, Oklahoma: Oklahoma Folklore Society, 1931.

"Southern Cop." *Partisan Review* 3 (October 1936): 201.

"Southern Road." In *Book of American Negro Poetry*. Edited by James Weldon Johnson. New York: Harcourt, Brace and Co., 1931.

"Sporting Beasley." In *Southern Road*. Boston: Beacon Press, 1974.

"Strange Legacies." *Crisis* 40 (August 1928): 242.

"Strong Men." In *Book of American Negro Poetry*. Edited by James Weldon Johnson. New York: Harcourt, Brace and Co., 1931. Reprinted in *United Asia* 5 (June 1953): 150.

"Thoughts of Death." *Opportunity* 6 (August 1928): 242.

"To a Certain Lady in Her Garden." In *Caroling Dusk*. Edited by Countee Cullen. New York: Harper and Brothers, 1927.

"Uncle Joe." In "Sixteen Poems of Sterling Brown." Folkway Recording, FL 9794, 1973.

"When de Saints Go Ma'ching Home." *Opportunity* 5 (July 1927): 48.

"The Young Ones." *Poetry* 3 (1938): 189–90.

Short Stories

"And/Or." In *American Negro Short Stories*. Edited by John Henrik Clarke. New York: Hill and Wang, 1966.

"Words on a Bus." *South Today* 7 (Spring 1943): 26–28.

Essays on Culture and Society

"Athletics and the Arts." In *The Integration of the Negro Into American Society*. Edited by E. Franklin Frazier. Washington, D.C.: Howard University Press, 1951.

"The Atlanta University Summer Theater." *Opportunity* 12 (October 1934): 308–9.

"Chronicle and Comment." *Opportunity* 7 (December 1930): 375.

"Concerning Negro Drama." *Opportunity* 9 (September 1931): 284–88.

"Count Us In." In *What the Negro Wants*. Edited by Rayford W. Logan. Chapel Hill: University of North Carolina Press, 1945. Also in *Primer for White Folks*. Edited by Bucklin Moon. Garden City, New York: Doubleday, 1945.

"Folk Values in a New Medium." Co-author, Alain Locke. In *Folk-Say*. Vol. 1. Edited by B. A. Botkin. Norman, Oklahoma: University of Oklahoma Press, 1930.

"Georgia Nymphs." *Phylon* 6 (Autumn 1945): 363–67.

"Georgia Sketches." *Phylon* 6 (Summer 1945): 225–31.

"Literary Scene." *Opportunity* (February 1931): 53–54.

"The Muted South." *Phylon* 6 (Winter 1945): 22–34.
"Out of Their Mouths." *Survey Graphic* 31 (November 1942): 480–83.
"Signs of Promise." *Opportunity* 10 (September 1932): 287.

Critical Reviews

"Alas the Poor Mulatto." Review of Geoffrey Barnes, *Dark Luster*. (New York: Alfred H. King, 1932). *Opportunity* 11 (March 1933): 91.

"Amber Satyr." Review of Roy Flannagan, *Amber Satyr* (New York: Doubleday, 1932). *Opportunity* 10 (November 1932): 352.

"American Epoch." Review of Howard Odum, *An American Epoch, Southern Portraiture in the National Picture* (New York: Holt, 1930). *Opportunity* 9 (June 1931): 187.

"Arcadia, South Carolina." Review of Doris Ullman and Julia Peterkin, *Roll Jordan Roll* (New York: R. O. Ballou, 1933). *Opportunity* 12 (February 1934): 59–60.

"As to Jungle Ways." Review of William Seabrook, *Jungle Ways* (New York: Harcourt, Brace and Co., 1931). *Opportunity* 9 (July 1931): 219, 221.

"Banana Bottom." Review of Claude McKay, *Banana Bottom* (New York: Harper, 1934). *Opportunity* 11 (July 1933): 217, 222.

"Biography." Review of Benjamin Brawley, Paul Laurence Dunbar, *Poet of His People* (Chapel Hill: University of North Carolina Press, 1936). *Opportunity* 15 (September 1937): 216–17.

"Black Genesis." Review of Samuel Stoney and Gertrude Shelby, *Black Genesis* (New York: Macmillan, 1930). *Opportunity* 8 (October 1930): 311–12.

"Black Ulysses at War." Review of Howard Odum, *Wings on My Feet* (New York: Bobbs-Merrill Co., 1929). *Opportunity* 7 (December 1929): 383–84.

"Book Reviews." Review of Benjamin Brawley, *Negro Genius* (New York: Biblo-tanner Booksellers Publishing, Inc., 1966. Reprint of the 1937 ed.). *Opportunity* 15 (September 1937): 280–81.

"Caroling Softly Souls of Slavery." Review of Louis Hughes, ed., *Thirty Years a Slave* (New York: Books for Libraries, 1931. Reprint of the 1897 ed.). *Opportunity* 9 (August 1931): 251–52.

"Come Day, Go Day." Review of Richard Coleman, *Don't You Weep, Don't You Moan* (New York: Macmillan, 1935). *Opportunity* 13 (September 1935): 279–80. Also review of Roark Bradford, *Let the Band Play Dixie* (New York: Harper, 1934). *Opportunity* 13 (September 1935): 279.

"Fabulist, Felossofer." Review of Roark Bradford, *Ol' Man Adam and His Children* (New York: Harper, 1928). *Opportunity* 6 (July 1928): 211–12.

"First Negro Writers." Review of Benjamin Brawley, *Early Negro American Writers* (New York: Books for Libraries, 1968. Reprint of the 1935 ed.). *New Republic* 86 (6 May 1936): 376.

"From the Inside." Review of Richard Wright, *Uncle Tom's Children* (New York: Harper and Row, 1938. *Nation* 16 (April 1938): 448.

"From the Southwest." Review of J. Frank Dobie, *Tone the Bell Easy* (Dallas: Southern Methodist University Press, 1965. Reprint of the 1932 ed.). *Opportunity* 11 (October 1933): 333. Also review of John Mason Brewer, *Negrito: Negro Dialect Poems of the Southwest* (San Antonio, Tex.: Naylor Printing Company, 1933. *Opportunity* 11 (October 1933): 313.

"God Sends Sunday." Review of Arna Bontemps, *God Sends Sunday* (New York: Harcourt, Brace and Co., 1931). *Opportunity* 9 (July 1931): 191.

"Imitation of Life: Once a Pancake." Review of Fannie Hurst, *Imitation of Life* (New York: Harper, 1933). *Opportunity* 13 (March 1935): 87–88.

"Insight, Courage and Craftsmanship." Review of Richard Wright, *Native Son* (New York: Harper and Row, 1940). *Opportunity* 18 (June 1940): 185–86.

"Joel Chandler Harris." Review of Julia C. Harris, ed., *Joel Chandler Harris: Editor and Essayist* (Chapel Hill: University of North Carolina Press, 1931). *Opportunity* 10 (April 1932): 119–20.

"John Brown: God's Angry Man." Review of Leonard Ehrlich, *God's Angry Man* (New York: Simon and Schuster, 1932). *Opportunity* 11 (June 1933): 186–87.

"Local Color or Interpretation." Review of Julia Peterkin, *Bright Skin* (Dunwoody, Georgia: Norman S. Berg, 1932). *Opportunity* 10 (July 1932): 223.

"Lock Is a Fortune." Review of Zora Neale Hurston, *Their Eyes Were Watching God* (Philadelphia: J. B. Lippincott, 1937). *Nation* 145 (October 1937): 409–10.

"Mamba's Daughters." Review of DuBose Heyward, *Mamba's Daughters* (New York: Doubleday, 1929). *Opportunity* 7 (May 1929): 161–62.

"Mississippi, Old Style." Review of Stark Young, *So Red the Rose* (New York: Scribner, 1934). *Opportunity* 12 (December 1934): 377–78.

"More Odds." Review of Edwin R. Embree, *Brown America, The Story of a New Race* (New York: Viking, 1931). *Opportunity* 10 (June 1932): 188–89.

"Never No More." Review of James Knox Miller, *Never No More* (play). *Opportunity* 10 (February 1932): 55–56.

"Never No Steel Driving Man." Review of Roark Bradford, *John Henry* (New York: Harper, 1931). *Opportunity* 9 (December 1931): 382.

"The New Secession—A Review." Review of Julia Peterkin, *Black April* (Indianapolis: Bobbs-Merrill, 1927.) *Opportunity* 5 (May 1927): 147–48.

"A New Trend." Review of Welbourne Kelley, *Inchin' Along* (New York: Morrow, 1932). *Opportunity* 11 (February 1933): 56. Also review of Scott Nearing, *Free Born, An Unpublishable Novel* (New York: Urquhart Press, 1932). *Opportunity* 11 (February 1933): 56. Also review of George Spivak, *Georgia Nigger* (Montclair, New Jersey: Patterson Smith, 1969, Reprint of the 1932 ed.). *Opportunity* 11 (February 1933): 56.

"Not Without Laughter." Review of Langston Hughes, *Not Without Laughter* (New York: Knopf, 1930). *Opportunity* 8 (September 1930): 279–80.

"Our Book Shelf." Review of Gordon Casserly, *Dwellers in the Jungle* (New York: F. A. Stokes Co., 1927). *Opportunity* 6 (March 1928): 91–92.

"Poor Whites." Review of George Milburn, *Oklahoma Town* (New York: Harcourt, 1931). *Opportunity* 9 (October 1931): 317. Also review of Erskine Caldwell, *American Earth* (New York: Scribner, 1931). *Opportunity* 9 (October 1931): 317. Also review of John Fort, *God in the Straw Pen* (New York: Dodd, 1932). *Opportunity* 9 (October 1931): 317.

"Pride and Pathos." Review of Members of the Society for the Preservation of the Spirituals, *The Carolina Low Country* (New York: Macmillan, 1931). *Opportunity* 9 (December 1931): 381, 384.

"Prize Winning Stories." Review of Richard Wright, *Uncle Tom's Children* (New York: Harper and Row, 1938). *Opportunity* 16 (April 1938): 120–21.

"Realism in the South." Review of Erskine Caldwell, *Kneel to the Rising Sun* (New York: Viking, 1935). *Opportunity* 13 (October 1935): 311–12.

"A Review of Kingdom Coming." Review of Roark Bradford *Kingdom Coming* (New York: Harper and Brothers, 1933). *Opportunity* 11 (December 1933): 382–83.

"A Romantic Defense." Review of Twelve Southerners, *I'll Take My Stand: the South and the Agrarian Tradition* (New York: Harper and Brothers, 1930). *Opportunity* 9 (April 1931): 118.

"Satire of Imperialism." Review of Winifred Holtby, *Mandoa, Mandoa!* (New York: Macmillan, 1933). *Opportunity* 12 (March 1934): 89–90.

"Shadow of the Plantation." Review of Charles S. Johnson, *Shadow of the Plantation* (Chicago: University of Chicago Press, 1934). *Journal of Negro History* 21 (January 1936): 70–73.

"Signs of Promise." Review of Kenneth T. Rowe, *University of Michigan Plays* (Ann Arbor, Michigan: George Wahr, 1932). *Opportunity* 10 (September 1932): 287.

"Six Plays for a Negro Theatre." Review of Randolph Edmonds, *Six Plays for a Negro Theatre* (Boston: Walter H. Baker, 1934). *Opportunity* 12 (September 1934): 280–81.

220   Selected Bibliography

"Smartness Goes Traveling." Review of Evelyn Waugh, *They Were Still Dancing and Black Mischief* (New York: Farrar and Rinehart, 1932). *Opportunity* 11 (May 1933): 154, 158.
"South on the Move." Review of Jonathan Daniels, *Southerner Discovers the South* (New York: Macmillan, 1938). *Opportunity* 16 (December 1938): 366. Also review of Herman Nixon, *Forty Acres and Steel Mules* (Chapel Hill: University of North Carolina Press, 1938). *Opportunity* 16 (December 1938): 367.
"Southern Cross Sections." Review of Berry Fleming, *Siesta* (New York: Harcourt, 1935). *Opportunity* 13 (December 1935): 380, 385. Also review of Frederick Wright, *South* (New York: Farrar and Rinehart, 1935). *Opportunity* 13 (December 1935): 380, 385.
"Three Ways of Looking At the South." Review of William A. Percy, *Lantern on the Levee* (New York: Knopf, 1941). *Journal of Negro Education* 14 (Winter 1945): 68–72. Also review of Anne Kendrick Walter, *Tuskegee and the Black Belt* (Richmond, Virginia: Dietz Press, 1944). *Journal of Negro Education* 14 (Winter 1945): 68–72. Also review of Arthur Raper and Ira De A. Reid, *Sharecroppers All* (Chapel Hill: University of North Carolina Press, 1941). *Journal of Negro Education* 14 (Winter 1945): 68–72.
"Truth Will Out." Review of Frederic Bancroft, *Slave Trading in the Old South* (Baltimore: J. H. Furst Co., 1931). *Opportunity* 10 (January 1932): 23–24.
"Two African Heroines." Review of David Garnett, *The Sailors Return* (New York: Knopf, 1925). *Opportunity* 4 (January 1926): 24–26. Also review of Louis Charbonneau, *Mambu et Son Amour* (Paris: J. Ferenczi et Fils, 1924).
"Two Negro Poets." Review of Arna Bontemps, *Black Thunder* (New York: Macmillan, 1936). *Opportunity* 4 (July 1936): 216–20. Also review of Frank M. Davis, *Black Man's Verse* (Chicago: Black Cat Press, 1935). *Opportunity* 14 (July 1936): 216, 220.
"Weep Some More My Lady." Review of Louis Untermeyer, *American Poetry, From the Beginning to Whitman* (New York: Harcourt, Brace and Co., 1931). *Opportunity* 10 (March 1932): 87.

Essays on History

"Negro American." In the *Encyclopedia Britannica*, XVI, co-authors Sterling A. Brown, John Hope Franklin, and Rayford Logan. Chicago: William Benton, 1969.
"The Negro in American Culture." In "Carnegie-Myrdal Study of Blacks in America." New York: Schomburg Library.

Selected Bibliography   221

"The Negro in the American Theatre." In *Oxford Companion to the Theatre*. Edited by Phyllis Hartnoll. London: Oxford Press, 1950.
"The Negro in Washington." *Washington: City and Capital*. Federal Writers' Project. Washington, D.C.: United States Government Printing Office, 1936.
"Saving the Cargo: Sidelights on the Underground Railroad." *Negro History Bulletin* 4 (April 1941): 151–54.

Essays on Literature and Folklore

"The American Race Problem as Reflected in American Literature." *Journal of Negro Education* 8 (July 1939): 275–90.
"The Approach of the Creative Artist to Studies in Folklore." *Journal of American Folklore* 54 (October 1946): 506–7.
"The Blues as Folk Poetry." In *Folk Say*. Vol. 1. Edited by Benjamin A. Botkin. Norman: University of Oklahoma Press, 1930.
"Blues, Ballads and Social Songs." *Seventy-five Years of Freedom*. Washington, D.C.: Library of Congress Press, December 18, 1940, pp. 17–25.
"A Century of Negro Portraiture in American Literature." *Massachusetts Review* 7 (Winter 1966): 73–96. Also in *Black and White in American Culture*. Edited by Jules Chametzky. Amherst: University of Massachusetts Press, 1969.
"Chronicle and Comment." *Opportunity* 8 (December 1930): 375.
"Contributions of the American Negro." In *One America*. Edited by Francis J. Brown and Joseph S. Roucek. New York: Prentice-Hall, 1945.
"A Literary Parallel." *Opportunity* 10 (May 1932): 152–53.
"The Literary Scene." *Opportunity* 9 (January 1931): 20.
"Mississippi, Alabama: New Style." *Opportunity* 13 (February 1935): 55–56.
"The Negro Character As Seen by White Authors." *Journal of Negro Education* 2 (April 1933): 179–203. Also in *When People Meet*. Edited by Bernard J. Stern and Alain Locke. New York: Progressive Education Association, 1942.
"The Negro in American Literature." In *A Biographical Sketch, James Weldon Johnson*. Nashville: Fisk University, 1938.
"The Negro in Fiction and Drama." *Christian Register* 114 (14 February, 1935): 111–12.
"Negro Literature—Is It True? Complete?" *Durham Fact Finding Conference*. Durham, North Carolina: Fact Finding Conference, 1929, pp. 26–28.
"The Negro Writer and His Publisher." *Quarterly Review of Higher Education Among Negroes* 9 (July 1941): 140–46.
"The New Negro in Literature (1925–1955)." In *The New Negro Thirty Years*

Afterward. Division of Social Sciences Graduate School. Washington, D.C.: Howard University Press, 1955.

"Our Literary Audience." *Opportunity* 8 (February 1930): 42–46, 61.

"A Poet and His Prose." *Opportunity* 10 (August 1932): 256.

"The Point of View." *Opportunity* 9 (November 1931): 347–50.

"Problems of the Negro Writer." In *Official Proceedings, National Negro Congress*. Washington: National Negro Congress Publications, 1937.

"Seventy-Five Years of the Negro in Literature." *Jackson College Bulletin* 2 (September 1953): 26–30.

"Unhistoric History." *Journal of Negro History* 15 (April 1930): 134–61.

Essays on Music

"The Blues." *Phylon* 13 (Autumn 1952): 286–92.

"Blues, Ballads and Social Songs." *Seventy-Five Years of Freedom*. Washington, D.C.: Library of Congress Press, December 18, 1940.

"Farewell to Basin Street." *The Record Changer* 3 (December 1944): 7.

"Negro Folk Expression." *Phylon* 11 (Autumn 1950): 318–327.

"Negro Folk Expressions: Spirituals, Seculars, Ballads and Work Songs." *Phylon* 14 (Winter 1953): 45–61.

"Spirituals, Blues and Jazz—The Negro in the Lively Arts." *Tricolor* 3 (April 1945): 62–70.

"Stray Notes on Jazz." *Vassar Brew* 27 (June 1946): 15–19.

Introductions

"Foreword." In *Place America*. Thomas Richardson. New York: National Association for the Advancement of Colored People, 1940.

"Introduction." In *Rearing Children of Good Will*. Edited by Edith Neissen. New York: National Conference of Christians and Jews, 1954.

I am indebted to Robert G. O'Meally's "An Annotated Bibliography of the Works of Sterling A. Brown" printed in *CLA Journal*, December 1975 and the "Bibliography of Works By and About Sterling A. Brown" included in *Sterling A. Brown: A UMUM Tribute*, edited by the Black History Museum Committee, Philadelphia, Pennsylvania.

WORKS CONSULTED

Books

The American Negro Writer and His Roots: Selected Papers From the First Conference of Negro Writers, March 1959. New York: American Society of African Culture, 1960.

Anderson, George Kumler, and Watson, Eda Lou, eds. *This Generation: A Selection of British and American Literature from 1914 to the Present with Historical and Critical Essays.* Chicago: Scott, Foresman and Co., 1939.

Baker, Houston A. *Long Black Song: Essays in Black American Literature and Culture.* Charlottesville: University of Virginia Press, 1972.

Barksdale, Richard K., and Kinnamon, Keneth, eds. *Black Writings of America: A Comprehensive Anthology.* Riverside, N.J.: Macmillan, 1972.

Bell, Bernard. *The Folk Roots of Contemporary Afro-American Poetry.* Detroit, Michigan: Broadside Press, 1974.

Black History Museum Committee, ed. *Sterling A. Brown: A UMUM Tribute.* Philadelphia: Black History Museum UMUM Publishers, 1976.

Bogan, Louise. *Achievement in American Poetry.* Chicago: Henry Regnery Co., 1951.

Bone, Robert A. *The Negro Novel in America.* Rev. ed. New Haven: Yale University Press, 1965.

Bontemps, Arna, ed. *American Negro Poetry.* New York: Hill and Wang, 1963.

Botkin, Benjamin, ed. *Lay My Burden Down: A Folk History of Slavery.* Chicago: University of Chicago Press, 1945.

Brawley, Benjamin Griffith. *The Negro Genius.* New York: Dodd, Mead and Co., 1937.

Bronz, Stephen H. *Roots of Negro Racial Consciousness.* New York: Libra Publishers, Inc., 1964.

Brooks, Cleanth. *A. E. Housman: A Collection of Critical Essays.* Englewood Cliffs, N.J.: Prentice Hall, Inc., 1968.

Brown, Sterling N. *My Own Life Story.* Washington, D.C.: Hamilton Printing Co., 1924.

Butcher, Margaret. *The Negro in American Culture.* New York: Knopf, 1956.

Calverton, Victor Francis. *The Liberation of American Literature.* New York: C. Scribner's Sons, 1932.

Chapman, Abraham, ed. *Black Voices.* New York: New American Library, 1968.

Charters, Samuel. *Poetry of the Blues.* New York: Oak, 1963.

Coffman, Stanley K., Jr. *Imagism: A Chapter for the History of Modern Poetry*. Norman: University of Oklahoma Press, 1951.

Coleridge, Samuel Taylor. *The Best of Coleridge*. Edited by Earl Leslie Griggs. New York: Roland Press Company, 1935.

Courlander, Harold. *Negro Folk Music USA*. New York: Columbia University Press, 1963.

Cowley, Malcolm. *Exile's Return: A Literary Odyssey of the 1920's*. New York: Viking Press, 1951.

Cunard, Nancy, ed. *Negro: An Anthology*. First published in 1934 under title *Negro Anthology*. New York: Frederick Ungar Publishing Company, 1970.

Davis, Arthur P. *From a Dark Tower: Afro-American Writers*. Washington, D.C.: Howard University Press, 1974.

Davis, Arthur P., and Peplou, Michael W. *The New Negro Renaissance: An Anthology*. New York: Holt, Rinehart and Winston, 1975.

Davis, Arthur P., and Redding, Saunders, eds. *Cavalcade: Negro American Writing from 1760 to the Present*. Boston: Houghton Mifflin Company, 1971.

Dett, R. Nathaniel. *Religious Folk Songs of the Negro*. Hampton, Virginia: Hampton University Press, 1927.

Dollard, John. *Caste and Class in a Southern Town*. New Haven: Yale University Press, 1937.

Dreer, Herman. *American Literature by Negro Authors*. New York: Macmillan Co., 1950.

Education for Freedom: A Documentary Tribute to Celebrate the Fiftieth Anniversary of the Election of Mordecai W. Johnson as President of Howard University. Washington, D.C.: Moorland-Spingarn Research Center, Howard University, 1976.

Ellison, Ralph. *Shadow and Act*. New York: New American Library, 1966.

Emanuel, James Andrew, and Gross, Theodore L. *Dark Symphony: Negro Literature in America*. New York: Macmillan Company, 1968.

Federal Writers' Project. *American Stuff: An Anthology of Prose and Verse by Members of the Federal Writers' Project*. New York: Viking Press, 1937.

————. *Mississippi: A Guide to the Magnolia State*. New York: Viking Press, 1938.

————. WPA. *Washington: City and Capital*. Washington, D.C.: Government Printing Office, 1937.

Fisher, Miles Mark. *Negro Slave Songs in the United States*. New York: Russell and Russell, 1968.

Fry, Gladys-Marie. *Night Riders in Black Folk History*. Knoxville: University of Tennessee Press, 1975.

Gaines, Francis Pendleton. *The Southern Plantation: A Study in the Develop-

ment and Accuracy of a Tradition. New York: Columbia University Press, 1924.

Gayle, Addison, Jr., ed. *The Black Aesthetic*. New York: Doubleday, 1971.

——. ed. *Black Expression: Essays By and About Black Americans in the Creative Arts*. New York: Weybright and Talley, 1969.

Gloster, Hugh Morris. *Negro Voices in American Fiction*. Chapel Hill: University of North Carolina Press, 1948.

Gregory, Horace, and Zaturenska, Marya. *A History of American Poetry, 1900–1940*. New York: Harcourt Brace and Co., 1946.

Gross, Seymour L., and Hardy, John Edward, eds. *Images of the Negro in American Literature*. Chicago: University of Chicago Press, 1966.

Henderson, Stephen. *Understanding the New Black Poetry: Black Speech and Black Music as Poetic References*. New York: William Morrow and Company, Inc., 1973.

Hentoff, Nat, and McCarthy, Albert J., eds. *Jazz*. New York: Rinehart and Company, 1959.

Hicks, Granville. *The Great Tradition: An Interpretation of American Literature Since the Civil War*. New York: Macmillan Company, 1935.

Housman, A. E. *A Shropshire Lad*. New York: Henry Holt and Company, 1922.

Huggins, Nathan Irvin. *Harlem Renaissance*. New York: Oxford University Press, 1971.

——. *Voices from the Harlem Renaissance*. New York: Oxford University Press, 1976.

Hughes, Glenn. *Imagism and the Imagists: A Study in Modern Poetry*. Stanford, California: Stanford University Press, 1931.

Hughes, Langston. *The Weary Blues*. New York: Alfred A. Knopf, Inc., 1926.

Hughes, Langston, and Bontemps, Arna, eds. *The Book of Negro Folklore*. New York: Dodd, Mead, and Company, 1958.

Hyman, Stanley Edgar. *The Promised End*. Cleveland: World Publishing Co., 1963.

Jackson, Blyden, and Rubin, Louis D., Jr. *Black Poetry in America: Two Essays in Historical Interpretation*. Baton Rouge: Louisiana State University Press, 1974.

Johnson, James Weldon, ed. *The Book of American Negro Poetry*. New York: Harcourt, Brace and World, Inc., 1922; reprint ed., 1959.

Johnson, James Weldon. *God's Trombones: Seven Negro Sermons in Verse*. New York: Viking Press, 1927; reprint ed., 1969.

Johnson, James Weldon, and Johnson, Rosamond, eds. *The Book of American Negro Spirituals*. New York: Viking Press, 1925.

Jones, LeRoi. *Blues People: Negro Music in White America*. New York: William Morrow and Company, 1963.

Keil, Charles. *Urban Blues*. Chicago: University of Chicago Press, 1966.

Kent, George E. *Blackness and the Adventure of Western Culture*. Chicago: Third World Press, 1971.

Kerlin, Robert T. *Negro Poets and Their Poems*. Washington, D.C.: Associated Publishers, Inc., 1923.

Krehbiel, Henry Edward. *Afro-American Folksongs: A Study in Racial and National Music*. New York: Frederick Ungar Publishing Co., 1962.

Laws, G. Malcolm. *Native American Balladry*. Philadelphia: American Folklore Society, 1964.

Locke, Alain, ed. *The New Negro*. New York: Albert and Charles Boni, Inc., 1925; reprint ed., New York: Atheneum, 1970.

Locke, Alain. *Negro Art: Past and Present*. Washington, D.C.: Associates in Negro Folk Education, 1936.

Lomax, John. *Adventures of a Ballad Hunter*. New York: Macmillan Co., 1947.

Lomax, John, and Lomax, Alan. *American Ballads and Folk Songs*. New York: Macmillan Co., 1935.

Mangione, Jerre. *The Dream and the Deal: The Federal Writers' Project, 1935–1943*. Boston: Little, Brown and Company, 1972.

Mays, Benjamin. *The Negro's God as Reflected in His Literature*. New York: Atheneum, 1968.

Murray, Albert. *The Negro and The Blues*. Columbia: University of Missouri Press, 1973.

Nelson, John Herbert. *The Negro Character in American Literature*. College Park, Maryland: McGrath Publishing Co., 1926.

Odum, Howard W., and Johnson, Guy B. *The Negro and His Songs: A Study of Typical Negro Songs in the South*. Chapel Hill: The University of North Carolina Press, 1925; reprint ed., New York: New American Library, Inc., 1969.

Ottley, Roi, and Weatherly, William J., eds. *The Negro in New York: An Informal Social History, 1926–1940*. New York: Praeger Publishers, 1967.

Redding, Jay Saunders. *To Make a Poet Black*. Chapel Hill: University of North Carolina Press, 1959.

Ricks, Christopher. *A. E. Housman: A Collection of Critical Essays*. Englewood Cliffs, N.J.: Prentice-Hall, Inc., 1968.

Roberts, Evelyn H. *American Literature and the Arts Including Black Expression*. New York: Heath Cote Publishing Co., 1977.

Scott, Wilbur S. *Five Approaches of Literary Criticism*. New York: Collier Macmillan Publishers, 1962.

Silverman, Jerry. *Folk Blues*. New York: Macmillan Co., 1958.

Smith, Bernard. *Forces in American Criticism: A Study in the History of American Literary Thought*. New York: Harcourt, Brace and Co., 1939.

Talley, Thomas W., ed. *Negro Folk Rhymes*. New York: Macmillan Co., 1922.

Tischler, Nancy M. *Black Masks: Negro Characters in Modern Southern Fiction*. University Park, Pa.: Penn State University Press, 1969.

Untermeyer, Louis. *American Poetry Since 1900*. New York: Henry Holt and Co., 1923.

———. ed. *Modern American Poetry: A Critical Anthology*. New York: Harcourt Brace and Co., 1921.

Van Doren, Mark. *Edwin Arlington Robinson*. New York: Literary Guild of America, 1927.

Wagner, Jean. *Black Poets of the United States: From Paul Laurence Dunbar to Langston Hughes*. Translated by Kenneth Douglas. Urbana, Ill.: University of Illinois Press, 1973.

Welleck, Rene, and Warren, Austin. *Theory of Literature*. New York: Harcourt, Brace and Company, 1949.

Williams, Sherley Anne. *Give Birth to Brightness: A Thematic Study in Neo-Black Literature*. New York: Dial Press, 1972.

Writers' Project of Virginia, FWP. *The Negro in Virginia*. New York: Hastings House, 1940.

Zyla, Wolodymr T. and Wendell M. Aycock, eds. *Proceedings: Comparative Literature Symposium, Ethnic Literature Since 1776: The Many Voices of America*. Lubbock: Texas Tech University Press, 1978.

Journal and Magazine Articles

Anderson, Jervis. "Our Far-Flung Correspondents: A Very Special Monument." *New Yorker* 20 (March 1978): 93–121.

Aubert, Alvin. "Black American Poetry, Its Language, and the Folk Tradition." *Modern Black Literature*. Edited by S. Okechukwu Mezu. Buffalo: Black Academy Press, Inc., 1971.

Bell, Bernard. "Folk Art and the Harlem Renaissance." *Phylon* 36 (June 1975): 155–63.

Benston, Kimberly W. "Sterling Brown's After Song: 'When De Saints Go Ma'ching Home' and the Performance of Afro-American Voice." *Callaloo* Nos. 14 & 15, 5 (February-May 1982): 37.

Bontemps, Arna. "Negro Poets, Then and Now." *Phylon* 11 (Winter 1950): 355–66.

Brawley, Benjamin. "The Negro in American Fiction." *Dial* 60 (1910): 449.

Brooks, Gwendolyn. "Poets Who Are Negroes." *Phylon* 13 (Winter 1952): 13.

Chapman, Abraham. "The Harlem Renaissance in Literary History." *CLA Journal* 11 (1967): 38–58.

Daniel, Jack L., and Smitherman, Geneva. "How I Got Over: Communication Dynamics in the Black Community." *Quarterly Journal of Speech* 62 (February 1976): 26–39.

Davis, Allison. "Our Negro Intellectual." *The Crisis* 35 (August 1928): 268–69.

Dover, Cedric. "Notes on Coloured Writing." *Phylon* 8 (Fall 1947): 213–24.

Ekaete, Genevieve. "Sterling Brown: A Living Legend." *New Directions: The Howard University Magazine* 1 (Winter 1974): 5–11.

Fox, Daniel M. "The Achievement of the Federal Writers' Project." *American Quarterly* 13 (Spring 1961): 3–19.

Gates, Henry Louis, Jr. "Songs of a Racial Self," *New York Times Book Review* (11 January 1981): 11, 16; rev. & exp. *Black American Literature Forum* (Summer, 1981): 39–42.

Henderson, Stephen. "Sterling Brown: A Living Legend." *New Directions: The Howard University Magazine* 1 (Winter 1974): 5–11.

[Holmes], E.[ugene] Clay. "Sterling Brown: American Peoples' Poet." *International Literature* 2 (June 1934): 117–22.

Hughes, Langston. "My Adventures as a Social Poet." *Phylon* 8 (Fall 1947): 205–12.

———. "Some Practical Observations: A Colloquy." *Phylon* 13 (Winter 1952): 307–11.

Lee, Ulysses. "Criticism at Mid-Century." *Phylon* 11 (Winter 1950): 328–37.

Locke, Alain. "American Literary Tradition and the Negro." *Modern Quarterly* 3 (1926): 215–22.

Lomax, Alan. "Conference on Character and State of Studies in Folklore." *Journal of American Folklore* 59 (October-December 1946): 507–10.

Neal, Larry. "The Ethos of the Blues." *The Black Scholar* 3 (Summer 1972): 42–48.

"The Negro in Art." *The Crisis* (April 1926): 278.

"The Negro in Art." *The Crisis* (August 1926): 193.

"The Negro in Art: How Shall He Be Portrayed?" *The Crisis* (March 1926): 219.

"The Negro in Art: How Shall He Be Portrayed?" *The Crisis* (February 1926): 165.

O'Meally, Robert. "Reconsideration." *New Republic*. (11 February 1978): 35.

Randall, Dudley. "Black Aesthetic in the Thirties, Forties, and Fifties." *Modern Black Poets*. Edited by Donald Gibson. Englewood Cliffs, N.J.: Prentice-Hall, Inc., 1973.

Rowell, Charles H. "Sterling A. Brown and the Afro-American Folk Tradition." *Studies in the Literary Imagination* 7 (Fall 1974): 131–52.

Stuckey, Sterling. "Through the Prism of Folklore: The Black Ethos in Slavery.'' *New Black Voices*. Edited by Abraham Chapman. New York: New American Library, 1972.

Thurman, Wallace. ''Fire Burns.'' *Fire: A Quarterly Devoted to the Younger Negro Artists* 1 (November 1926): 47–48.

———. ''Negro Poets and Their Poetry.'' *Bookman* (July 1928): 555–61.

Turner, Darwin T. ''Introductory Remarks About the Black Literary Tradition in the United States of America.'' *Proceedings: Comparative Literature Symposium, Ethnic Literature Since 1776: The Many Voices of America*. Edited by Wolodymyr T. Zyla and Wendell M. Aycock. Lubbock: Texas Tech University Press, 1978.

Tykulsky, Evelyn. ''Six Howard University Professors.'' *Our World* (January 1949): 50.

Walker, Margaret. ''New Poets.'' *Phylon* 11 (Winter 1950): 345–54.

Winston, Michael R. ''Through the Back Door: Academic Racism and the Negro Scholar in Historical Perspective.'' *Daedalus* 100 (Summer 1971): 678–719.

Wolfe, F. Bernard. ''Uncle Remus and the Malevolent Rabbit.'' *Commentary* 8 (July 1949): 31–34.

Interviews and Speeches

Baraka, Amiri. Lincoln University, Pa. Interview, 15 March 1979.

Brown, Sterling. Howard University, Washington, D.C. Transcribed speech, 18 May 1972.

———. 1222 Kearney Street, Washington, D.C. Transcribed interview, 4 May 1973.

———. Founders Library, Howard University, Washington, D.C. Interview, 10 May 1973. Interviewers, Steven Jones and Stephen Henderson.

———. 1222 Kearney Street, Washington, D.C. Transcribed interview, 14 May 1973. Interviewer, Steven Jones.

———. 1222 Kearney Street, Washington, D.C. Transcribed interview, 8 June 1975. Interviewer Steven Jones.

———. Howard University, Washington, D.C. Interview, 19 May 1978. Interviewers, James Early and Ethelbert Miller.

Cook, Mercer. Museum of African Art, Washington, D.C. Speech, 1 May 1979.

Davis, Athur P. 3001 Veazey Terrace, Washington, D.C. Interview, 31 August 1978.

Kent, George E. University of Chicago, Chicago, Ill. Interview, 10 May 1978.

Turner, Darwin T. University of Tennessee, Knoxville, Tenn. Interview, 30 November 1978.

Winston, Michael R. Moorland-Spingarn Center, Howard University, Washington, D.C. Interview, 7 March 1979.

Newspaper Articles

"A Son's Return: 'Oh Didn't He Ramble.' " *Kujichagulia*. Published by Williams Black Student Union, November 1973, pp. 4–6.
West, Hollie. "The Teacher . . . Sterling Brown, the Mentor of Thousands." *The Washington Post*, 16 November 1969, pp. F1–F3.

Dissertations

Blue, Ila Jacquith. "A Study of Literary Criticism By Some Negro Writers, 1900–1955." Ph.D. dissertation, University of Michigan, 1959. Ann Arbor, Mich.: University Microfilms, 1971.
Collier, Eugenia. "Steps Toward a Black Aesthetic." Ph.D. dissertation, University of Maryland, 1976.
Kifer, Allen Francis. "The Negro Under the New Deal, 1933–1941." Ph.D. dissertation, University of Wisconsin, 1961; Ann Arbor, Mich.: University Microfilms, Inc., 1971.

Memoranda

Brown, Sterling A. Memo to Dr. (Benjamin A.) Botkin. 1 June 1938. File "Memos," Negro Studies, National Archives, Record Group 69.
———. Memo to Gorham Munson. 9 January 1940. File "Memos," Negro Studies. National Archives, Record Group 69.
———. "Editorial Report." 11 April 1940. File "Memos," Negro Studies. National Archives, Record Group 69.
———. Memo to State Directors. File "General Letters," Negro Studies. National Archives, Record Group 69.
———. "Report from the Editor on Negro Affairs." February 1937. File "Letters from State Directors," Negro Studies. National Archives, Record Group 69.
———. Memo to Henry G. Alsberg. 17 June 1938. File "Memos," Negro Studies. National Archives, Record Group 69.
———. Memo to Director of Georgia Project. 16 August 1939. File "General Letters," Negro Studies. National Archives, Record Group 69.
———. Memo to Alsberg. 8 June 1937. File "Memos," Negro Studies. National Archives, Record Group 69.

Cronyn, George W. Letter to Myrtle Miles. 5 November 1936. File "General
    Letters," Negro Studies. National Archives, Record Group 69 (copy).
Miles, Myrtle. Letter to Henry G. Alsberg. 4 March 1937. File "Incoming
    Letters by State," Negro Studies. National Archives, Record Group 69.
Montgomery, Mabel. Letter to Henry G. Alsberg. 4 May 1937. File "Beau-
    fort," Negro Studies. National Archives, Record Group 69.

INDEX

About the Author

JOANNE V. GABBIN is Associate Professor of English at Lincoln University in Pennsylvania. Her earlier works include numerous editorials in the *Black Conference on Higher Education Journal* and articles in *The Dictionary of Literary Biography* and *The Black American Literature Forum.*